Language Education Throughout the School Years: A Functional Perspective

WILEY-
BLACKWELL

Language Learning Monograph Series

Mary J. Schleppegrell, Series Editor
Nick C. Ellis, General Editor

Schumann:
The Neurobiology of Affect in Language

Bardovi-Harlig:
Tense and Aspect in Second Language Acquisition: Form, Meaning, and Use

Kasper and Rose:
Pragmatic Development in a Second Language

Seedhouse:
The International Architecture of the Language Classroom: A Conversation Analysis Perspective

McNamara and Roever:
Language Testing: The Social Dimension

Young:
Discursive Practice in Language Learning and Teaching

Bigelow:
Mogadishu on the Mississippi: Language, Racialized Identity, and Education in a New Land

Christie:
Language Education Throughout the School Years: A Functional Perspective

Language Education Throughout the School Years: A Functional Perspective

Frances Christie
Emeritus Professor of Language and Literacy Education,
the University of Melbourne, and Honorary Professor of
Education and Linguistics, the University of Sydney

WILEY-
BLACKWELL

Blackwell Publishing was acquired by John Wiley & Sons in February 2007. Blackwell's publishing program has been merged with Wiley's global Scientific, Technical, and Medical business to form Wiley-Blackwell.

Registered Office
John Wiley & Sons Ltd, The Atrium, Southern Gate, Chichester, West Sussex, PO19 8SQ, United Kingdom

Editorial Offices
350 Main Street, Malden, MA 02148-5020, USA
9600 Garsington Road, Oxford, OX4 2DQ, UK
The Atrium, Southern Gate, Chichester, West Sussex, PO19 8SQ, UK

For details of our global editorial offices, for customer services, and for information about how to apply for permission to reuse the copyright material in this book please see our website at www.wiley.com/wiley-blackwell.

The right of Frances Christie to be identified as the author of the editorial material in this work has been asserted in accordance with the Copyright, Designs and Patents Act 1988.

Library of Congress Cataloging-in-Publication Data

Christie, Frances.
    Language education throughout the school years : a functional perspective / Frances Christie.
        p. cm. – (Language learning monographic series)
    Includes bibliographical references and index.
    ISBN 978-1-1182-9200-6
    1. Children–Language. 2. Language and languages–Study and teaching. 3. Language and education. I. Title.
    LB1139.L3C458 2012
    372.6–dc23
                                        2012000111

A catalogue record for this book is available from the British Library.

Set in 10/13 pt TimesNRPS by Aptara
Printed in the U.S.A. by The Sheridan Press

01—2012

**Language Education Throughout
the School Years:
A Functional Perspective**

Contents

Series Editor's Foreword

Education faces daunting new challenges around the world today. Complex contexts of literacy use in adult life require that students develop advanced competencies in all school subjects. At the same time, global migration has increased the diversity of classrooms around the world, where many children now learn in a language not their mother tongue. Teachers are expected to support all children in reaching the high standards needed for participation in society, and in this context, it is timely that education is offered a turn toward linguistics and what a focus on language can offer. In this *Language Learning* monograph, Frances Christie offers a welcome new linguistic perspective on how language develops as children and adolescents engage in learning across school subjects and shows how this perspective suggests better ways to support them in that learning.

Two aspects of this work are particularly noteworthy. One is the conception of language development as extending beyond the years of early childhood and primary education. Christie argues and provides evidence for the position that language learning is a central aspect of learning school subjects throughout schooling. She describes developments in the grammar that children and adolescents need to take up if they are to meet the challenges and expectations of the tasks set them in speaking and writing at each new phase of learning. In careful detail she lays out the linguistic features of many of the genres students engage with, illustrating how these linguistic features are intrinsic to making the meanings that the tasks and disciplines call for.

The second major contribution of this monograph is the use of a functional grammar that offers new ways of describing and assessing these challenges and expectations. Drawing on systemic functional linguistics (e.g., Halliday, 1994), Christie illustrates the power of a meaning-focused grammar in connecting content knowledge, enactment of interpersonal relationships, and the various organizational approaches that characterize the texts children and adolescents are asked to read and expected to produce in their speech and writing. Halliday has suggested that students encounter language in three ways throughout their schooling: they *learn language, learn through language,* and *learn about language* (Halliday, 1980/2004). It is the last of these, learning about language, to which Christie's work here makes another innovative contribution. She has been a major figure for decades in developing pedagogical innovations based in functional grammar. Her early work (e.g., Christie, 1985) identified language as the *hidden curriculum* of schooling, and her subsequent research on pedagogic discourse (e.g., Christie, 1999) and classroom discourse analysis (Christie, 2002) informed both theory and research methods for exploring how knowledge in different subject areas is constructed and reflected in the discursive choices made by speakers and writers. Through her work on register and genre and an extensive set of pedagogical and teacher education materials too numerous to mention here (but see references at the end of this volume), she has offered teachers and teacher educators concrete tools and approaches for supporting students as they engage with language in new ways at school. Her pioneering descriptions of trajectories of writing development (Christie & Derewianka, 2008) demonstrate how particular language choices are functional for achieving the goals for learning in different subjects, and yet draw on grammatical features that are often far removed from the everyday experiences of children with language outside of school. Her most recent work continues to break new ground in illuminating discipline-specific features of the language used to teach and learn (e.g., Christie & Maton, 2011).

In this volume, Christie shows how functional grammar can be a tool for describing, assessing, and supporting language development across the school years and across subject areas. The focus on disciplinarity is especially timely, given recent interest in content-based instruction in North America (Stoller, 2004) and Content and Language Integrated Learning in Europe (Dalton-Puffer, 2011). Language educators are increasingly recognizing the need to situate language learning in subject area classrooms, and in this work Christie offers guidance for supporting content-specific language learning that will undoubtedly inspire new curricular innovations.

The monograph begins with an introduction to systemic functional grammar that provides the basis for the analyses Christie develops in subsequent chapters, each of which describes challenges that schooling presents at different stages of development: in early childhood (Chapter 2), late childhood to early adolescence (Chapter 3), midadolescence (Chapter 4), and late adolescence to adulthood (Chapter 5). Throughout, Christie instantiates the theory through analysis of students' oral and written language drawn from her research in Australia and Indonesia. The final chapter then offers recommendations for pedagogical practices that enable students of all ages to become more aware of the multifunctionality of language and more conscious about the choices available to them in making meaning.

Christie clearly demonstrates how the language of schooling in English develops across the years as students move from using language that serves them well in talking about their everyday experiences into using the increasingly challenging and dense formulations needed to construe abstract disciplinary knowledge in the humanities and sciences. As the data illustrate, successful students draw on increasingly abstract and technical lexis and nominalization as well as sophisticated use of modality to present judgment and attitude. Control of these language resources depends on development of systems of reference, thematic structuring, and a range of clause types that enable information to be densely presented. Throughout the book, Christie summarizes key features of language development at each stage, offering recommendations for supporting literacy in history, science, and language arts across 13 years of schooling.

In this volume, Frances Christie has written a monograph that will undoubtedly stimulate interdisciplinary research on language development, literacy, and assessment, as educators, applied linguists, and others interested in the relationship between language and learning find inspiration for thinking in new ways about the challenges of schooling. By outlining developmental pathways into the valued genres of schooling, this monograph provides teachers, teacher educators, and literacy researchers with theoretical and pedagogical tools for supporting all students in participating in those genres. In the challenging educational contexts in which young people participate today, the volume promises to offer new ways forward in providing all students with more explicit guidance in developing the language resources they need for success.

With this issue I assume the editorship of the *Language Learning* monograph series. I want to extend my deep appreciation to Lourdes Ortega, former editor, for her generosity of time and advice in helping me get started in this role. She has again and again responded to questions large and small, providing information and guidance to smooth the transition. I also want to thank Catherine O'Hallaron for her careful editorial work, as well as the anonymous reviewers who provided insightful comments and suggestions on an earlier version of the manuscript.

Mary J. Schleppegrell
University of Michigan, Ann Arbor

References

Christie, F. (1985). Language and schooling. In S. Tchudi (Ed.), *Language, schooling and society* (pp. 21–40). Upper Montclair, NJ: Boynton/Cook.

Christie, F. (Ed.). (1999). *Pedagogy and the shaping of consciousness: Linguistic and social processes*. London: Continuum.

Christie, F. (2002). *Classroom discourse analysis: A functional perspective*. London: Continuum.

Christie, F., & Derewianka, B. (2008). *School discourse: Learning to write across the years of schooling*. London: Continuum.

Christie, F., & Maton, K. (Eds.). (2011). *Disciplinarity: Functional linguistic and sociological perspectives*. London: Continuum.

Dalton-Puffer, C. (2011). Content-and-language integrated learning: From practice to principles? *Annual Review of Applied Linguistics, 31*, 182–204.

Halliday, M. A. K. (1994). *An introduction to functional grammar* (2nd ed.). London: Edward Arnold.

Halliday, M. A. K. (2004). Three aspects of children's language development: Learning language, learning through language, learning about language (1980). In J. Webster (Ed.), *The language of early childhood* (Vol. 4, pp. 308–326). London: Continuum.

Stoller, F. (2004). Content-based instruction: Perspectives on curriculum planning. *Annual Review of Applied Linguistics, 24*, 261–283.

Acknowledgments

I am very grateful to Mary Schleppegrell, who invited me to write this monograph. The invitation was a quite unexpected honor, and it has allowed me to reflect on a great deal of research in which I have been involved over the last 25 to 30 years. I must also thank four anonymous reviewers who generously read drafts of all the chapters and made very constructive and detailed comments on what I had written. I very much appreciated their advice on many matters. Finally, and as always, I must record my thanks to the many teachers and children whose classroom work I have been allowed to scrutinize, analyze, and discuss. Without them there would be no book at all.

Frances Christie
Sydney
September 2011

Language Learning   ISSN 0023-8333

CHAPTER 1

A Language Theory for Educational Practice

1.1 Introduction

Over the last century a great deal of research and educational theory contributed to the general professional understanding of the nature of language and its role in living and in learning. The research was various, drawing at times on peda- gogical theories, at other times on psychological and literary theories, at times on a range of linguistic theories, structural, transformational or functional, as well, in more recent times, as various poststructuralist theories and theories of multiliteracies. Sometimes, of course, the research has sought to move eclecti- cally across theories, drawing selectively on more than one orientation. Much of the research and associated theory has been useful, addressing matters as various as the spelling and writing systems; grammar and its teaching; speak- ing, listening, reading, and writing development for L1 and L2 students;[1] literature and its values; the teaching of composition; and pedagogies for teach- ing the students. However, relatively few studies have sought to articulate a theory of language and an associated theory of language and literacy develop- ment for all the years of schooling from kindergarten to Year 12 or its equivalent. Rather, their tendency has been to focus on aspects of language and literacy for the early or the middle years and, though often less consistently, for the secondary years. Few have addressed the whole of schooling. This book seeks to repair the omission. It outlines a functional theory of language that draws on the systemic functional linguistic (SFL) theory of Halliday and his colleagues (e.g., Halliday & Matthiessen, 2004; Hasan, Matthiessen, & Webster, 2005, 2007; Halliday & Webster, 2009; Martin & Rose, 2007b), and it goes on to out- line an account of the developmental processes by which young people move from childhood, aged about six or seven, when they commence schooling, until they pass out of school aged about 17 or 18, going on to enter further education or the workforce.

Such an account is timely. One of the more remarkable developments of the 20th and early 21st centuries has been the steady advance of educational provision for all. Whereas at the start of the 20th century many children in the English-speaking world did not complete even a primary education, by the commencement of the 21st, most were achieving, or at least attempting, not only a primary but also a secondary education, continuing until age 16 years, and in many cases to 17 or 18 years. Overall, a strong community expectation now holds in the English-speaking world that young people should have an education for the years of childhood and adolescence. It is easy to forget how historically recent such a development has been, or how significant are the years through which young people pass. A child of six or seven, for example, has had very different developmental and life experiences from one of 10, and the life experiences and developmental changes of the 16- or 17-year-old differ again. Change and adjustment are regular features of the years involved, whereas the school subjects children and adolescents actually study are quite various. One factor at least remains constant over the years of schooling: Language is the fundamental resource in which teachers and students work together. Language is the principal semiotic or meaning-making resource available to students, and their success in learning depends quite crucially on the extent to which they master language, engaging with the many ways in which it varies and changes, depending on context and purpose. Such a statement applies even in the multimodal world of the 21st century in which many verbal or visual resources are used in teaching and learning.

We need a theory of language that, on the one hand, offers a model of the English language system and, on the other hand, provides a model for tracing developmental change in language and literacy across the years of schooling. This book argues that such a theory, once articulated, provides a solid basis on which to plan curriculum and pedagogy for the school years, enabling teachers to provide appropriate support at the different stages, to anticipate potential learning difficulties, and to offer challenges in dealing with emerging tasks over the years of schooling.

This chapter outlines the functional theory of language that informs the book, briefly introducing the SF grammar developed in its name. The discussion is intended both to explain the theory and to suggest ways in which that theory can be used by teachers and teacher educators in tracing school language development in English across the years of schooling. I argue that such development occurs in four broad phases from childhood to late adolescence and adulthood. The first phase, in early childhood, involves children in learning relatively simple, even commonsense, discourses as they master aspects of classroom talk and take their first steps in learning literate language. The second phase, in late childhood to early adolescence, sees children meet new demands in various discourse patterns as they come to terms with the new knowledge of the changing curriculum, most visibly marked by the move from the primary to the secondary school. The third phase, in midadolescence, involves learning often difficult and dense school discourses requiring analysis, evaluation, and interpretation. The last phase, by late adolescence into adulthood, demands high levels of abstraction, judgment, evaluation, and interpretation in the discourses of the school.

These four phases are to be interpreted flexibly, in that not all children progress at the same rates or in the same ways, though they provide a broad basis for interpreting language development in school. The phases might be thought to be self-evident, in that they follow the conventional patterns by which schooling in English-speaking countries is divided into the primary and secondary years and into stages within these. However, I would argue that they are not self-evident, at least with regard to the linguistic demands in learning and using the discourses of schooling, which are the concerns of this book. That is because many children still falter and fail in trying to move through their schooling, their failures too often not understood in terms of mastering the patterns of school discourses, whose nature often remains invisible beyond the first years of school. In fact, an implicit policy often applies that the oral language and literacy skills are understood as taught in the first years only, after which these early skills are seen as sufficient, functioning in some unproblematic way to deal with the knowledge of school, endlessly recycled as it were to learn new information. Knowledge in these terms is seen as "content," learned in some sense independently of language and literacy. As the linguist Reddy (1993) pointed out some years ago, this view sees language as no more than a neutral conduit in which meaning or content is carried, rather than created. The fact is that meaning in language does not exist independently of the resources in which it is expressed.[2] School meaning is shaped quite fundamentally in the linguistic resources that teachers and students constantly use, and the discourses they create over the years of schooling change to deal with the expanding range of meanings that an education involves. By achieving a linguistic description of the nature of the changes over the years of childhood, adolescence, and young adulthood, we have a powerful tool with which to address students' development in schools.

1.2 A Functional Theory of Language

Most people, whether linguists or not, would accept that language serves functions, though they would perhaps not always agree about ways to conceptualize such functions. Moreover, most people would agree that language is significant for its role in social interaction. However, the theory proposed by Halliday is unusual in that a very intimate connection is claimed of language function and social process, such that there is a "systematic relationship between the social environment on the one hand, and the functional organization of language on the other" (Halliday & Hasan, 1985, p. 11). Language is as it is because of the way it has evolved over the millennia, both shaping and shaped by the nature of social experience (see discussions in Williams & Lukin, 2004).

Deep in the organization of all natural languages, it is argued, three *meta-functions*[3] have evolved, their presence accounted for by the broad set of purposes for which all people use language: the *ideational* (having to do with the experience or "content" involved in using language), the *interpersonal* (having to do with the relationship of participants in using language), and the *textual* (having to do with the organization of the language to create coherent messages). As we use language, all three metafunctions are simultaneously engaged: That is, we simultaneously express some information or experience, negotiate some relationship, and organize the language in order to create coherent meaningful text. (See further discussion below.)

Moreover, language is to be understood as functioning on three different *strata*: a *semantic or meaning stratum*, which is realized in a second stratum, the system of wording, technically the *lexicogrammar*, and this is in turn realized in the third stratum, the *phonology*, though for the purposes of literate language, we recognize a *graphology* (see Figure 1.1). The term lexicogrammar is preferred, incidentally, because lexis and grammar are seen as complementary, and not distinct phenomena, as most formal linguistic descriptions would imply (see Halliday & Matthiessen, 1999). Equally, semantics or meaning is not seen as independent of language: On the contrary, it is fundamental to the language, and knowable because of the other two strata in which it is realized. The concentric circles in the figure suggest the way each stratum or level provides an environment in which another emerges in a relationship of *stratification*: Thus "the lexicogrammar appears in the environment of semantics and provides the environment for phonology" (Halliday & Matthiessen, 1999, p. 4). The bidirectionality implied in the two-headed arrow is intended to suggest the very intimate association of all three strata: The one is known only because of the presence of the others.

To engage with language in such terms is, among other matters, to see language as discourse or *text* in some context of use, never as isolated or fragmented words. A text is "any instance of living language that is playing some part in a context of situation" (Halliday & Hasan, 1985, p. 10), and it follows

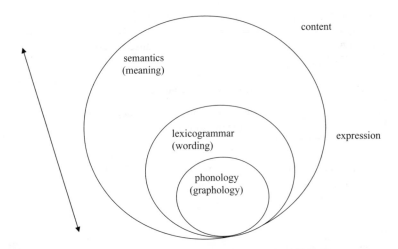

Figure 1.1 Language as a tri-stratal system (Halliday & Matthiessen, 1999, p. 5).

that any attempt to study and understand language will focus on instances in use. The point is an important one for education: children learn language in contexts of use, so that a language and literacy pedagogy for schooling should acknowledge and work with this as a general principle, creating and developing meaningful opportunities for learning.

Such a theory represents a radically different interpretation of language from more mainstream linguistic theories, including, for example, that of Chomsky (e.g., 1962, 1974, 2002, 2006), whose influential structuralist theory of language proposes, among other things, that syntax and meaning are separable. For him, linguistics is a branch of cognitive psychology, and its interest is to understand the "universal grammar" that he claims exists in the human brain, its presence responsible for the fact that people learn to speak language. The preoccupation with the study of syntax in Chomsky's work requires that issues of meaning, and even of purpose in using language, are set aside. Though he has expressed an interest in semantics, his principal concern has been to develop a linguistic theory that "deals with idealization, namely an ideal speaker-hearer in a homogeneous speech community" (Chomsky, 1974, p. 40), in order to establish basic principles underlying language. To this end, Chomsky, unlike Halliday, has not sought to examine instances of language in use, for in his terms they are irrelevant to the enterprise of establishing the general principles that underlie the functioning of language. Moreover, and unlike Halliday, Chomsky (1981) has quite specifically stated that his linguistic theory has little

Table 1.1 The metafunctions found in all natural languages

Metafunction		What is realized or expressed
Ideational {	Experiential	
	Logical	The knowledge, content, or activity
Interpersonal		The relationship of speaker or writer to listener or reader
Textual		The organization of the message

to offer educational practice, for linguistic theory, at least as he proposes it, is not concerned with language in social contexts of use.[4]

1.2.1 The Metafunctions

The functional grammar (Halliday & Matthiessen, 2004), to be explained more fully below, is briefly introduced here to demonstrate the working of the metafunctions.

As Table 1.1 is intended to suggest, the *ideational metafunction* involves the information or ideas represented in language. This metafunction is made up of two other metafunctions: the *experiential* and the *logical*. The experiential metafunction refers to the experience(s) expressed in language, especially as they are expressed within clauses; the logical metafunction refers to the logical meanings created between clauses, normally expressed in conjunctive relations, and giving different meanings to the nature of the experiential meanings expressed within clauses. Experiential meanings are expressed in the range of possible *process* types, which are realized in verbs; their *participants* are realized in noun groups, or noun phrases; and their *circumstances* are realized in prepositional phrases or adverbial groups.

Consider, for example, the writing of a young child who was just learning to write. She produced two clauses (double slashes indicate clause boundaries):

> *On Saturday we went to visit my grandma //* and she gave me a new dress for my birthday.*

Using the functional grammar we may display these two clauses thus:

On Saturday	*we*	*went to visit*	*my grandma*
circumstance (prepositional phrase)	participant (noun group)	process (verbal group)	participant (noun group)

and	she	gave	me	a new dress	for my birthday
(conjunction)	participant (noun group)	process (verbal group)	participant (noun group)	participant (noun group)	circumstance (prepositional phrase)

Looking at the first clause we can note that

- **Experientially**, this clause builds some simple personal information about a family member, expressed in a verb creating a *material process* (*went to visit*) that creates action, grammatical participants[5] expressed in noun groups (the pronoun *we* and *my grandma*) and some circumstantial information expressed in a prepositional phrase (*on Saturday*).
- **Interpersonally**, through its declarative mood choice, the clause establishes the relationship of speaker or writer to listener or reader: It is that of one who informs.
- **Textually**, the clause presents and orders both experiential and interpersonal information, representing them together as a message. To do this, it starts with the prepositional phrase (*on Saturday*) making this the opening *theme*. Theme is what the clause is about, sometimes also referred to as the point of departure for the message. In English, but not in all languages, the normal or *unmarked* way theme is expressed is in the subject of the verb, as in *we went to visit my grandma on Saturday*. However, the child chose to create a *marked theme*, by putting the circumstantial information first.

Turning to the second, dependent clause, we can note that

- **Logically**, a conjunction of addition introduces the dependent clause, for it builds a logical relationship between the meanings of the two clauses, hence adding to the meanings made.[6]
- **Experientially**, the process in this clause is also material (*gave*), and the participants are expressed again in noun groups (*she, a new dress*), and a prepositional phrase (*for my birthday*) creates another circumstance.
- **Interpersonally**, the clause again uses the declarative mood, establishing the relationship of speaker or writer to listener or reader: It is that of one who informs.
- **Textually**, the opening conjunction (*and*) realizes a *textual theme*, whereas the *topical or experiential* theme is realized in the subject of the clause (*she*), which refers to a participant in the previous clause, helping to create texture. Themes, thematic development, and reference are important features of language, oral and written, about which I say more later.

Overall, as even this brief example has sought to demonstrate, all the metafunctions are at work in creating the two clauses I have introduced. Indeed, this is true of any stretch of text, ensuring that meaning is made experientially, logically, interpersonally, and textually.

1.2.2 The Notion of Register

Above, we noted that a text is said to function in a context of use. It follows that language changes, depending on context of use, though we need a principled means of explaining the sources of the differences. Here SFL theory borrows from the work in particular of the anthropologist Malinowski (1923, 1935/1977), who proposed that any instance of language must be understood both in its immediate *context of situation* and in its broader *context of culture* (Halliday & Hasan, 1985). Most cultures, for example, have contexts of situation in which people trade (e.g., for food, clothing, and so on), though these contexts differ, depending on the broader context of culture in which they occur.

Turning in particular to the notion of *register* (a term borrowed from music theory), SFL theory proposes that language differs from one context of situation to another in terms of three *register variables*:

- √ The *field of discourse*—The nature of the social activity; what it is that participants are engaged in. Fields are infinitely various, including, for example, having an evening meal with one's family, teaching and learning about some subject in a classroom, playing football, running a shop, participating in parliamentary debate, or giving a public lecture. For the purposes of written discourse, be the example a novel, a newspaper article, a political tract, or an account of a scientific experiment, the topic involved is the field. All these involve different contexts, having distinctive discourses with characteristic lexis or vocabulary.

- √ The *tenor of discourse*—The nature of the relationships of participants; their roles and status vis-à-vis one another. Relationships are also various, and they bring very different roles having consequences for the ways interactants use language. For example, members of the family at dinner speak to each other differently from teachers and students in classrooms, or from players on a football field, or from vendors to customers in a shop, or from the lecturer who addresses an audience of students. In addition, the nature of written language is such that the writer takes a different relationship with readers depending on whether he or she tells a story, guides behavior, as in a recipe, or seeks to persuade the reader of a point of view as in a political tract.

Table 1.2 The relationship of register and the metafunctions in a context of situation

Register	Realized by	Metafunction
Field: social activity or content	⟶	Ideational (experiential and logical): representing experience
Tenor: role and status of persons	⟶	Interpersonal: enacting relationships
Mode: the role of language in activity	⟶	Textual: organizing experience

✓ The *mode of discourse*—The role language plays in the situation. This includes whether it is spoken or written and whether it is a part of action, as in playing a game, or constituting action, as in a written text. Where language accompanies action in speech (as in the football game), or a diagram in writing (as in a scientific explanation), it is said to be *ancillary* to, or complementary of, the other semiotic modes. Where meanings are expressed wholly in language, as in much writing, the text is said to be *constitutive* of the meaning (Halliday & Hasan, 1985). In the contemporary world of Information Communication Technologies, the clear distinction between language as constitutive or ancillary is no longer completely satisfactory, because in many instances the meanings in texts function in an interplay of several resources, verbal and visual (see discussions in Unsworth, 2008). Nonetheless, the distinction continues to have some value for pedagogical purposes, as it is relevant to teaching children to read and write.

Table 1.2 sets out the relationship of the metafunctions and register. Thus, the experiential and logical metafunctions (together creating the ideational metafunction) are primarily involved in realizing the *field*. The interpersonal metafunction is primarily involved in realizing the *tenor* of relationship, and the textual metafunction is primarily involved in realizing the *mode*. There is, in other words, a connection between choices in the grammar and the meanings of any context of situation with respect to field, tenor, and mode. The relationship of choices in the grammar and meanings in the social context is thus shown to be very intimate, much as Figure 1.1 is intended to suggest.

1.2.3 The Notion of Genre[7]
We noted above the distinction drawn by Malinowski between context of situation and context of culture. SFL theorists in the tradition of Martin and his colleagues (e.g., Martin & Rose, 2008) propose that whereas at the level of

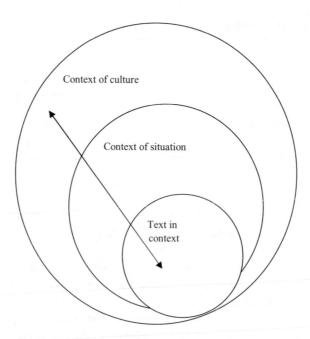

Figure 1.2 Text, context of situation, and context of culture (Martin & Rose, 2008, p. 10).

the context of situation, the above register variables apply, at the level of culture, different choices apply with respect to the wide range of genres available within the culture. Register and genre are said to operate on different planes of experience (Martin, 1985), such that whereas the language choices made with respect to field, tenor, and mode shape the meanings of the text at the level of context of situation, the choice of the overall *schematic structure* of the genre (its beginning, middle, and end sequencing) is drawn from the wider culture. A genre is a "staged, goal-oriented social process" (Martin & Rose, 2008, p. 9) through which people achieve some social purpose(s), and there are of course many genres found in English-speaking cultures (see Martin & Rose, 2008, pp. 8–18; Christie, 2008, 2010).[8] Figure 1.2 displays the model of text in context proposed, such that texts in context, context of situation, and context of culture are said to represent the different *strata* of language and social context. Text realizes context of situation, and context of situation realizes context of culture.

Genres in the SFL tradition have been extensively described in many contexts, and the activity of describing them will no doubt continue, as by their nature they evolve. The discussion in coming chapters makes use of several different types of genres while tracing development primarily in control of literacy, though some discussion of oral language are given as well. However, no attempt is made to discuss a comprehensive body of genre types. Instead, examples are selected to illustrate aspects of development in language and literacy at different stages.

Now that I have offered a brief overview of the functional theory and its key concepts, I want to turn more directly to the functional grammar itself, as an understanding of this will inform all the discussions in the coming chapters in this book.

1.3 Functional Grammar

Of the metafunctions, the ideational metafunction is perhaps the one closest to most people's intuitions about language and what it is for: it is for getting things done in the world, whether we mean the active world of interaction with others, or the inner world of thought and imagination. It is for this reason that I commence this discussion by considering the ideational metafunction. More specifically, I commence by considering the experiential metafunction: that is, the manner in which experience is represented in language, for this takes us into the study of process types. I then go on to discuss the logical metafunction, the interpersonal metafunction, and finally the textual metafunction.

1.3.1 The Experiential Metafunction

As I already indicated briefly above, the experiential metafunction concerns the meanings that are constructed within clauses, which are the basic units of analysis. The *transitivity process*, to give it its full name, is said to consist of

- o the process itself (expressed in a verb)
- o the participants (expressed in nouns or noun groups)
- o circumstances (expressed in prepositional phrases and adverbial groups).

Processes
Table 1.3 summarizes the process types in English.

Quite a bold claim is made in the name of the functional grammar regarding transitivity: namely, that all the many meanings realized in verbs in the language can be understood as belonging to one of the six broad groupings of process types displayed in Table 1.3. *Material*, *mental*, and *relational* are the main types of process, because they are used more often than the others: They deal, respectively, with actions in the world; thought, perception, and imaginative experience about the world; and states of being, having, and identifying in the

Table 1.3 A summary of process types in English

Process types	The type of experience	Examples (taken from texts in this book)
Material	Acting in the world	We *switched* on the electricity but also: Other factors *influenced* Hitler's rise to power
Behavioral	Physical and psychological behavior	So we*'ll write* it, shall we? *I read* the book "Sister of the South"
Mental	Thinking (cognition)	Nelson *believed* that both races should live in harmony
	Feeling (affect)	I *liked* this book
	Perceiving (perception)	It was the most amazing movie I *had* ever *seen*
Verbal	Saying, symbolizing	[Nelson Mandela] *said*, "During my lifetime I have dedicated myself to the struggle of the African people" but also: Many situations throughout the book *show* the children's reactions and emotions
Relational	Being (attributive)	He's in a water sac
	Having (possessive)	We *have* an incubator
	Naming (identifying)	He *is* my hero
Existential	Existing	There *were* many weaknesses to the Weimar Republic There *is* quite a deal of material available on Sparta

world. Although the various process types are distinct, they also tend to shade into each other, as Figure 1.3 reveals. Its circular structure reflects the actual subtleties of language in the ways it represents experience. Meanings can shade into others, and although this is apparent in the many ways in which people go about using language in their daily lives, language and meaning are perhaps not always thought of in these terms.

Material processes commonly include a large range of actions (e.g., *he kicked the ball*), though the actions are sometimes of a more abstract kind, such as the instance in Table 1.3, *other factors influenced Hitler's rise to power*. Other similarly abstract instances found in texts cited in this book are *religion occupied an important place in Spartan life* or *most cases of hemophilia can be and are diagnosed at an early age*.

Figure 1.3 The grammar of experience: Types of process in English (Halliday & Matthiessen, 2004, p. 172).

Behavioral processes are part action and part mental, so that, as Figure 1.3 reveals, they lie between material and mental processes. They can include behaviors, such as *he is laughing*, and others, such as *he is reading to the children*.

Mental processes cover a large range having to do with thinking (e.g., *I understand the problem*), feeling (e.g., *she loves her children*), and perception (e.g., *I can hear the music*).

Verbal processes include a range having to do with saying (e.g., *he told a story* or *the clocks tells the time*), though they also include more abstract instances, as in the example in Table 1.3: *Many situations throughout the book show the children's reactions and emotions*, or *this quote* [from the novel *Catcher in the Rye*] *shows that Holden is not taking this advice seriously*.

The English language has an enormous range of relational processes, most commonly realized in the verb *to be*, but there are many other examples (e.g., *he gets sick when he goes to sea*, or *the patient remains in a stable condition*) where these two create an attribute or characteristic. Others are identifying (e.g., *he is my hero*, or *Barack Obama is the President of the USA*). Relational processes also include those of possession (e.g., *we **have** an incubator*, or *he **owns** a large house*).

Finally, existential processes occur when we have expressions in which there is a dummy subject, as in *there **were** many weaknesses to the Weimar Republic*. In these cases *there* is the grammatical subject of the clause, but the content is expressed in the participant, in this case *many weaknesses*.

A detailed discussion of transitivity is offered in Halliday and Matthiessen (2004), and a more introductory account is offered by Thompson (2004). Several other introductory accounts relevant for educational purposes are now available in various books on the functional grammar (e.g., Coffin, Donohue, & North, 2009; Derewianka, 2011; Droga & Humphrey, 2002; Humphrey, Love, & Droga, 2011).

Participants[9]

The participants in processes are various, though as we saw above, they are typically realized either in pronominal expressions or in nouns:

We	*switched on*	*the electricity*
participant	process: material	participant

but also in larger noun groups as in:

The first part of mechanical digestion	*happens*	*in the mouth*
participant	process: material	circumstance

Sometimes a participant is expressed in an embedded clause (always shown with double squared brackets):

[[What Luhrmann has created]]	*is not*	*just a modern transformation of Romeo and Juliet*
participant	process: relational (attributive)	participant

and sometimes there is an embedded clause within the noun group, expanding meaning:

The most important thing [[I learned]]	was	[[that the convicts weren't always kept in jails]]
participant	process: relational (identifying)	participant

The capacity to expand the noun group is one of the very powerful tools possessed by English for compressing a great deal of experiential information, and it is exploited a great deal by successful writers of the language. Young children, as we shall see in later chapters, rarely exploit the resource of noun group expansion to the fullest. Hence, one of the interesting developmental markers in early writing is the emergence of expanded noun groups using embeddings:

The zoo	is	a place [[where there are lots of animals]]
participant	process: relational (attributive)	participant

Where young children start to create such expressions, they reveal some developing appreciation of the potential of noun groups for making meaning. Where older children do not create such expressions, they reveal some difficulty in controlling the resources of English and will need assistance.

Circumstances

If we think of the process itself as providing the nucleus or the center of some "going on" in the world and the participants as providing the entities involved, then the circumstances provide the associated circumstantial information (though of course not all processes have circumstances). Table 1.4 summarizes common examples, which are found in the data used in this book.

Like the noun groups that create participants, the prepositional phrases and adverbs are very important in building experiential information. The first circumstances to appear in young children's language are typically those of *time* and *place*, expressed in prepositional phrases:

> **On the holidays** *(time) Robyn and me went* **to our friends' house** *(place)*.

though those of *matter* also appear early:

> *It is a scary book* **about a boy king [[who is on a quest]]**.

Table 1.4 Some common circumstances and their realization

Circumstances	Example: prepositional phrase	Example: adverbial group
Time	*In the past the convicts would stumble out*	*Now a film has been released*
Place	*Robyn slept in Craig's room*	*And then it came down*
Matter	*This is a story about a boy [[called Lief]]*	
Accompaniment	*It's getting bigger with long feathers*	
Manner	*The film has been created under the mask of 'making the story appeal to a younger audience'*	*Scout was talking to them rationally*
Purpose	*The nutrients are used for growth and tissue maintenance*	
Concession	*Despite the religious overtones of the more ordinary rituals the difference in status of the monarch and people is obvious*	
Extent	*Throughout the court scene it becomes more and more evident that he didn't do it*	
Role	*Nelson Mandela can be recognized as a hero*	

All three types of circumstance have very much to do with positioning young children in terms of time, place, and the "aboutness" of things, and this probably explains their early emergence in infancy and early childhood. The other circumstances appear to emerge as life opportunity requires them. However, as I argue in later chapters, the various adverbial groups that express circumstantial information tend to emerge later—in late childhood to adolescence, in fact—at least for the purposes of children's writing development. That is because adverbial groups have a role in expressing evaluation, as in:

> *Ever since Australia was colonized Aborigines have been treated extremely poorly.*

Of course simple evaluative expression itself emerges quite early, typically in mental processes of affect and of cognition, as in the following by a young writer:

*I **liked*** (affect) *this book and I **think*** (cognition) *it was well written* (from Christie & Derewianka, 2008, p. 65).

The extent to which adverbial groups are used to express evaluative information differs considerably, depending on the field of knowledge being constructed as well as the genre type. For example, adverbial groups are less common in school science texts than in the texts of subject English or history (see Christie & Derewianka, 2008). This reflects the fact that scientific fields and their associated genres are required to foreground the experiential information and the methods used to establish it, whereas history and English studies require overt evaluation. Although it is not the case that adverbial groups uniquely express evaluation, it is clear that a significant proportion are used for this purpose. There is, however, another sense in which adverbial expressions contribute to evaluative expression in close association with the subject and finite in a clause,[10] perhaps intruding some sense of the urgency of some action:

*I **immediately** rocketed out of the bedroom*

or the likelihood of an action:

*Herodotus provide accounts of other similar events, which **almost certainly** led to mockery by other states.*
*The convicts **even** slept with rats in their beds and with their filthy clothes on.*

In such cases the adverbs are part of the mood system, contributing to the expression of the interpersonal metafunction, to be discussed below.

1.3.2 The Logical Metafunction and Clause Interdependencies
Where the experiential metafunction is realized in the transitivity processes found within clauses, the logical metafunction is involved in the creation of meanings between clauses. The interdependencies between clauses contribute to overall meanings in many ways. Sometimes a clause can stand alone:

We all had fun.

More commonly, clauses are linked, sometimes in a relationship of equality:

We went to see the lost dogs' home // and I saw a cat // and I saw a dog.

Sometimes clauses are linked in a relationship of inequality:

While the little chick is in the egg // it is floating in a water sac.

Table 1.5 summarizes a set of common conjunctions in English.

Table 1.5 Some common conjunctions linking clauses in equal and unequal relationships

Equal relationship	Unequal relationship
and	*when*
but	*while*
so	*unless*
otherwise	*until*
and yet	*although*
moreover	*whereas*
furthermore ———	*if*
	therefore
	as a result

Although young children tend, initially, to write simple clauses linked by *but* or *and*, they move on to creating clause complexes, often with dependent clauses of time:

> **When he dries out** *he is soft and fluffy*

and a little later, of reason:

> *In my opinion this is a great book for older children* **because it is scary and exciting**

whereas they master nonfinite clauses[11] of purpose quite early:

> *We used an incubator* **to keep the eggs warm**

though other uses of nonfinite clauses are more typically a feature of later childhood and adolescence (Christie & Derewianka, 2008; Perera, 1984):

> *This connection . . . can be demonstrated* **by investigating the life and death of kings and others in Spartan life.**

The full range of dependent clauses appears in successful children's writing in late childhood to adolescence, as we shall see in forthcoming chapters, including nondefining relative clauses:

> *Nelson Mandela was a freedom fighter in South Africa,* **who struggled to relieve the people of apartheid**

Such clauses are not to be confused, by the way, with embedded clauses, some of which appeared above. Another example of an embedded relative clause is as follows, where, within the embedding, there are three clauses, whose boundaries are noted:

The digestive system is a system [[that helps break down food // (and) absorb the nutrients from food // as well as eliminate waste]].

Compression of other clauses within embeddings is not uncommon, at least in the written texts read and written by adolescents, and such compression is also very much a part of the discourse of much adult literate language.

As children and adolescents mature, they learn to read and write many texts with embeddings of the kind just displayed, for embedding is one of the resources English uses to compress a great deal of information. Where children show limited understanding of embedded clauses and their meanings, they need assistance in exploring the meanings and in learning to construct such meanings themselves.

To turn to one other type of clause interdependency, we should note that where speech or thought is reported:

*Ross **said** // he might fix it.*
*Nelson **believed** that . . . both races should live equally and in harmony.*

The relationship of the clauses is said to be one of *projection*: That is, the first clause in these two cases "projects" the other.

Into adolescence, when young people show some confidence in writing they can create strings of interconnected clauses in their discourses:

People with mild cases of hemophilia sometimes use desmopressin (also called DDAVP) // which is a synthetic hormone [[that forces the production and release of certain factors in the blood // to aid clotting for a short period of time]].

Possessed of such confidence, they can also start to compress meanings within clauses, by using a resource called *grammatical metaphor*, about which more is said below. First, I turn to the interpersonal metafunction.

1.3.3 The Interpersonal Metafunction and Evaluative Language More Generally

Using the functional grammar, both Halliday (1975) and Painter (1999, 2009) have documented how control of the basic resources of language allows young children to learn "how to mean" in the preschool years; very young children use it to negotiate relationships, build a sense of knowledge about their world, express imaginative experience, and generally enter into an understanding of many matters important to their lives and their well-being. The first of the basic grammatical systems young children master to achieve these things is the *mood system* (Halliday, 1975), for it is with this that they learn to interact with others and to shape their sense of their world. In fact, the mood system is fundamental to the interpersonal metafunction, and we use it constantly all our lives to achieve participation in family, community, and the wider world. Without a mood system we could not enter into dialogue with others, and the nature of social life as we know it would be inconceivable.

To use some made-up examples, consider how the mood system allows us to offer information:

I have a book about chickens.

to offer a service:

Would you like to read a book about chickens?

to ask for information:

Where is the book about chickens?

or to command:

Let's read the book about chickens!

All the above meanings about chickens are said to have *positive polarity*, though we can also have *negative polarity*, creating opposite meanings:

I don't have a book about chickens.
I would not like to have a book about chickens.
I don't know where the book about chickens is.
Don't read the book about chickens.

Of course, between the two positive and negative poles, we can always intrude various shades of meanings, identified by Halliday and Matthiessen (2004) as aspects of the system of *modality*, enabling us to grade our meanings:

I may have a book about chickens.
You must read the book about chickens!
I am determined to read the book about chickens![12]

The resources of modality are very rich in English, for they are expressed in modal verbs (*may, might, must*), modal adjectives (*possible, certain, likely, definite*), and a large range of modal adverbs, to which I alluded above. Where such adverbs appear in association with the subject and finite in a clause, they are known as *modal adjuncts*, because they express some judgment by the speaker or writer about the message involved. Some examples from the data used in this book include

> We **soon** left the barracks to drive back to school
> It was **only briefly** mentioned
> They **also** made sacrifices
> Spartan soldiers were **simply** to be wrapped in their red cloaks

Modality appears quite early in young children's oral language (typically in modal verbs, e.g., *can*, *might*, and so on), though it emerges rather later in their written language (Christie & Derewianka, 2008), and it is a resource that can cause difficulties for second language learners of English of all ages. According to Ventola (1997), speakers of English as a second or foreign language at university levels, for example, experience particular difficulties in handling modality in their academic writing, although she acknowledges there are other sources of difficulty as well. As Hood (2010) demonstrates, modality is only one of the resources in which the meanings of academic discourse in different disciplines are expressed. As I argue in later chapters, the discourses of the various subjects children and adolescents read and write about in schools involve a great deal of evaluative language, although evaluation is expressed rather differently in the various disciplines from which school subjects are drawn. Moreover, evaluative language becomes more significant as children grow older, evident in the developmental challenges they face as they enter adolescence and need to appraise events and phenomena of many kinds. Capacity to handle evaluation in the different subjects thus becomes one of the markers of young people's progress in controlling the resources and the meanings of written English.

The general term *appraisal* has been proposed by Martin and his colleagues to refer to the evaluative resources of English discourse (e.g., Hood, 2010; Hood & Martin, 2007; Macken-Horarik, 2003; Martin & White, 2005). They argue that evaluation always involves expression of attitude of some kind, where that can be feeling or affect:

> It was fun.

or appreciation of some event or phenomenon:

> It was the most amazing movie I had ever seen.

or judgment about the propriety or perhaps the justice of some behavior:

> Heroes try to make things right and fight injustice where it can be found.

Attitudinal expressions draw on many resources in the discourse, including evaluative lexis (*fun*; *amazing movie*; *injustice*) and intensity (***most** amazing*), though other resources are often involved, depending on the register and genre values that apply. These may include modal adjuncts (see above), modal verbs, and some uses of negative polarity:

> *Nelson Mandela is a hero . . . . He **was determined** (modal verb) **not** (negative adjunct) to give up and **determined** (modal verb) to abolish apartheid, so that all people **could** (modal verb) live freely.*

Interpersonal or attitudinal meanings, or both, are sometimes made thematic, as in

> ***In my opinion** this is a good book.*

This brings us to consideration of theme, the basic resource that is most directly involved in expressing the textual metafunction.

1.3.4 The Textual Metafunction

The textual metafunction helps organize the clause as a message, giving order to the ideational and interpersonal meanings. I noted above that in English we make what comes first in the language thematic, though that is not the case in all languages. In usual or unmarked situations, the experiential or topical theme is expressed in the subject of the verb:

> ***We** have an incubator.*
> ***That**'s the water sac.*

English speakers learn quite early in life to vary what they make thematic, creating what are termed marked themes:

> ***On the holidays** Robyn and me went to our friends' house* (expressed in a circumstance of time)
> ***When Brian was getting the rubbish bins** he found this box of old stuff* (expressed in a dependent clause of time)

In such cases the normal order, by which in the first case the circumstance would be placed at the end of the clause:

> *Robyn and me went to our friends' house on the holiday*

and in the second case, the dependent clause would be placed after the clause on which it depends:

Brian found this old box when he was getting the rubbish bins

is reversed. This is because an added value is given in foregrounding the information of interest to the speakers, in each case in positioning themselves and the events in their tales in the manner they want.

One other method of creating a marked theme is found in expressions like this, where a dependent clause is displaced from its usual place, creating what is called an enclosed clause (in double angle brackets):

I just saw Superman for the first time and «after I'd seen it» I thought I could fly

The speaker could have said:

I just saw Superman for the first time and I thought I could fly after I'd seen it

The effect, as in the above examples, is to emphasize the information, thus bringing the information to the attention of one's listener or reader. These enclosed clauses tend to emerge in speech in childhood, but their appearance in writing is a later development, more typically of late childhood to early adolescence.

Marked themes in speech can emerge quite early:

If he tried to peck that . . . that egg *the water would burst like a balloon*

However, young children typically write their first texts using simple unmarked themes, often creating a repetitive series of interlinked topical themes:

***We** went to see the lost dogs' home*
*and **I** saw a cat*
*and **I** saw a dog.*

The first unmarked themes to emerge in writing are generally those of time, and this largely reflects the fact that the first efforts at writing often involve simple retelling of experiences, as is true of the two examples given above.

Over time, writers develop facility in constructing series of theme choices that unfold over sequences of clauses, giving direction and order to the text. Thus, in a scientific text on the human digestive system the opening element starts with this clause, whose theme is shown in bold:

***The digestive system** is a system [[that helps break down food // and absorb the nutrients from food // as well as eliminate waste]].*

Now note next how the item *nutrients*, which appears relatively late in this clause, is reinstated as theme in the next sentence

> **The nutrients [[that are absorbed from your food]]** *are used for growth and tissue maintenance, or burnt off as energy.*

Then note that in the third clause, the writer revisits the opening theme, though in a slightly different way, helping to bring the first element of the text to its close:

> **The main parts of the digestive system** *are the mouth, esophagus, stomach and the two intestines (small and large).*

Thus is overall direction and development given to the text.

Where young people develop with confidence they will, well into adolescence, be able to read and write quite long sustained texts in which themes play an important part in ordering and shaping meanings. Capacity to follow thematic development is one important aspect of learning to read successfully, and where children and adolescents struggle to read difficult and dense texts, they will need constant scaffolding by their teachers in order to follow the ordering by which the texts unfold. The dense passages can be managed by "chunking" them: breaking them into meaningful units to assist comprehension and interpretation (Perera, 1984). Here the sound of the teacher's voice can be helpful in breaking up passages, allowing pauses to discuss them. Equally, in learning to write, young people can be assisted to learn how to sequence series of clauses to create order as they write, often in group or guided situations.

Apart from the topical themes I have been discussing, there are also interpersonal theme choices, including the one cited above:

> **In my opinion** *this is a good book.*

and other examples in the data in this book are:

> **Unfortunately** *my brother had to go to the local hospital for a week.*
> (expressed in a modal adjunct)
> **What** *can you tell me about the yolk?* (expressed in a WH- interrogative)

These are all termed interpersonal theme choices because they make prominent an aspect of the speaker's or writer's interpersonal relationship with the listener or reader.

As indicated earlier, textual themes are expressed in the whole cluster of conjunctive relations that are involved in linking clauses as part of the logical metafunction. Examples found in the data used in this book include

*We didn't have a mother hen // **so** we used an incubator to keep the eggs warm.*
*The kings were buried outside the city // **because** it was thought safer // **if** the spirit of the dead king was removed from close association with the living.*

One further resource relevant to the textual metafunction, also mentioned above, should be mentioned: that of *reference*. The term refers to the ways items once introduced into a text are then reintroduced later, building ongoing texture. In Chapter 2 I examine a text extract in which young children are talking about a book on the growth of chickens. A young child points to a picture of a chicken with its egg tooth visible, and says:

Here's a little egg tooth.

to which another responds:

And that helps him.

This kind of reference, out of the text that is being spoken and into the context the children share, is called *exophoric* because it points out. But in writing about the chicken's development under the teacher's direction, the children are assisted to write, in part

The little chick *looked like a dot.*
It *stays in the egg for twenty-one days.*

Where reference is built in such a manner, building internal unity within the text, it is termed *endophoric* reference because it builds references within. Like all other language matters I have reviewed in this discussion of the functional grammar, this one is relevant to an understanding of the language and literacy development of children and adolescents. Even native speakers have some difficulty in controlling endophoric reference in writing, and the problem is made the more acute if they are reluctant or poor readers. However, the problem is a more serious one for many students of English as a second or foreign language. That is because many other languages do not have the pronominal system that English does, having quite different ways to introduce various entities into texts and then to sustain reference to them through the discourse. Control of reference is thus a relevant issue to be examined in reviewing aspects of the language and literacy development of children and adolescents.

Finally, before leaving this discussion of matters thematic, I introduce two terms, relevant for tracking the progress of topical themes across texts: *new information* and *given information*. A very common feature in the unfolding of texts over a series of clause is to introduce information toward the end of one clause (referred to as new information) and then reinstate it in theme position in the next clause, where it is now given information:

> *The digestive system is a system that helps break down food and absorb <u>the nutrients from food</u>, as well as eliminate waste.*

> <u>*The nutrients that are absorbed from your food*</u> *are used for growth and tissue maintenance, or burnt off as energy.*

Although this is not the only means by which texts unfold and build their meanings in coherent ways, it is a very common one, and important in the development of long passages of written language.

1.4 Grammatical Metaphor

When children first learn to talk and, later on, learn to write, they use the simplest forms of English grammar to express their meanings, as in these examples from Painter's study of her two boys' early language development in the preschool years:

> *All horses have tummies don't they?*
> *Snakes and worms, they don't have legs.*
> *I saw a cowboy on a horse.* (All selected from Painter, 1999, pp. 101–118)

In all such cases, the grammar is said to be *congruent*, in that all the language items fulfill congruent or characteristic roles in making meaning:

- o nouns create entities, things, phenomena (*horses, tummies, snakes, worms, legs*);
- o verbs create doing, being, having, thinking, and so forth (*have, saw*); and
- o prepositional phrases create associated information (*on a horse*).

Furthermore, we should also note that where conjunctions occur, they link clauses simply as in the following written text, from another source:

> *We went to the lost dogs' home // **and** I saw a dog // **and** I saw a cat.*

We all make extensive use of congruent grammar for all our lives, especially in speech, for it is very adequate for many situations throughout our lives. But we can also change the usual grammatical patterns by which meanings are expressed, creating what Halliday (1985) has termed *grammatical metaphor*. Consider the following made-up example:

The soldiers invaded the town // and they destroyed the buildings // and stole many precious artifacts.

This could be reexpressed thus:

The soldiers' invasion of the town caused the destruction of the buildings and the theft of many precious artifacts.

The congruent version consists of three clauses, whereas the second, *noncongruent* version consists of only one clause. Furthermore, several grammatical items have changed: *invaded* becomes *invasion*, *destroyed* becomes *destruction*, and *stole* becomes *theft*. The process by which such verbal expressions become nouns is known as *nominalization*. In addition, we should note that the connections between the events expressed in the conjunction *and* are now buried in the newly created verbal group *caused*, which is said to realize a causative process.[13] In summary, the actions expressed using a congruent grammar in the original three clauses have been reexpressed in a noncongruent or grammatically metaphorical way.

In his original edition of the *Introduction to Functional Grammar*, Halliday (1985) proposed that grammatical metaphor is a feature that emerges in children's language by about age nine. Considerable research since then (e.g., Aidman, 1999; Christie & Derewianka, 2008; Derewianka, 2003; Painter, 2009; Painter, Derewianka, & Torr, 2007) has confirmed that it is indeed a development of late childhood to early adolescence. Young children aged nine years can use nominalization, as in

*After an hour of **trudging** through the dark and depressing forest . . .*
(from Christie & Derewianka, 2008, p. 35; written by a boy aged nine)

More congruently this would read

After they had trudged through the dark and depressing forest . . .

Grammatical metaphor is discussed in some detail in Simon-Vandenbergen, Taverniers, and Ravelli (2003).

Grammatical metaphor is very relevant to the concerns of this book for at least two reasons. First, grammatical metaphor is an essential tool with which we shape many of the significant meanings of scholarship and ideas, and although it is used in adults' speech, it is used most extensively in shaping written discourse. It is therefore important for school learning. The second reason grammatical metaphor is relevant to this book is that its emergence in late childhood to adolescence is an important feature of the language and literacy development of young people. Although it is true that it emerges in late childhood in many children, its emergence is uneven across groups of children, so that many children do not achieve a good grasp of grammatical metaphor or of the discourses it helps to construct. Teachers need an understanding of the nature of grammatical metaphor and its significance in shaping meanings in written discourse the better both to scrutinize students' progress and to identify teaching strategies to deal with the problems that arise in its absence. Such problems tend to arise most acutely in the childhood to adolescent years and, correspondingly, in the movement from the primary to the secondary school.

1.5 A Model of Language Development for Schooling

In the opening pages of this chapter I outlined an account of language and literacy development over the years of schooling, and I proposed that this be thought of in four overlapping phases. In the first phase, involving the initial years of schooling, young children use a functional grammar to shape ideas and information, and it is with this that they take their first steps in mastering the discourses of schooling, including its literate discourses. In these years they deal mostly with familiar or commonsense experience, albeit already shaped by the requirements of schooling in terms of beginning to understand some abstract ideas, including those having to do with learning literacy. By late childhood, the start of the second phase, the discourses begin to change, facilitated by a gradual expansion of language resources, so that children can make meanings in new ways. The shift from late childhood to early adolescence is marked, ideally, as we have seen above, by achieving some early control of a noncongruent grammar. The emergent control of grammatical metaphor, both in reading and writing, enables enhanced development in understanding the increasingly uncommonsense discourses of the different school subjects. The third phase, by midadolescence, sees some consolidation and expansion of the gains made, and the later years—the final phase—see further expansion, in terms of achieving control of abstraction, generalization, and evaluation, all of them required in the different registers and genres of the various school subjects. The end of schooling at about age 18 does not, of course, mark the end of development. On the contrary, it merely paves the way for future development.

Children and adolescents progress at different rates and in different ways, so that the boundaries between the phases are blurred. Moreover, for reasons having to do with social class positioning in some cases and, in other cases, for reasons having to do with language background, children and adolescents inevitably proceed very differently. In developing the arguments to be made in later chapters, I draw on my own research using the functional grammar over the last 25 years, and documented in many places, including a number of funded research reports (Christie, 1991, 1994, 1995b, 1995c, 1996, 1998, 1999a, 2000; Christie & Derewianka, 2007) and a number of publications (e.g., Christie, 1984, 1985, 1990, 1993, 1995a, 1999b, 2000 2001, 2002, 2003a, 2003b, 2004a, 2004b, 2005, 2006, 2007a, 2007b, 2008; Christie & Derewianka, 2008; Christie & Martin, 2007; Christie & Maton, 2011; Christie & Misson, 1997; Christie & Simpson, 2010; Christie & Soosai, 2000–2001; Christie & Unsworth, 2005). I should also acknowledge the contributions of two former doctoral students, now colleagues, Brian Gray and Marina Aidman, whose work I have drawn on in Chapter 2. My debt to others in the SFL tradition will be obvious as the book unfolds.

The data I draw on has been amassed over the years in one of two broad types of case studies. In the first type, I sought to investigate and document actual classroom practices by observation of classroom groups and collection of associated data, enabling me to acquire a sense of teacher expectations and of children's development in language and literacy over sustained periods of time (normally at least a school term, but more commonly over several years, in both primary and secondary schools). The other broad type of study involved me in overt intervention into classroom practices, working with teachers to make selective use of the functional grammar and genre-based pedagogies. Data used in this book are drawn from both types of study, and as the succeeding chapters unfold I introduce texts from different studies, indicating in each case details of the contexts from which they are drawn.

Chapters 2 to 4 provide discussions of the phases of school learning I have identified. I trace the developmental changes that occur, particularly in literate development, arguing a gradual shift from the immediate and the common-sense to the more distant and uncommonsense in the discourses of schooling, as children and adolescents are required to come to terms with increasingly abstract information and ideas. The grammatical organization of the discourses of different subjects changes considerably, and I illustrate some of the changes by reference to texts from subjects English, science, and social studies or history. These school subjects each draw on different knowledge bases, hence building different knowledge structures, whose features are most marked or foregrounded in the years of adolescence and as young people reach the last years of schooling. The pedagogical implications of this account of language and literacy development for mother tongue and second language users are discussed at various points in these first four chapters, and a final chapter explores more fully the implications of the account for a language theory for educational practice.

Notes

1 The terms *L1* and *L2* refer, respectively, to native speakers of a language and second language speakers.

2 It is not suggested, of course, that meaning is not expressed in other ways. Meaning is expressed in all semiotic systems, such as movement, gesture, dance, music, and the range of expressive arts. The interested reader would find it useful to read Reddy's paper in full.

3 Italics will be used the first time any technical term is introduced into the discussion.

4 It is of some interest to note in this context, that Halliday (2002) argues that because much linguistic inquiry, in the 20th century at least, was largely preoccupied with the study of idealized sentences in the manner of structuralist linguists like Chomsky, it avoided the study of language in use and hence also the study of meaning. One result was that studies such as pragmatics emerged as a separate field of linguistic research in an attempt to put meaning back into linguistic studies, often, paradoxically, without any interest in grammar at all. Halliday rejects the claims of pragmatics as a separate field of linguistics on the grounds that a robust linguistic theory must accommodate considerations both of structure and of meaning.

5 The term *participant* is a grammatical term, referring to any entity, phenomenon, or person realized in noun groups or their equivalents. It has no necessary association with people, as the term might suggest.

6 The notion that a conjunction expresses both a logical meaning and a textual meaning sometimes causes confusion. It is important to bear in mind that the theory here states that all linguistic items in clauses serve more than one function (e.g., *we* expresses the subject of the first clause and one grammatical participant in the process *we went to visit my grandma*). The linguistic item *and*, a conjunction, has two functions, one as part of the logical metafunction and one as part of the textual metafunction. In terms of the logical metafunction, the function has to do with the logical relationship between clauses. In terms of the textual metafunction, the function is to build connectedness between clauses, contributing to what is also called *texture*. Not all clauses have conjunctions, so they do not always have any logical relationship to other clauses. Not all clauses have textual themes either.

7 More than one model of genre is discussed in contemporary scholarship, and they have been quite extensively reviewed and debated in many contexts (see, e.g., Christie, 2006; Freedman & Medway, 1994a, 1994b; Hood, 2009, 2010; Hyland, 2000; Hyon, 1996; Johns, 2001; Martin, 2009, in press; Martin & Rose, 2008; Paltridge, 1997; Tardy, 2011). Although the traditions differ over many things, all are agreed that we can think of a genre as a social activity or process, whose purpose is to achieve important human goals.

8 Halliday and Hasan (e.g., Halliday & Hasan, 1985) have never accepted Martin's formulation, arguing that it is wrong to propose different planes of experience for register and genre, for indeed they would see genre and register as interchangeable terms functioning on the same plane of experience (see Hasan, 1995, 2004). Although the issue has been a lively one in many places, the fact remains that it is Martin's model of register and genre that has been most influential in educational discussions.

9 Different names are provided for the participants in all process types, and the interested reader will find these explained in Halliday and Matthiessen (2004).

10 Subject and finite together give mood in an English clause, whether that be *indicative* (hence either *declarative* or *interrogative*) or *imperative*. The grammatical test for finding subject and finite in a declarative clause, for example, is to use the tag question as in: *I immediately rocketed out of the room, **didn't I?*** As a general principle, the finite is expressed in a verb that gives tense (*I **rocketed** out of the room*) or in a modal verb (*I **might** rocket out of the room.*)

11 A nonfinite verb has no subject.

12 Halliday and Matthiessen (2004) regard *determined* as one of the considerable number of modal expressions that English verbs can create.

13 Causative processes are not shown in the earlier discussion of transitivity processes; they are less common than the others, and for that reason are not normally displayed in figures like Figure 1.3. I have identified them here because of their relevance to students' development in the senior years of schooling.

Language Learning   ISSN 0023-8333

CHAPTER 2

Early Childhood: The Initial Challenges of School Learning

2.1 Introduction

This chapter discusses language and literacy development in the first of the phases I have identified in school learning, covering the years from about age five or six to about age eight. This is the phase in which formal schooling commences, and children need to make many adjustments to learning the patterns of oral language characteristic of schooling in order to participate effectively in class work. In addition, children start to learn literacy. The visible manifestations of literacy inevitably come to the fore, as children come to terms with the spelling and writing systems, though the demands of learning literacy involve more than spelling and writing, important as they are. Learning literacy takes children into relatively abstract experience as they grapple with new terms and ideas like *word*, *letter*, *alphabet*, whereas the larger challenge of mastering the grammar of written as opposed to spoken language, commenced in the first years, will last well beyond childhood into adolescence. Indeed, the initial demands in learning to handle writing are so considerable that children "typically regress in semiotic age by anything up to three years" (Halliday, 1993, p. 110). The first school years are developmentally very important, and constant support and guidance are needed among even the relatively advantaged children who have had exposure to literacy and school-related practices before commencement of school. This chapter outlines developments in both oral language and literacy, arguing that the entry to schooling involves learning new ways to make meaning: new registers and genres in fact, all of which challenge young children to come to terms with school knowledge. I begin by outlining some aspects of oral language development before going on to examine aspects of growth in literate language, writing in particular.

2.2 Oral Language and Preparation for Schooling

Research in various parts of the world and from more than one tradition suggests that as parents and other caregivers interact with their children, so they encode various meanings and understandings about the nature of experience and relationship. The sociologist Bernstein (1971, 1975, 1990, 2000), for example, concerned to understand and explain the apparent failure of many working-class children in London to perform as well as their middle-class peers, proposed the operation of two different *codes* variously expressed in language: *restricted* and *elaborated*, the presence of which, he said, was established very early in life. Meanings that are localized and immediate to context tend to be restricted, whereas meanings that are built by expanding on or extending the experience of the immediate context, often also carrying some sense of personal evaluation or attitude, are elaborated. Elaborated codes, Bernstein proposed, were those most directly rewarded in schools, because they predispose possessors of the codes to engage in such things as exploration of ideas; explanation of phenomena; and expression of feelings, attitudes, and values, all of them relevant in an English-speaking society's educational system. Working-class children and their families, Bernstein suggested, tended to make greatest use of restricted codes, whereas middle-class children and their families tended to use both restricted and elaborated codes, depending on needs and purposes.[1] The differences between codes were not a matter of intelligence, nor were they a matter of dialect difference (Hasan, 1973/2005), though they were sometimes understood as one or the other of these. Moreover, codes were not to be confused with grammar: speakers draw on the same grammatical system to express meanings, but the meanings they create differ, depending on their social context. Overall, the theory proposed that codes involve variations in predispositions to make meanings (Bernstein, 1971), where these were an effect of social position and associated sociocultural values; they were learned, for the most part, quite unconsciously, fundamentally shaping a great many of the ways people interact and understand their world. Codes were learned from early in life from caregivers and others and as a necessary part of participating in the social processes of home, family, and neighborhood.

Code theory has been considerably refined and developed over some years in the light of ongoing research by Bernstein and his colleagues, becoming, in time, a major theory concerning cultural transmission (see, e.g., Christie & Martin, 2007; Christie & Maton, 2011; Maton & Moore, 2010; Morais, Neves, Davies, & Daniels, 2001; Moore, 2011; Muller, Davies, & Morais, 2004; Sadovnik, 1995; Young, 2008). Bernstein (1999) defined a code as "a regulative principle, tacitly acquired, which selects and integrates relevant meanings, forms of realization and evoking contexts" (p. 101).

Significant research in the SFL tradition developed by Hasan (1989, 1992, 2002, 2005, 2009) and her colleagues (Cloran, 1994, 1999; Williams, 1999, 2005a, 2005b, 2008) has extensively developed Bernstein's work, providing important linguistic evidence for the operation of the different meaning codes in different social groups, leading Hasan to describe what she termed *semantic variation* in the manner in which children and their families interact and make meaning, revealing differences in their "social locations" (Hasan, 2002). It will be important briefly to describe Hasan's study, because, using the functional grammar, she provided evidence in support of Bernstein's sociological theory.[2]

The study involved a very fine linguistic analysis of the talk collected in 24 mother–child dyads in families in Sydney, where the mothers were all native speakers of English and the average age of the children at the time of recording was 3 years, 8 months. Some investigation of family backgrounds enabled Hasan to group the 24 families from which the children came into equal numbers of two categories: those where the breadwinner (normally the father) had a Lower Autonomy Professional (LAP) occupation (e.g., carpenter or boilermaker) and those where the breadwinner had a Higher Autonomy Professional (HAP) occupation (e.g., engineer, financial consultant, or medical specialist). The terms LAP and HAP were intended to capture a sense of the relative independence or autonomy enjoyed by the breadwinners in their occupational settings. The linguistic analyses examined closely the discourse patterns of mother–child interaction in their daily lives, including, for example, patterns of questions and responses, who initiated talk and who elaborated, and the respective roles of the two in construction of the discourse. The evidence that emerged from the analysis of the talk supported Bernstein's proposals. For example, HAP mothers were shown to be more inclined to extend on and elaborate matters talked about than LAP mothers. It was not the case that LAP mothers did not talk to their children, for they did talk and, on the evidence, were loving parents. Rather, it was a matter of the kind of talk the HAP mothers tended to engage in and the kinds of contributions to the talk that their children were enabled to make. Thus, among other matters, their children tended not to repeat their questions, for the mothers tended to answer immediately. Furthermore, the HAP children were much more likely than LAP children "to ask *how/why* questions than *who/what/where/when* questions, or *is it/does it* kind of question(s)" (Hasan, 2009, p. 109). HAP children were also more likely to relate any questions they might ask to some other matter discussed, so elaborating on the question itself and extending its potential meaning. All such tendencies, Hasan argued, produced semantic variations in the manner in which HAP and LAP mothers and their children constructed meanings, tending over time to predispose the children involved to establish habits in using language with others in particular ways. The HAP ways tended to be those valued in educational contexts. The linguistic differences Hasan described accounted for the differences in codes described by Bernstein.

Hasan's was a linguistic study, conducted using a fine systemic functional analysis and Bernstein's sociological theory. It is of considerable interest to note that, although using very different research methods and orientations, American psychologists Hart and Risley (2002) undertook a major study leading to findings that paralleled those of Hasan. Their study was conceived against the background of the War on Poverty in the United States in the 1960s and in the light of their frustration at trying to understand the causes of educational failure among "low-income children" (Bloom in Hart & Risley, 2002, p. xiii). Thus, they investigated parents and young children talking with a view to establishing why many children failed in school. They collected and studied the "vocabularies" of 42 children from about age 1 to about 3 years, arguing that whereas some children learned vocabulary quickly, others were slow to learn, so that their educational performance tended to fall behind. Theirs is an impressive study, not least because of the extended period of time over which they followed the children. The study lacked the delicate linguistic analyses of Hasan and her colleagues, so that the focus on vocabularies seems by comparison a rather blunt instrument. They nonetheless produced some important findings, and it is a matter of some interest to this book and its concerns that as Hart and Risley developed their conclusions, they were perforce caused to discuss the discourse that parents and children produced, and not simply "vocabularies" as they originally claimed. They found that children of middle-class and poor families had similar everyday experiences as they went about the daily business of living, involving family and family activities and relationships, so that differences in talk were not to be explained by reference to these matters. However, they also found that children of middle class families experienced these things more often, so that the frequency of the interactions available was much greater than the frequency afforded the children from poorer families. Finally, and very tellingly in my view, they wrote:

> The data showed that when parents engaged children in more talk than was needed to take care of business, the content changed automatically. When parents began to discuss feelings, plans, present activities, and past

events, the vocabulary became more varied and the descriptions richer in nuances. (p. xx)

In other words, it was the middle-class parents who were more inclined than the poorer parents to involve their children in talk that did more than "take care of business," where the latter talk was similar to what Bernstein meant by his term *restricted codes*. Moreover, as the middle-class parents talked with their children of feelings, plans, present activities, and past events, they essentially moved the children into use of the elaborated code. In this sense, I suggest, Hart and Risley's conclusions provide general support for Bernstein's and Hasan's observations.

With yet different research orientations and addressing the concerns of poor American children—often Black—Delpit has written rather differently of codes. According to Delpit, there are "codes or rules for participating in power [which] relate to linguistic forms, communicative strategies, and presentation of self; that is, ways of talking, ways of writing, ways of dressing, and ways of interacting" (Delpit, 1995/2006, p. 25). Where poor children are not familiar with such codes, she argued, they are often locked out of the culture of schooling, with all the access to social power that it can confer. Heath (1983), reporting observations in two different American communities, also found evidence for the operation of different ways of meaning in different social groups. In the Australian context, studies involving Aboriginal children and their communities (e.g., Gray, 1985, 1999; Rose, 2004, 2010; Vinson, 2010) reveal similar patterns of difficulty experienced by children encountering the language patterns and expectations of schooling. It needs to be stressed, incidentally, that there is no suggestion that children unfamiliar with the coding orientations valued in schooling are necessarily deprived (although both Vinson and Rose, reflecting on the experience of young Australian Aboriginal children, consider them seriously deprived in many ways). Delpit (1995), for example, notes that many of the Black children in the United States that concern her "operate within perfectly wonderful and viable culture" (p. 25). For Bernstein, the issue of deprivation, or even of "deficit," did not arise: restricted and elaborated codes represented viable and socially valued orientations to making meaning, though possession of both conferred advantages in many situations, including those of schooling (see Bernstein, 1990, pp. 94–130). He wrote: "Clearly one code is not better than another; each possesses its own aesthetic, its own possibilities. Society, however, may place different values on the orders of experience elicited, maintained and progressively strengthened through the different coding systems" (1997, p. 135).

Schooling involves mastery of a range of new registers and genres, some realized in talk, others in written language, all representing new ways of making meaning. Such meanings typically go beyond the familiar toward less familiar, often remote meanings, as young children explore themes and ideas apart from those relevant to the shared immediate context of lived experience. They might, for instance, speculate about the lives of characters read about in books or recall and expand on class visits outside the classroom, such as excursions to zoos, or perhaps work with the teacher to talk about and plan future events or activities. Where such talk occurs, the information dealt with is not of the immediate context of the talk, and to that extent it is decontextualized. Painter (2007), for example, discussing the experience of her own two sons in the early years (growing up in a professional family), traces, among other things, how they prepared for school by moving from initial uses of language for achievement of immediate needs and goals toward capacity to talk about meanings of things less immediate, hence widening the ways things in the world could be understood. To do this, they dealt with the familiar experiences of daily life, but learned, with parental support, to engage in talk that took them beyond the immediate, toward ability to reflect on it and to generalize about it, hence building non-context-dependent meanings. For example, they developed understandings about what words "mean":

> Child (talking of wind): It's blowing and blowing out there. Can you hear it?
> Mother: Yes I can.
> Child: Hear it isn't mean a talk is it? Means listen to it, isn't it? Means listen to it, isn't it? It's two words, two words. (Produced at age 3 years 4 months; Painter, 2007, p. 142)

or about how things are classified:

> Child: What's a pet?
> Mother: A pet is an animal who lives in your house. Katy's our pet.
> Child: What's a pet called? (Produced at 2 years and 11 months; Painter, 2007, p. 140)

or about how to build generic categories:

> (Said while looking at a shared book)
> Child 1: Dog's not an animal.
> Mother: Yes it is [talk omitted] What is it then?
> Child 1: It's, it's just a dog.

Mother: Yes, but dogs are animals.

Child 1: No they aren't.

Mother: Well, what's an animal then?

Child 1: Um . . . giraffe's an animal.

Mother: Oh I see, you think animals is only for zoo animals.

Child: Yeah.

Mother: Dogs are animals too, they're tame animals. And cats, cats are animals too. Did you know that?

Child 2 [who is older]: And people, we're animals.

Child 1: We're not. (Produced at 3 years 8 months; Painter, 2007, p. 142)

All such activities are useful because, first, they build useful relatively abstract information, and second, they establish habits of using language to construct such information. Ways of dealing with experience are literally encoded in patterns of language use. All developments in language of the kind briefly revealed, so Painter writes, "enabled the discussion of meanings without reference to observed instances of the phenomena under attention" (2007, p. 153). In this sense, the two children prepared for school, though not all children are prepared for schooling in similar ways (Hasan, 2009; Williams, 1995, 1998, 2005b).

2.2.1 A Summary of Matters Discussed in This Section

To this point I have argued that

√ young children differ in terms of social positioning, where the latter term embraces social class and associated cultural values, ideologies, and beliefs;

√ hence, among other matters, young children function with different codes, involving different orientations to experience, differing modes and methods of interacting with others, and different ways of building a sense of their world;

√ such codes involve, on the one hand, capacity to expand on experience (the *elaborated code*) and, on the other hand, capacity to condense or constrain experience (the *restricted code*);

√ all such codes are valued and valuable, expressing a great deal of family and community membership as well as helping to maintain social cohesion;

√ schooling and school knowledge tend to reward those codes that facilitate elaboration of experience;

√ children possessed of elaborated codes tend to enjoy some advantage in dealing with school language and learning, whereas those not familiar with these codes are often disadvantaged in school; and

√ all children need assistance in coming to terms with school knowledge, and all children benefit from pedagogies that scaffold their learning, though those possessed mainly of restricted codes will need particular assistance.

2.3 Learning the Language of Schooling

In the first years of schooling a great deal of attention is devoted to initiating young children into the ways of working that constitute "doing school." These include, for example, learning to function in groups, to sit in classrooms in particular ways, to move about the rooms at different times in the school day for different activities, to take breaks and eat meals at supervised times, to participate in classroom talk, knowing when to speak and when to listen to the teacher or class peers, and learning how to read and write in a range of structured activities. Cazden (2001), Christie (2002), Green and Dixon (1994), and Mehan (1979) have all documented these details in different ways. The learning of these matters requires important adjustments for all young children, although those from middle-class or professional families tend to be better prepared than poorer children. In addition, where children are of non-English-speaking backgrounds, the tasks confronting them are often harder, as they are learning a language other than their own.

More than one set of register choices is involved, of course, and the genres of classroom talk also vary. In this discussion I consider two different, if familiar, early childhood activities, involving different language choices and generating different curriculum registers and genres. They both represent instances of early childhood curriculum genres (Christie, 2002), the first selected because it involves an activity intended to promote talking to learn, as well as early reading and writing behavior, the second, because it involves young children in narrating about some aspect of personal experience to a class group in a reasonably independent manner. Such a capacity is also valued in schooling. It will be noted that the language children use initially in coming to terms with the new registers and genres of school will involve a congruent grammar, noticeable both in their speech and in their first writing, though as pointed out above, the grammar of writing will be often simpler than that of speech.

2.3.1 An Instance of Classroom Talk for Learning and for Building Literate Behavior

Among the many activities generated early in schooling for young children are those in which they start to read and write. These typically commence when children enter the school, and a great deal of literate behavior is ideally modeled and practiced long before children are able to read and write independently. The text extract I use is taken from Gray (1999), who has spent many years working with disadvantaged Aboriginal children in several settings in Australia, and it is drawn from his doctoral work. The text selected involves a teacher working with a group of young Aboriginal children who, I have already noted, often experience difficulty participating in classroom talk. The children lived with their families in homes on the edge of town without water, sanitation, or electricity. They spoke nonstandard Aboriginal English, incidentally, although as Gray and others observed, when the classroom discourse emerged around a field of the kind considered here, supported by the reading of a book, they appeared to adopt the standard dialect with ease. Their older siblings had had a history of failure in school learning, so that for these children, as their teacher knew, much depended on establishing some positive learning experiences very early.

The teacher worked closely with Gray in developing a pedagogy intended to facilitate Aboriginal children's access to school language and to school learning. They used a term they took from Cazden (1977, 1983)—"concentrated encounter"—though they adapted it to create the notion of a "concentrated language encounter," around which to shape language-rich purposeful learning activities. Themes were selected for work with the children, and around these a range of activities was prepared and pursued over several weeks, so that the children had a constant opportunity to learn, practice, and revisit relevant language and build relevant knowledge. Joint negotiation of the necessary language and learning was a "key focus" of a concentrated language activity (Gray, 1999, p. 108), so that, over time, the children were enabled to develop independent control of matters dealt with, using relevant school language with which to progress to further new language and knowledge. The pedagogy was "strongly framed" (Bernstein, 1990, p. 37) in that the teacher controlled "the selection, organization, pacing (and) criteria of communication" that applied in the classroom, as well as the physical disposition of the children. The knowledge was also "strongly classified" (Bernstein, 1990, p. 36), so that it was clearly distinguished from the other areas of knowledge that might be taught at different times in the school day or week. In this, it differed from early childhood programs that tend toward an integrated curriculum, such that boundaries between areas of learning are not maintained (Bernstein, 1975). For example, in the instance considered here, the activity concerned the life cycle of chickens, so the knowledge at issue was scientific, and scientific meanings were foregrounded in the text. In these ways the pedagogy was focused, its goals made clear to the children as they jointly negotiated their work with the teacher.

The total curriculum activity extended over some weeks, so what is displayed here represents only a fragment of the whole. My purpose in displaying the extract is to illuminate how one successful teacher goes about building both oral language and literate behavior in a highly focused way. She and the children jointly construct a shared understanding of the knowledge of an important field of knowledge while also building a shared knowledge of how to talk and read for meaning and interpretation as well as how to construct a written text. The mode is dialogic, and the tenor is that of a supportive teacher to a group of young pupils as she guides their learning.

The teacher had earlier introduced fertilized eggs into the classroom in an incubator, and a range of activities over a series of prior lessons, including reading stories about chickens and cooking and eating eggs in the classroom, had already developed a shared knowledge of a great deal of the field of chickens. In guiding the talk in the extract here, the teacher made use of a little book, *Egg to Chick*, which had been consulted in earlier lessons; with this, she encouraged the children to follow the development of the chicks in the eggs, tracking progress each day by reference both to images and the verbal text. This extract occurred some days into the study. Grouping the children about her on the floor the teacher held up the book and the talk proceeded.

Though the pattern of talk may seem unremarkable, in that the teacher asks questions and the children respond, it should be noted that the familiar Initiation/Response/Evaluation (IRE) pattern (Christie, 2002; Mehan, 1979) does not really apply here. That is because the children are much more productively engaged in the talk than often occurs where the IRE functions.[3] They make constructive contributions to the shared knowledge building while the teacher is supportive of what they say. There is, in fact, a degree of shared pleasure, even excitement, in the way in which the talk unfolds. As Rose (2004) suggests, in this kind of teaching and learning context, earlier joint work and discussion have prepared the children to enter this instance of teaching with a shared basis for learning together. Thus, no child need have the negative experience of giving a wrong answer, and all can feel they have something to contribute.

Text 2.1 An early childhood curriculum genre (extract only). (By kind permission of Continuum International Publishing Group, a Bloomsbury company.)

Note that an ellipsis indicates a short pause in the discourse.

> T: *Ok, so day nineteen. Now let's have a look at our little science book* [holds it up] *and find out where we're up to. Now that was on Friday* [shows a page with "day 16" written on it] *because that was day sixteen.*

This one. [points to the number "16"] *Now we've got seventeen, eighteen* [turns the pages]. *What's the next day?*
Naomi: *Nineteen.*
T: *Day nineteen, and that's today isn't it? And have a look at our little chick now.*
[overlapping]
   Naomi: *It's getting bigger*
   T: *It's getting really big and*
   Naomi: *with long feathers*
T: *With long feathers. Good girl!*
[Three exchanges having to do with a query regarding the number of the page in the book are omitted]
T: *And what can you tell me . . . What can you tell me about the yolk?*
[overlapping]
   Naomi: *It's all gone.*
   David: *It's gone.*
   Naomi: *It's all gone.*
   David: *And he's in a water sac.*
T: *And he's in a water sac.*
Naomi: *If he tried to peck that . . . that egg the water would burst like a balloon.*
T: *That's right. The water bursts, right . . . . The water bursts like a balloon.*
Naomi: *I know what he's getting when he's hatched.*
T: *What?*
Naomi: *He's getting a little tooth.*
T: *Yes, he's getting a little egg tooth. Good girl.*
David: *Here . . . .* [points to picture] *Here's a little egg tooth.*
Jenny: *And that helps him.*
T: *That helps him to . . . That's right. That helps him to peck out of the . . .*
[overlapping]
   Naomi: *Egg*
   David: *Shell*
   Jenny: *Egg*
T: *Yes. Good girl.*
Sylvia: *Look. 'Cause he's getting a little beak there.* [points to picture]

A few minutes later, the talk led to discussion of the role of the incubator in the classroom, compared with that of the mother:

   [overlapping]

T: *'Cause the little chick has to be kept moving*
in the egg so he doesn't get all like . . .
Children: *Yeah*
T: *He needs a bit of exercise in there.* [A comment on the squashed image of the chick in its shell]
[overlapping]

   Jenny: *An' he don't die 'cause the mother hen . . .*
   Sylvia: *We don't have a mother hen. We have an incubator*
   Jenny: *An' he's not hurt in the . . . inside . . . inside the egg.*

T: *That's right. We have an incubator. That's right. That's the water* [points to picture in the book]. *That's the water sac. The water sac stops the little chick from getting hurt if it gets knocked.*
Sylvia: *We don't have mother hen.*
T: *Yeah we don't have*
Sylvia: *If mother hen kicks it, it's going . . . the little chick can't feel it.*
T: *Yeah. Why?*
Children: *Yeah because they're in the water sac.*
T: *Yes, because they're in the water sac.*

Several matters here are worthy of discussion. First, note the frequency with which the children contribute to joint construction of knowledge, so that there is a sense of equality and of a great deal of shared interest in the construction of meaning. In five instances in what is quite a short passage of dialogue, the children's contributions overlap, while there is a notable use of redundancy, apparent when children and teacher repeat each other, making frequent exophoric references to details found in the images in the book:

It's all gone [said three times]
And he's in a water sac
And he's in a water sac
. . . that egg the water would burst like a balloon.
That's right. The water bursts, right . . . The water bursts like a balloon.
He's getting a little tooth
Yes, he's getting a little egg tooth
We don't have a mother hen. We have an incubator
That's right. We have an incubator.
The water sac stops the little chick from getting hurt
Yeah, because they're in the water sac.
Yes, because they're in the water sac.

Redundancy is an important feature of successful classroom talk, involving a frequent revisiting of the information involved, as the discourse shifts from speaker to speaker, allowing meanings to be renewed or reinforced, or both, in different ways.

Another matter of interest in the text is the fact that the children are enabled successfully to handle the uncommonsense meanings and language of science,[4] so that they are learning to enter into some important school knowledge. This is apparent, for example, in several items of technical lexis having to do with the field (*incubator, water sac, mother hen, egg tooth*), but, more tellingly, it is also apparent in the successfully constructed sequences of talk, all of them employing a congruent grammar, consistent with the age group of the children, in which a number of process types are employed, building aspects of the scientific field. Thus, material processes create actions:

> *the water would burst*
> *the mother hen kicks*

and a number of relational processes create states of being related to the chicken:

> *it's getting bigger*
> *he's in a water sac*

The induction into scientific reasoning is apparent in other ways, as the children are enabled to build connectedness between events, creating explanatory observation by using two dependent clauses in marked theme position, each building conditional information:

> **If he tried to peck that . . . that egg** *the water would burst like a balloon*

and:

> **If mother hen kicks** *it, it's going . . . the little chick can't feel it*

whereas another clause builds a reason:

> *Yeah. Why?*
>
> *Yeah,* **because they're in the water sac.**
> *Yes,* **because they're in the water sac.**

Although chicken development is the immediate field of knowledge in construction, the children are also actively engaged in developing skills as readers, though they are not able to read or write independently at this stage of their schooling. The teacher's display of the book, the references to the pages and the numbers marking the days of chicken development in that book, and the uses of its images all constitute apprenticeship into appropriate reading behavior.

In fact, the activity of learning about chickens led to three subsequent lessons in which a written text was produced, and this involved shifts of register and genre. Although the field remained the same, the single most significant shift was with respect to mode, because the move was from the dialogic mode of speech to the monologic mode of written language. Here, learning to write was foregrounded, as the children learned something of the grammar of written language, where, among other matters, endophoric reference was invoked to build a unified coherent text. Even among children from literate households, where reading has been a frequent aspect of their preschool experience, learning to use reference in writing will require some effort, though for children without such a background the effort in learning it is much greater. The children in the classroom text discussed here, as I have already noted, were from Aboriginal families who possessed no books or print materials of any kind. The move into literate behavior was for them a momentous, if exciting, challenge.[5]

The written text was created by the teacher on large sheets of paper on which the children could watch the progress in writing it, assisting where they could as they sat grouped around her. At times the teacher involved them in helping create whole clauses or phrases and at times in spelling words or putting in full stops. Some examples will illustrate:

T [on the second day, pointing to the sheet written the previous day and planning to edit in some extra information]: *We're going to say this next: "His food is the . . .*

T/children together: *"Yolk."*

T: *All right, so we're going to put that little piece . . . we're going to put that little piece in . . . in here* [points to a section of the paper]. *All right so we'll write it in, shall we?*

T: *"His food* [writes as she says this]

Naomi: *"is"*

T: *"is the"* [writes this]

T/Children: *"Yolk."* [writes this]

A little later the teacher asks for help with spelling:

T: *Who can help me with egg? Egg. How do we write that?*

David: *I know.*

T: *Can you help me?*

David: *I know.*

Naomi: *I want to help. I want to help.*

T: *You see if you can write the word "egg."* [Hands the pen to Naomi]

T: *What's "tooth" start with?*
Jenny: *"To"* [an attempt to sound the letter]
Melissa and David: *"T."* [teacher writes "t"]
Naomi: *A "t."*

Later, once the text was completed, it was typed up and made into a classroom book, which the children could read and reread as the year progressed. The finished text, presented below, was a *procedural recount* genre, since it reconstructed the procedural sequence of events involved.[6] The elements of the genre are labelled, though the teacher did not use these labels.

Text 2.2 A procedural recount. (By kind permission of Continuum International Publishing Group, a Bloomsbury company.)

Introduction	We didn't have a mother hen so we used an incubator to keep the eggs warm. The incubator has a thermometer that tells how hot the eggs are. The orange light comes on every time the eggs start to get cold. When the arm* turns over it moves the eggs around to give the little chicks exercise.
Procedure	First, we switched on the electricity and put the eggs in. The little chick looked like a dot. It stays in the egg for twenty–one days. His food is the yolk. The little chick grows a little bit bigger. He grows a tiny head, a tiny heart, tiny eyes and tiny blood vessels. Then he grows tiny ears, tiny wings and tiny legs. Next he grows a tiny tail and a tiny beak. Then he grows tiny feathers and an egg tooth.
	While the little chick is in the egg it is floating in a water sac. When it is twenty–one days the little chick cracks open the egg with his egg tooth. It's hard work. At last the chick is out. He is all wet and weak and wobbly. When he dries out he is soft and fluffy.

*The reference is to the arm of the incubator

The written text constructs most of the details extensively modeled and rehearsed in the classroom talk, so that the experiential information, while simply created, is reasonably comprehensive.

The text uses exophoric reference in referring to class members (*we didn't have a mother hen*). Elsewhere, it successfully uses endophoric reference to build the internal unity required for the written mode here:

*When **the arm** turns over, **it** moves the eggs.*

and

*At last **the chick** is out. **He** is all wet and weak and wobbly.*

However, the overall unity of the text depends on several other resources as well, most notably its successful use of theme choices, sometimes retrieved as given information from a previous clause, as in:

We didn t have a mother hen so we used <u>an incubator</u> to keep the eggs warm.

<u>The incubator</u> has a thermometer . . .

and sometimes by use of a marked theme expressed in a dependent clause of time:

__While the little chick is in the egg__ it is floating in a water sac

or,

__When he dries out__ he is soft and fluffy.

All such theme choices serve to direct the discourse forward, whereas in the cases of the marked themes, they serve, in particular, to foreground important information for the subsequent unfolding of the events.

Overall, the children were inducted into ways of using language to talk about and construct simple scientific meanings while they were also inducted into ways of writing about these meanings. Moreover, they were enabled to do these things long before any of them were capable of doing these things independently. That was because the carefully planned and executed pedagogy supported or scaffolded the children toward a developing understanding of literacy, both its challenges and its possibilities.

The texts we have examined thus far were both constructed in dialogue, though the second—the procedural recount—when finished, was a monologic text, intended to stand alone as a relatively independent written text that could be revisited later on. Although schooling certainly requires capacity to operate in teacher-guided talk, it also values and rewards capacity to speak confidently to a group. Hence, we turn to an activity often found in early childhood classrooms and intended to foster children's capacity to talk in some sustained, relatively independent way. Here, children are encouraged to use language to perform for an audience, and the register and genre values are different from those applying in activities such as the one discussed above. Moreover, the pedagogy involved is very different from that applying in Texts 2.1 and 2.2.

2.3.2 An Instance of Classroom Talk for Performance

In English-speaking countries, a very common practice in the first 2 to 3 years of schooling is to have a morning activity, normally at the start of the day, in which individual children share some item(s) of news. It goes by a variety of names: Sharing Time, Show and Tell, News Time, or simply Morning News. I adopt the general term "Morning News" while noting that, in fact, the activity can involve children in producing one of several genres (Christie, 2002), most of which I do not consider here.[7] The practice of holding activities such as Morning News has been variously justified. Cazden (2001) wrote that sharing time

> may still be the only opportunity during the official classroom "air time" for children to compose their own oral texts, and to speak on a self-chosen topic that does not have to meet criteria of relevance to previous discourse. Sharing time may also still be the only time when recounting events from personal, family, and community life is considered appropriate in school. (p. 11)

Morning news and related activities have also been recognized as sites in which children rehearse the language of early writing, as they are typically involved in narrating about experience in a manner similar to the language of much early writing (Michaels, 1986).

In his study of very early language development, Halliday (1975, 1993) proposed that of the functions for which young children developed an early language—or *protolanguage*—the last to emerge was the "informative" function, because this involved children in telling information to others who were not present at the events described. Painter (2009) recorded a similar observation. A very young child needs mentoring and scaffolding of appropriate language for such an activity. Children who enter school aged five, six, or seven are, of course, long past the protolinguistic stage. Nonetheless, narrating about experience—in particular, telling one's interlocutors about events that occurred when the latter were not present—is a developmentally demanding task, and not all children can do it well. Morning News activities in early childhood education no doubt emerged as a means of assisting young children in learning to handle the language of narration of experience.

The morning news giver is required to address the class group with confidence, normally standing (or sitting in a special chair) in a central position before the other children, who are typically seated on the floor (at least this is true in the Australian experience). One important registerial feature marking the activity as different from classroom activities like that discussed above in Text 2.1 is that the field of discourse is selected by the child from out-of-school experiences, and it potentially covers a wide range of matters. It is in this sense that the pedagogical fields selected are "loosely framed," meaning that the teacher exercises little control over what is selected. However, certain unacknowledged constraints often apply to what can be talked about. The events selected are ideally celebratory, such as a birthday party, the arrival of a baby, a visit to one's grandparents, a family holiday, getting a new toy, and so on.[8] Skilled morning news givers, nonetheless, often select experiences that suggest a degree of naughtiness. The pleasure in telling of such things lies in an appeal to a shared sense of what adults might punish, or at least disapprove, in one's behavior and an associated sense of managing to "get away" with that behavior, as illustrated in the example below.

The example of morning news giving I cite is unusual, in that the text was jointly constructed by two boys who were close friends. In my experience, teachers do not normally allow joint construction in such an activity, because the aim is that an individual gives news (Christie, 2002, pp. 28–62, offers a detailed discussion of Morning News). However, in the instance here, the nominated news giver—Aaron—was very proficient, having proved his skill many times before, and because the teacher was aware of this, she no doubt did not consider the involvement of the second speaker—Stephen—to be an impediment. A great deal of casual storytelling, even in the adult world, involves joint construction (Eggins & Slade, 2005), for the participants enjoy its intersubjective character, and the ease with which the two boys talked in our example was evidence of their shared pleasure. The two boys were aged 6 years, and they were members of a class of about 25 children.

The genre constructed in Aaron and Stephen's morning news giving is an example of what in the SFL tradition has been termed an *anecdote*. This was first described by Plum (1988) in analyzing oral storytelling in adults, and it has been subsequently described and discussed by others, including Martin and Rose (2008). In the SFL tradition, there are several types of story, all having different structures as they achieve different social purposes. A narrative, for example, has a series of events leading to a complication, which is then resolved in some way. The distinctive feature of an anecdote, in contrast, is that it while it also unfolds some event(s) leading to a crisis, or at least an unexpected incident, it is the storyteller's emotional reaction to this crisis that gives "point" to the tale. Although the event and emotional reaction can sometimes be unpleasant, among young children like those reported here, they are normally pleasurable. Here, the tenor of the boys' talk was marked by a strong sense of equality and solidarity in the warmth of their friendship with each other and with their classmates. Their teacher, who was present and standing to the side of the room, was, of course, the authority figure in the situation, though her only contribution to the episode was that she smiled, revealing that she understood the enjoyment of the boys.

I identify the elements of structure in the anecdote as Plum (1988) originally recognized them, though Martin and Rose, cited above, handle them a little differently. The elements here where ^ indicates sequence, are

(Orientation) ^ Events ^Crisis ^ Reaction ^(Completion).

The essential elements are the Event, the Crisis, and the Reaction. The Orientation introduces a person or persons in some setting, of either time or place, in order to initiate the tale. On occasion, the storyteller will commence without an Orientation (hence the brackets around it indicate it is optional), moving immediately to the Events. Typically, the genre finishes with the Reaction, leaving listeners laughing, gasping, or perhaps gesturing in some way. In the text here, a Completion is provided, bringing the text to a close, though this is an optional element, also indicated by the brackets. (Ellipses again indicate pauses in the talk.) A marked theme is shown in bold.

Text 2.3 An anecdote.

Orientation	A: **When Brian was getting the rubbish bins**, *he found this box of old stuff, and he saw this racing car, and he gave it to me. He gave it to me, and the wheel's broken*
Events	*and Stephen came over to my house on Saturday and he saw it* [overlapping] S: *So did Mirko* A: *And Mirko and the car* S: *We got toys down at the creek and um, we was taking it up the hill and rolling it down* [overlapping] A: *Rolling it down* S: *And then we jumped on it* [laughter]
Crisis	S: *and then it came down and rrm! Splash! It had gone down to the river!* [laughter]
Reaction	S: *I didn't even get in trouble when I was soaking wet!* [said on a high rising tone] [laughter]
Completion	A: *And it's up at Ross's place, 'cause I was going to bring it, except Ross said he might try and fix it.* Another Child: *Ross?* A: *Yes, Jodie's dad. My brother's friend.*

The story was very successful in that the whole class laughed loudly, particularly at the Reaction. Wherein lies the success? It lies in the appeal to the shared understandings, first, that young children who take risks by playing near water and getting wet also risk incurring adult reproof and, second, that there is joy to be felt in avoiding such reproof and, as I noted earlier, "getting away with it." Thus, after establishing the context for his tale using a marked theme:

> ***When Brian was getting the rubbish bins*** // *he found this box of old stuff* // *and he saw this racing car*// *and he gave it to me*

Aaron goes on to create a series of Events leading to the Crisis:

> *and then it came down, and rrm! Splash! It had gone down to the river!*

Here the child's excitement is apparent in the emphatically high rising tone of his voice and in the onomatopoeic item *rrm*, followed by *Splash!*, both creating a sense of the speed of the car as it plunged into the creek.

The text is grammatically very simple, for it uses a congruent grammar, creating a series of clauses that, for the most part, are linked additively:

> *He gave it to me* // *and the wheel's broken*// *and Stephen came over to my house on Saturday*// *and he saw it*

The Reaction is constructed through two shifts in the grammar: they are the adoption of negative polarity (*didn't*) where elsewhere the text uses positive polarity, and the use of the modal adjunct (***even***):

> *I **didn't even** get in trouble when I was soaking wet!*

and the other children's reaction of laughter proves the success of the story.

In jointly constructing their tale, Aaron and Stephen were showing themselves already skilled at producing a genre found in the wider context of culture they shared as English-speaking boys growing up in Australia. In that their classmates responded as warmly as they did, they too revealed familiarity with the genre, though they did not necessarily always produce such a genre as well, at least not in the classroom context identified here. Given the simplicity of the genre and its register choices, it would be difficult to claim that children reluctant or unable to produce such a genre "lacked the necessary language," if, by that, for example, we refer to such things as capacity to use negative modality or a modal adjunct, both identified above in the Reaction element. In particular, this is not a matter of dialect, for code and dialect are quite different things (Halliday, 1995; Hasan, 1973/2005; Sadovnik, 2008), though children's difficulties in talking in school are sometimes explained in terms of dialect and the problems of nonstandard dialects. The issue here is one of meaning, to return to issues we addressed earlier: Meanings are encoded in language choices, and individuals select from the meanings available to them in terms of their experience and social location (Hasan, 2002). The two boys involved in joint construction of the genre had a shared understanding of the events they described and a shared sense of the attitudinal significance attached to them, and they could also deploy the necessary language resources to express these matters.

Many children perform well in Morning News, though such an activity is just one of several possible strategies worth pursuing to develop ability to narrate about experience. In practice, Morning News tends to reward those children who are able to take the simple events of out-of-school and family life and elaborate on these in a lively way. Not all children can do this, even those whose mother tongue is English, and second language users often have additional problems. Sometimes the reluctance of children to speak may be a matter of individual difference: Some are more interested or willing than others to be involved. However, for other children, even an activity as apparently simple as reconstruction of personal experience for the purposes of schooling involves particular orientations to making meaning that they do not necessarily possess. That is to say, the activity involves working with certain meaning "codes" that predispose children to select events and shape them in ways that express values and attitudes of a desired, or at least an acceptable, kind (Christie, 2002).

One further observation I would make on Morning News as I have described it is that in that children need to select and talk about personal events beyond school, the teacher, not normally aware of the details of those events, is often unable to help children who struggle to produce coherent discourse for public performance or to identify the values and attitudes expected of them. Teacher efforts to scaffold talk among children who want to share information about activities outside of school often flounder because of this, leaving teachers reduced to creating an interview situation (Christie, 2002), seeking to elicit information about events not shared, where the talk often becomes unproductive. It was because of these problems, among others, that Gray (1999), whose work I cited above, adopted other strategies, more dialogic in character, in working with such children, like those used by the teacher above in the lessons about chickens. The critical issue for Gray, in developing capacity to narrate about experience in a sustained way, was that the teacher and children should share events such as class visits or class activities, reconstructing them in talk, frequently revisiting them over weeks and months, and constantly modeling how to talk about them, so that capacity to narrate about them independently was built over time. The teacher's role in guiding and sharing activity and talk was critical, and eventually many children did develop the facility to offer independent accounts of activities.

It is relevant in this context that Feez (2010), an authority on Montessori educational principles, has noted that activities like "Show and Tell" (her term) are not typically part of the Montessori approach to early childhood education, though strategies to promote oral language are very much part of the tradition. That is because Montessori activities to promote talk are developed in ways involving teacher and student participation, so that they are typically more dialogic than traditional "Show and Tell" activities. Such activities might at times engage children in independent talk of personal experiences, but only after a great deal of opportunity to engage in shared talk, often over some periods of time. A very important principle applies in all these contexts: As a child uses and learns language, so too the child learns how to mean. Capacity to present information to others in a coherent and lively way is an important skill and one well worth cultivating among very young children in the first years of schooling. I have shown one instance of a jointly constructed story told in Morning News in which appropriate register and genre choices were successfully selected and deployed.

2.3.3 A Summary of Matters Discussed in This Section

I have argued that for very young children,

- √ there are important tasks in learning oral language for schooling;
- √ some of these tasks involve learning to participate in teacher-guided class discussion;
- √ other tasks involve learning to talk with a degree of independence in constructing information and ideas;
- √ teacher-guided talk ideally facilitates language learning through joint negotiation of information, creating opportunity for children to contribute to and develop shared understandings of hitherto unfamiliar or uncommonsense knowledge; and
- √ engagement in well-directed class talk prepares young children for the important task of learning literacy.

2.4 Learning Literate Practices

The spoken language, learned in the critical preschool years, is the primary symbolic system for making meaning, and it provides the essential tool for learning with which children enter school and commence a formal education.

It thus necessarily provides the basis on which young children learn "the second order symbolic system" of literacy (Halliday, 1993, p. 109), which develops a new consciousness about the nature of language. The new consciousness involves understanding that knowledge, whether of personal or researched experience, may be taken and essentially reconstructed in the processes of writing about it. An emergent understanding of the uses of a writing system in the human species generally had profound consequences, for it opened up the capacity to record information and communicate it across space to persons in other places and across time, including to future generations. An emergent appreciation of the significance of writing also represents a very significant shift in the understanding of young children. It takes some years before children fully master the writing system.

2.4.1 Some Rudimentary Early Writing

The move into attempting independent writing often accompanies drawings, and because, historically, writing emerged from drawing and painting (Halliday, 1985), it may be that children should be actively encouraged to draw or paint when they first write. Kress (1997) certainly concludes that drawing is one important precursor of early writing. Where children are encouraged to draw and write in school they sometimes produce texts such as Text 2.4, created by a boy called Christopher in his first year of school and aged 6 years. Christopher worked in a classroom in which the teacher encouraged writing about personal experiences, so that the fields for writing, unlike those in the classroom alluded to above in Texts 2.1 and 2.2, were loosely classified, and the directions for writing were also loosely framed, to use Bernstein's terms again. Text 2.4 depicts a green football oval, two figures playing football, and a picture of a little cart. Hence, in terms of mode, the text is written but ancillary to the image.

When he had finished the drawing and the writing he told his teacher that he had written, "Look at me. I'm playing football. I might make a motor cart." (The uncorrected spelling is shown on the image). I note incidentally, that the choice of the opening here, *"Look at me. I'm ..."* was borrowed from some very simple reading books the teacher and her colleagues had created in the classroom as models for the children to read. Hence, it is clear that in this instance Christopher relied on the models available to him, though the rest of the text was his own invention. The child already showed some grasp of the writing and spelling systems, evident in his correct construction of several letters, his awareness of the phonemes many represent (as in his spelling of "fotbol"), his awareness that these are deployed to create words on the page, and in his understanding that the text is to be created by moving from left to

Text 2.4

right across the page. The field is that of football playing, the tenor is intimate, as of a friend to a friend, and the mode is written language accompanying an image.

Another simple text by a classmate called Veronica is found in Text 2.5, written independently after a class visit to an animal shelter. Her teacher had told the class to write about their visit to the animal shelter. The text was written a little later than Text 2.4, and it shows some evidence of development when compared with the latter. Thus, it consists of three equal clauses, linked additively, and, though rudimentary and lexically thin, it is clear and coherent (the spelling is corrected). In mode terms, the language is constitutive of the text, and indeed it needs no image to make its meanings clear.

Text 2.5

We went to see the lost dogs' home // and I saw a cat // and I saw a dog.

Veronica, who was a cheerful, talkative little girl, was capable of much more informative and sustained language production in speech at the time she wrote this. The rather minimal nature of her text tends to support Halliday's claim, referred to above, that children's language regresses for a time as they come to terms with the effort of mastering writing.

2.4.2 Some Later Developments

With time and support, young children learn to produce longer texts, such as Text 2.6, a recount, written by Robyn, in the same class as Christopher and Veronica, though it was written later in the school year. Its field is drawn from out-of-school experience, and its tenor is also intimate and informal; its mode is written language, and language is again constitutive of the text. The text represents a considerable advance on the two previous texts, evident in several ways, and worth noting for their developmental significance: Textually, the recount is well organized, making use of several marked themes to order and progress the text forward; experientially, it expresses more experiential information than the earlier texts, much of that experience found in the range of circumstances Robyn selects, though of course other items have a role; logically, its clauses are linked for the most part by conjunctions of time or addition, both characteristic of the kind of genre produced and the field being dealt with; and interpersonally, it builds an intimate relationship with the intended reader, even selecting some lexis to express attitude.

Although the teacher did not use the term "recount" when encouraging the children to write, the patterns of class talk in Morning News and related activities became a model that Robyn and others used in their writing. The elements of structure of a recount are as follows:

Orientation ^ Record of Events ^ (Reorientation).

The Orientation establishes a person or persons in a setting of either time or space, or perhaps of both. The Record unfolds the events that occurred, and the Reorientation, which is optional, typically rounds the text off.

Text 2.6

Orientation	**On the holidays** Robyn and me went to our friends' house to sleep over for two nights.
Record	Robyn slept in the fold up bed and I slept in the stretcher. Robyn slept in Craig's room. I slept in Ally's room. We all had fun. **When we played in the back yard in the cubby house** we played mothers and fathers. **When it was dark** we put Foot Loose on and turned it up and danced.
Reorientation	Then we went to bed.

This text includes three marked themes, the first of which (expressed in a circumstance of time: *on the holidays*) opens the text, and the other two of which (expressed in dependent clauses of time: *when we played in the back yard in the cubby house*; *when it was dark*) help shape the directions taken in the unfolding of events. These are quite fundamentally involved in creating the overall structure of the text as a recount genre. Experientially, most processes are material (*went*, *slept*, *played*), as is characteristic of recounts, and several circumstances of time and place "flesh out" the meanings expressed in each clause:

- In the Orientation:
  on the holidays: circumstance of time
  to our friends' house: circumstance of place
  for two nights: circumstance of extent

- In the Record:
  in the fold up bed: circumstance of place
  in the stretcher: circumstance of place
  in Craig's room: circumstance of place
  in Ally's room: circumstance of place
  in the back yard: circumstance of place
  in the cubby house: circumstance of place

- In the Reorientation:
  to bed: circumstance of place

Circumstances of time and place are very commonly found in texts by young writers, and this reflects the fact that in their first writing they often recreate personal experience, where matters of spatial and temporal setting tend to be important. Developmentally, nonetheless, the presence of so many circumstances represents an advance on texts such as those in Texts 2.4 and 2.5, because they provide a great deal of experiential information of a kind not found in the other texts. They also add to the lexical density that slowly emerges as a characteristic of written language as children grow older.

One other matter of some developmental interest is the presence of the single clause sentence in the Record: *We all had fun*. Here, using simple lexis (*fun*), the child intrudes into the text a simple evaluation of the events described, providing the reader with a sense of their significance for herself. Attitudinal expression is, of course, more relevant in some genres than in others: It was not so relevant in Text 2.2 above, because that concerned creation of scientific knowledge. It is relevant in a personal recount, though not all young writers include it. As we shall see in later chapters, achieving adequate control of attitudinal expression takes some years, involving mastery of various linguistic resources for writing not yet available to a child as young as the writer of Text 2.6.

Attitudinal expression can be actively cultivated by teachers, as in the example below of an activity in which young children, aged seven and eight, were involved in reading selected storybooks from the school library and in learning to write reviews of these.

2.4.3 Learning to Play with the Grammar for Writing and Expand Meaning

By about age seven or eight, successful children display a growing confidence in control of the grammar of writing, particularly where their learning has been carefully structured toward clear goals. In a classroom in a Sydney primary school, the teacher followed a genre-based approach to teaching writing while she also actively encouraged wide reading and discussion of books from the school library. Among the range of genres considered over the school year for writing, she introduced a *book review*. Genre-based pedagogy in the SFL tradition has been described in several contexts (e.g., Martin, 2009), and I return to it in discussing pedagogical matters more fully in Chapter 6. Suffice it to note at this stage that in a genre-based pedagogy in the SFL tradition, there are equally important goals having to do with teaching the field of knowledge for writing and the target genre for writing. Hence, a great deal of attention is devoted—normally over several lessons—to building the language and the field of knowledge. It is only after some substantial work has gone into this phase, preparing the learners to understand the knowledge they need, that a later phase of discussing and modeling the target genre is introduced. At this stage, an example of the genre is introduced and deconstructed, its elements each considered, and their role in the overall organization or schematic structure of the genre is discussed. A subsequent phase involves joint negotiation and construction of an example of the genre, whereas field knowledge is always in construction. A later phase leads to independent construction of a genre, though only when the teacher judges the children sufficiently skilled to do this.

In the classroom described here, the teacher adopted a simple schematic structure for a book review as follows:

Publishing details ^ Introduction to the novel ^ Description of the novel ^ Judgment of the novel.

The teacher explicitly modeled this book review structure, involving the children in discussing its various elements and their purposes. The children then jointly wrote a book review with their teacher before going on to write independently. They were free to select any novel they liked, so to that extent the children had a degree of independence in their writing. However, because the character and purpose of the target genre were clearly established, to this extent the activity was strongly framed.

Text 2.7, written by Tracey, is about a children's story, *The Sister of the South*, by one of Australia's popular writers for children, Emily Rodda. The text is of interest for several reasons, having to do with the developmental progress that Tracey had made, evident both in her growing grasp of the grammatical organization of written English and in her capacity to express attitude. Here I would draw attention to several noun groups that are expanded through the resource of embeddings and the presence of one marked theme expressing attitude.

Text 2.7

Publishing details	Title: The Sister of the South
	Author: Emily Rodda
	Illustrator: Marc McBride
	Year: 2004
	Place: Sydney
Introduction	I read the book "Sister of the South" by Emily Rodda. It is a chapter book. It is a scary book about a boy king [[who is on a quest]].
Description	This is a story about a boy [[called Lief]]. He is a King. He went on a quest with Jasmine and Barda. The quest is [[to destroy the last of the four sisters]]. They succeed. Then grey slime flooded Lief's Kingdom. Lief calls seven dragons: the dragons of the Diamond, Emerald, Lapus Lazuli, Topaz, Opal, Ruby and Amethyst. The dragons got into a circle in the air and breathed fire into the centre of the circle. It bounced down to the grounds and burnt the grey slime.
Judgment	**In my opinion** this is a great book for older children because it is scary and exciting.

Tracey enjoyed the writing activity, and she took pride in her book review, not least because she had enjoyed the book she selected and wanted to write about it. Like the other texts that emerged in the class, hers was typed up by her teacher for display in the classroom.

It will be noted that here, as in Text 2.6, the grammar is congruent, though there is at least one notable development in the expression not found in the earlier texts we have examined so far. It is the presence of embedded clauses, already alluded to above. In the usual manner in which an English clause functions, it has noun groups within it, as in

I read the book "Sister of the South" by Emily Rodda.

or

It is a chapter book.

However, where a clause appears that is compressed within a noun group, it is said to have a reduced or down-ranked status. It serves a function in compressing relevant information into the noun group, thus expanding its meaning as in

It is a scary book about a boy king [[who is on a quest]].
This is a story about a boy [[called Lief]].

The emergence of such clause embeddings marks an important step in learning to exploit the resources of language. Such a development, according to Painter (1990) and Derewianka (2003), may be thought of as "proto-metaphorical," because it reveals developing capacity to play with language, and it may represent a first step toward metaphorical usage. Moreover, it tends to dispose children toward greater use of abstraction as they grow older. (See also Christie & Derewianka, 2008.) In the two cases I have cited, the clause embeddings are very typically those that emerge first in young writers, for they are used as part of introducing characters in stories and are familiar from stories read to children.

A third instance of an embedding is of interest because it is part of a clause building abstraction, as it defines, using a relational identifying process to do so:

The quest is [[to destroy the last of the four sisters]].

The noun "quest" is of course an abstract noun, whose meaning had been discussed in class and understood from a reading of the book. However, it is clear that the effort to write about it effectively disposed the writer to create quite an abstract expression. Thus may even quite young writers be encouraged to handle abstract meanings.

The latter is an important observation, for it points to a relevant pedagogical issue: The ability to create abstract meanings, like other meanings, needs to be cultivated and developed in significant learning experiences. Children need assistance in creating speculative and abstract meaning. In discussing stories, for example, they need to learn to be helped to explore questions having to do with meanings, values, and purposes (e.g., Christie, 2005, pp. 91–107). This will enable them in time to start to shape abstract ideas, and about this I say a little more below.

To turn to other features of Text 2.7, touching upon matters of the textual metafunction and theme that were discussed earlier, we can note that in the longest element (the Description), the text uses a *presenting reference* to introduce a character:

*This is a story about **a** boy called Lief,*

followed by *presuming references,* so called because they build on what has been presented (Martin, 1992, pp. 93–156):

***He** is a king.*
***He** went on a quest with Jasmine and Barda.*

Even in such a simple way young children are learning to build the endophoric reference needed to give written language a degree of internal unity and cohesion.

The series of theme choices is unmarked, and this is characteristic of such an element, because the object is to identify some phenomenon and describe it. Thus, some items repeat previous theme choices, whereas others retrieve an item from given information in a previous clause, as here, where again a presenting reference is followed by a presuming once:

He went on a quest with Jasmine and Barda.

The quest is to destroy the last of the four sisters

One of the significant tasks of the first phase of literate development is achieving successful control of reference so that texts are appropriately coherent. In fact, reference in English often causes confusion even to native speakers once they start to write texts of any length (Perera, 1984). Moreover, reference is a particular source of difficulty to students of English as a second language, whose languages are different in character, and many of which do not use referential items such as deictics. Speakers of Indonesian, for example, find English reference quite difficult as do speakers of several other Asian and South East Asian languages.

Turning to the clauses in Text 2.7, these are simple, and for the most part they are equal, being linked additively, and some create single clause sentences:

He is a king.
They succeed.

More varied and complex clause interconnectedness will be a later development in the writing of this child.

Although there is some attitudinal expression in the Introduction, attitude appears most fully in the Judgment, where the interpersonal theme choice, *in my opinion*, had been modeled by the teacher, as had been the verb *recommend*. The child states her view, using a clause of reason to enhance it: *In my opinion this is a great book // because it is scary and exciting.*

There is, incidentally, a degree of confusion about tense in the text, evident in the Description element (*He is a king. He went on a quest . . .*). Such confusion appears in writing by older writers too, because English tense is difficult to control in writing, and lapses in texts by such a young writer are not unusual. Tense is itself an interesting aspect of young children's writing in this early phase of schooling, for despite their capacity to handle other tenses in speech, in their writing, at least, young children select either simple present or simple past. The various gradations of other tense choices are not typically found in the writing of the very young. This is another measure of the challenge felt by young children up to eight or nine years in handling written language.

In being encouraged by her teacher to write Text 2.7, Tracey was developing resources for expressing reflection on books read and some evaluation of them. As we have seen, the effort to do this had even taken her into building some abstract meaning. The ability to formulate and express reflection on the details of a novel can be cultivated. Thus, teacher-guided talk should develop around several readings of a shared book, involving consideration of

o the characters in the book and what they did;
o how the characters felt about events that happened and why they felt and acted as they did;
o what was meant by any abstract word like *quest* (or others depending on the book);
o whether the book was a *scary* one and what made it so; and
o why the book had its particular title.

Later talk should then turn to considering

o why people write book reviews;
o what details about a book might be included in a review;
o deconstruction of a model book review, examining its elements and their functions; and
o joint writing of a review about a shared book.

Joint construction will provide the basis for children to move on to later independent construction. Rose (2004), who acknowledges a debt to Gray in his work with disadvantaged Australian Aboriginal children, explains how principles of scaffolding work in teaching Aboriginal students. A related account is given by Martin and Rose (2007a).

2.4.4 Learning to Build Abstraction

Above, we have noted that the young writer of Text 2.7 demonstrated an ability to handle an abstract meaning in her explanation of the "quest" in the book she reviewed. Abstraction can be cultivated and appear in children's writing in many other ways and by reference to various fields of knowledge. Emergent control of abstraction in reading and writing is ideally a development of late childhood. Consider the example of Anna, a child for whom English was a second language (Aidman, 1999). She was, in fact, a bilingual speaker of Russian and English and the daughter of a professional family. She commenced her schooling already confident in her use of Russian and English, though she knew little of the writing systems of either language. With considerable parental support as well as support from her teacher, she developed an early interest in writing English (and her mother encouraged her in mastering the Russian writing system as well).

Educated in a different part of Australia from Tracey, Anna was early interested in the school science program. At age seven and a half, after a class visit, she wrote a short *Report* on the zoo, Text 2.8.

Text 2.8 The zoo.

General Statement	The zoo is a place [[where there are lots of animals]].
Description	The biggest animal [in the zoo] is an elephant.
	The tallest animal [in the zoo] is a giraffe.
	Lots of tourists visit the zoo.

As befits a factual text reporting on the zoo, the tenor of the text is quite formal: the identity of the writer is not revealed, and the *general referents* used to refer to animals and people (***lots** of animals,* ***lots** of tourists*) show the writer seeks to deal with general phenomena rather than personal or specific entities or phenomena. Furthermore, no attitudinal expression is involved in her writing. The text consists of only four single-clause sentences. The first uses an embedded clause and a relational identifying process to build simple definition:

The zoo is a place [[where there are lots of animals]].

The next two sentences use embedded phrases to expand the noun groups, as well as other relational identifying processes to provide descriptive detail:

The biggest animal [in the zoo] is an elephant[9]
The tallest animal [in the zoo] is a giraffe

whereas the last sentence, using a material process, provides detail of another kind:

Lots of tourists visit the zoo.

Text 2.8 does not, of course, deal in abstraction, though it reveals a writer aware that she is *generalizing* about aspects of experience rather than dealing with specific or individual aspects, so that she is achieving some control of elements of a scientific register, relevant to later developments in achieving scientific abstraction. It is of interest to see what the same child wrote a few months later, when she had just turned eight. Text 2.9 emerged from a class study of soil erosion, a significant problem in many parts of rural Australia.

Text 2.9 Erosion.

General Statement	*Erosion is the gradual wearing away of the soil by wind, running water, waves and temperature.*
Description	*Rabbits cause a lot of damage to the land. Removing all the trees causes the soil to become loose and it is easily blown or washed away.*

The text, although very short, reveals much greater abstraction, this time achieved with an example of a nominalization. It will be recalled that the expression "nominalization" refers to those instances where meanings typically expressed in verbs in the English grammar are changed to express them as nouns or noun groups, thus creating phenomena about which we can develop discussion. This is a form of grammatical metaphor. The example given by Anna appears in her opening General Statement:

Erosion is the gradual wearing away of the soil by wind, running water, waves and temperature.

The nominalization in *the gradual wearing away of the soil by wind, running water, waves and temperature* represents an abstraction, used to introduce and define a technical term—*erosion*. Expressed as speech, much as probably applied in the classroom talk preparatory to writing, this would be:

"Wind, running water, waves and temperatures wear away (or erode) soil. This is called erosion."

Turning to the Description element, we find an opening causative process in the first sentence:

*Rabbits **cause** a lot of damage to the land*

The second sentence makes use of another causative process, and there is another instance of grammatical metaphor here in the three clauses involved:

> *Removing all the trees **causes** the soil to become loose // and it is easily blown // or washed away.*

Expressed as speech the whole sentence would be as follows, creating four separate clauses rather than the three in the written text:

> *"If you remove all the trees // the soil becomes loose // and it is easily blown away by the wind // or washed away by water."*

Note how the conditional clause *if you remove all the trees* disappears in the grammatically metaphorical expression, its meaning buried in the verbal group *causes*.

It is by deconstructing grammatically metaphorical expressions in this way that we can see why they are often difficult for children to comprehend. The reasoning and interpretation that would otherwise be expressed in clauses linked by conjunctions creating logical connectedness between events are removed, even buried in the grammatically metaphorical form. Interpretation and comprehension of meanings are thus often made very difficult for learners, whether advantaged or not. As already noted in Chapter 1, grammatical metaphor appears, at the earliest, by late childhood, typically by about age nine, though in many children it emerges much later, and others struggle to come to terms with it at all (Christie & Derewianka, 2008). Early evidence of some emergent capacity to handle abstraction expressed in grammatical metaphor is one useful measure of children's developmental growth in control of literacy. Equally, its apparent absence in the language of learners becomes a measure of their learning difficulties.

Thus, in guiding the reading of any new and unfamiliar texts teachers should

o prepare the learners initially by providing relevant information about the field of information to be read, using unfamiliar and technical vocabulary items in speech, to establish in advance something of their sound and their meanings;

o establish goals in reading the text, indicating the kinds of information to be gathered from the text;

o jointly read the passages from the text, stopping frequently to discuss meanings of words; and

o identify any instances of grammatical metaphor (and of abstract nouns and technical terms) and express their meanings in the more familiar or commonsense language of speech, encouraging the learners to talk about the meanings, achieving familiarity with them.

Conversely, in guided writing of texts teachers should

- o prepare the learners by active exploration of the field of information as well as the target genre for writing;
- o work with the learners in joint writing about the field, constructing the genre, its elements and its various sentences; and
- o build uses of technical language by exploring and contrasting grammatically metaphorical and nonmetaphorical ways to express meanings, even playing with spoken versions and exploring how to turn these into more written forms.

2.4.5 A Summary of Matters Discussed in This Section

I have argued that

- √ the entry to literate behavior marks a significant challenge for young learners, involving the need to learn the spelling and writing systems as well as some aspects of the grammar of writing;
- √ so great is the challenge that the early writing that children produce is grammatically simpler than their speech and their language actually regresses for a time;
- √ their first efforts in writing rely very heavily on the models available to them in speech;
- √ with appropriate scaffolding and modeling of relevant language patterns, children gain a developing confidence in both reading and writing;
- √ in writing they move from grammatically simple to more complex texts, apparent in capacity to express a growing volume of information, expressed both in prepositional phrases that create circumstances and in embeddings within noun groups;
- √ among successful children, by late childhood emergent control of writing brings with it some capacity to express abstraction, evident in some control of nominalization.

2.5 Conclusion

In this chapter I have outlined major developments in young children's learning of oral language and literacy in the first years of schooling. I commenced the discussion with some reflections on the differential preparedness of young children for the language of schooling, noting that children of some "social locations," to use Hasan's (2002) term, function better than others in schooling. I thus noted the need for teachers to be alert to social differences, actively scaffolding children's learning of relevant language in speech and in literate language. I went on to argue, with respect to oral language, that young children have important tasks for schooling, some of which involve learning to participate in teacher-guided class discussion, contributing to and developing shared understandings of hitherto unfamiliar knowledge, and others of which involve learning to talk with a degree of independence in constructing information and ideas.

Both sets of activities involve taking up relevant language choices in terms of all the metafunctions. Classroom talk like that reviewed in Text 2.1, for example, is dialogic, where the teacher's role in asking questions and guiding talk is important, though the roles of the children are also important: They are enabled to contribute to the discourse, both shaping responses to questions and offering relevant information, as they learn to handle the language of an unfamiliar field of uncommonsense knowledge. In a monologic situation, in which a child becomes a giver of news—whether in the formal activity of Morning News or some other—the child takes up a different role. Here the role is to (re)create personal experiences for the audience of one's class peers. This involves selection of a field of experience and constructing and shaping the information in such a way that the talk is intelligible and ideally entertaining, or at least interesting.

Engagement in class talk also prepares young children for the important task of learning literacy, a challenge that looms large in the first years of school. Here again there are developments across all metafunctions and their associated linguistic features. Thus, some sense of text unity and text direction is achieved through mastery of theme and thematic progression, coupled with emergent control of reference. Some sense of ways to create and link clauses appears, initially by means of deploying equal clauses linked by additive conjunctions; a little later, dependent clauses that enhance meaning are deployed, typically introduced by temporal (*when*) and some reason conjunctions (*because*), though much depends on the fields and genres involved. The experiential information expressed within clauses is expressed in the transitivity elements of participants, processes, and any circumstances: Participants (realized in noun groups) tend to expand by means of embedded clauses or embedded phrases, processes (expressed in verbal groups) remain reasonably simple, whereas circumstances, initially very sparse, tend to emerge a little later, expressed in prepositional phases, typically of time (*on the holidays*) and place (*in the back yard*). Interpersonally, relevant mood choices are mastered fairly readily by most children, though associated resources having to do with expression of attitude are normally expressed in simple lexis such as *we had fun*. However, where, as in the book review I discussed, resources for attitudinal expression are modeled by the teacher, interpersonal themes (*in my opinion*) can be introduced. Equipped with all the facility they should have achieved by about age eight to nine, children who move successfully into late childhood and early adolescence—the second of the phases I have proposed—show significant developments in their control of oral and literate language, as we shall see in Chapter 3.

Notes

1 As some readers of this volume will be aware, when the terms "restricted" and "elaborated" codes were first proposed by Bernstein some years ago, they sparked an often heated controversy, some legacy of which remains in some places even today. Critics attacked his work for a variety of reasons. However, the principal one was that the notion of a "restricted code" was understood to suggest a "deficit theory"—some kind of cognitive deficit or failure among those who used the code. It was held to diminish the often poor children understood to use the code while also denying the actual capacities in life such children possessed. Critics included Labov (1969), Rosen (1973), Stubbs, (1983), and Trudgill (1983), among others. However, the criticisms rested on a serious misreading of the very carefully explained research that Bernstein and his colleagues had provided, in at least two senses. First, he had proposed that all speakers, working-class and middle-class, used both codes, and the restricted code was frequently used in the intimate interplay of familial and communal life. However, middle-class speakers, he suggested, also used an elaborated code not readily available to many working-class speakers. The second sense in which the critics confused the issue was that code has nothing to do with intelligence or cognition anyway; rather, it depends on the social positioning of people, where this certainly embraces aspects of social class, but it also embraces aspects of cultural values, beliefs, and ideology. A brief response to the critics may be found in Christie (1999b), and more detailed responses are offered by Bernstein (1990, pp. 94–130), Hasan (2005, 2009), and Moore (in press).

2 Such a rigorous and exhaustive study is not easy to summarize quickly. See, in particular, Hasan (2009) and Williams (1999, 2005a) for detailed discussions.

3 In fact, I would argue that IRE is a defensible element of classroom talk, which can usefully occur in sequences of talk where it functions along with other patterns (Christie, 2002; Gibbons, 2004; Wells, 1993).

4 I introduced the notion of commonsense experience in Chapter 1 when writing of the tendency of young children and their tendency to build largely familiar and commonsense experience. The notions of commonsense and uncommonsense experience are taken from Bernstein (1975), who wrote, "In a sense, educational knowledge is uncommonsense knowledge. It is knowledge freed from the particular,

the local, through the various languages of the sciences or forms of reflexiveness of the arts which make possible either the creation or the discovery of new realities" (p. 99).

5 Adams (1994, p. 8) stated that "in the typical American home, parents read to their preschoolers daily—resulting in hundreds and thousands of hours of literacy exposure prior to school entry": No doubt a very similar observation could be made of many children in Australia. The disadvantages experienced by children who lack such exposure are thus very obvious.

6 The term "procedural recount" is found in discussions of genres in several places (e.g., Christie & Derewianka, 2008; Martin & Rose, 2008; Unsworth, 2000, 2002). There are variations in the manner in which such a genre is described, though its essential component will be an element that involves reconstruction of a procedure, as in a science experiment. In the classroom studied here, the teacher worked with a range of factual texts that she distinguished from stories and other text types.

7 For example, the genres may include more than one type of story (e.g., narrative, anecdote), whereas activities of "show and tell" typically involve display of toys and other items, where narration of event is not an issue.

8 Michaels (1986) cites an instance of a child telling of a sad event, though in my observation such things are uncommon. However, I note that one of the anonymous reviewers who read and wrote useful comments on a draft of this manuscript, stated that in her experience (I assume it was a woman!) talk of such matters is not unusual in American early childhood classrooms today.

9 Embedded phrases, as distinct from embedded clauses, can be displayed using single brackets: []. I do not make a regular practice of displaying them, though I do so now to demonstrate that they represent yet another means of expanding relevant information in language.

CHAPTER 3

Late Childhood to Early Adolescence: Some Transitional Years

3.1 Introduction

This chapter discusses language and literacy development from late childhood to early adolescence, when children are about 9 to 12 or 13 years of age. These are the years of transition from the upper primary to the junior high school, when the nature of the school curriculum changes, as the claims of different school subjects emerge, building what are sometimes called "subject-specific literacies" (e.g., Unsworth, 2002). The character of the school day also changes, with children needing to adjust to working with several subject specialists as their teachers, rather than with the individual teacher who is typically found in the primary classroom. Children must learn to construct new, more abstract meanings, where these involve mastering new registers and genres and, necessarily, the grammatical patterns in which these are realized. Schooling represents an initiation into many things valued in an English-speaking culture: forms of knowledge; ways of asking and answering questions about such knowledge; ways of evaluating knowledge, information, experience, and ideas; and habits of reasoning and analytic practices of various kinds, depending on the school subject studied.

All these many forms of knowledge, procedures, and practices—creating subject specialisms—are expressed in language, sometimes in the constitutive sense, in that language alone realizes what is involved, and sometimes in an ancillary sense, in that language is ancillary to, or complementary of, other semiotic modes, like graphs, images, tables, diagrams, and so on. As I noted in Chapter 1, in the contemporary world of multiliterate practices, meaning in many texts resides in an intimate interplay between verbal and nonverbal resources, so that a clear distinction between texts that are constitutive of language and others that are not is not always valid. There are considerable challenges in learning to read, manipulate, and create images, diagrams, formulas, graphs, and figures. These are matters discussed by Kress (2003), Unsworth (2008), Chan and Unsworth (2011), and Daly and Unsworth (2011), among others. Nonetheless, as Macken-Horarik (2008) has also shown, at least with respect to senior English studies, the requirement to read, view, and interpret a range of multimodal resources often leads to the need to produce a written text that is constitutive of meaning. She refers to English examination papers for senior students in the Australian state of New South Wales, in which they are required to interpret such things as photos, a comic strip, and even a speech by a new member of parliament, making some kind of connection between such disparate resources. The point to be noted, according to Macken-Horarik, is that although the reading challenge is considerable, there remains a fundamental challenge to produce a written essay. Control of writing continues to be a critical issue even in the multiliterate world of the 21st century.

Of course, the move into meaning making beyond the immediacies of local or commonsense experience commences in the primary years. However, the transition from the primary to the secondary school initiates a more fundamental apprenticeship into the subject specialisms. It is quite profound in its consequences, for it takes young people increasingly into the realms of uncommonsense experience and knowledge, where they must come to terms, in time, with abstraction, generalization, interpretation, evaluation, and judgment, all of them involving meaning making that is increasingly abstract and "free of localistic assumptions and dependencies" of the kind associated with familiar commonsense experience (Butt, 2004, p. 218). Moreover, once possessed of capacities to handle knowledge and experience in the terms suggested, the meaning-making potential available to individuals will need to be "transportable" (Butt, 2004, p. 218), in that it can be used in a range of complex and often unseen future situations, for the complex contemporary global world requires nothing less than significant transportable skills.

It is because the challenges of learning in the late childhood to early adolescence transition are so considerable that many young people struggle and fall behind, their oral language and literacy not strong enough to deal with the apparently invisible demands. It is in literate skills in particular that school performance is increasingly measured and where children flounder; this is often because they fail to master the discursive and grammatical features of written language, where these are either encountered in their reading or required in their writing. The children involved may, and often do, present with a degree of proficiency in face-to-face interaction, so that the depth of their difficulties is to that extent somewhat obscured. Their difficulties arise from dealing with the more abstract written language of the uncommonsense knowledge of school subjects, and although the children involved are often students for whom English is a second language (Gibbons, 2004), many others include those I alluded to in Chapter 2, whose social backgrounds and out-of-school experiences do not always equip them well to deal with school learning. Thus, they are at times native speakers of English, yet they function with meaning codes other than those rewarded, or at least foregrounded, in the practices of schooling. A pedagogy for deliberate intervention and guidance is required, deconstructing and modeling the kinds of text types that children need to speak, read, and write and teaching a relevant metalanguage where this is useful. In this context, both Delpit (2006) and Sadovnik (2008), referred to in Chapter 2, have noted the apparent success of schools in the United States that use explicit, rather than implicit, pedagogies and which are concerned to create a structured curriculum experience in which knowledge is strongly defined, the various areas of the curriculum clearly delineated.

I commence this discussion by considering grammatical differences between speech and writing, for though I have mentioned this topic in earlier discussions, it is appropriate now to look more directly at the issue because of its relevance for the transitional years I have identified. I argue that because the differences between the two become more marked as children grow older, it is important for teachers to be aware of them, the better to assist their students' learning. As a general principle, written language moves away from the immediacies of speech, allowing the expression of increasingly abstract meanings, often of an uncommonsense kind. Speech is dynamic and "grammatically intricate" (Halliday, 1985, p. 87), in that it creates its meanings through strings of interconnected clauses as we speak. Written language, on the other hand, is static and lexically dense, expressing its meanings through dense passages of writing. Neither speech nor writing is "better" than the other, for they serve different purposes. However, the fact remains that for the purposes of schooling, control of the written mode is critical, and nowhere is this more apparent than in secondary school learning, where an adequate grasp of the grammar of writing is essential.

Aspects of the grammatical differences between speech and writing having been established, I go on in later sections of this chapter to examine in some detail developmental changes in the transitional years of late childhood to early adolescence. I develop the discussion around texts selected from three broad curriculum areas, all found in English-speaking cultures, though their character no doubt differs from place to place. They are social studies (a general term used here to cover such subjects as history, geography, and, in the Australian context at least, environmental studies), English, and science. These are selected partly because they throw light on the "subject-specific specialisms" I have alluded to above and partly because they show several students coming to terms with the increasingly abstract meanings that a secondary schooling requires. The texts used in this discussion are drawn from Australian experience, more specifically my own research over a number of years, already referred to in Chapter 1, and the discussion and analysis are, in addition, informed by a great deal of SFL research in Australia (e.g., Martin & Rose, 2008; Rose, 2009) and in other parts of the English-speaking world, including work by Coffin (1997, 2004, 2006), who writes of subject history in both Australia and the United Kingdom, and Schleppegrell, who writes of a range of school subjects, including English, history, and mathematics in the American school context (2004, 2007, 2011; Schleppegrell, Achugar, & Oteíza, 2004; Fang & Schleppegrell, 2008).

3.2 Differences between Speech and Writing

In his discussion of the differences between speech and writing Halliday (1985) observed that in the history of the human species "writing evolves in response to needs that arise as a result of cultural changes" (p. 39). Such changes included, for example, the move away from nomadic lifestyles toward those involving more settled communities, where, among other things, provision and exchange of goods and services occurred and divisions of labor appeared. The settled lifestyle encouraged the emergence of many new social and cultural practices, including those for recording information and ideas and communicating these to others over space (e.g., in different towns, cities, and even countries) and over time (e.g., in creation of permanent records and advice for future generations). These developments, over quite long periods of time, led to the emergence of writing systems. Just as language as speech had evolved over the millennia, so too did language as writing evolve, though much later in time, both being part of the processes of *phylogenesis* of language in the human species.

The processes of the *ontogenesis* of language and literacy in children bear some parallel to those of phylogenesis, in at least two senses. First, there is a parallel in that considerable proficiency in the spoken mode needs to be established before children start to learn literacy, and, as we saw in Chapter 2, much of what they write at first has features of the grammar of speech. The other sense in which there is a parallel lies in the fact that children need to accumulate sufficient life experiences in order to develop an awareness of the meaning potentiality available to them in literacy: this enables them to enter into many social and cultural practices that would be otherwise closed to them. Although learning these practices starts early in life, particular challenges emerge, as I have already suggested, in the late childhood to the years of early adolescence, as young people start to mean in new ways.

At this point, we turn to the school experience of a student called David, 12 years old and in his first year of a secondary schooling. He was one of a class of students in an inner city high school in Melbourne, and he was a native speaker of English. His English teacher had initiated a major unit of study on stories and storytelling. One aspect of the study involved all the children in the class in telling a story about some personal event, which could be embarrassing, frightening, or funny, in which they had been involved. After devoting two lessons to hearing all the stories, the class teacher asked the students to create written versions of their stories. He intended that they should eventually discuss the differences, with a view to bringing to consciousness some of the choices the students made in creating their tales as they did in the two modes.

Text 3.1 represents David's oral story, and analysis of the text reveals that it is an instance of an anecdote genre, an example of which we have already examined in Chapter 2. It will be recalled that anecdote is a name adopted in the SFL genre tradition (e.g., Martin & Rose, 2008; Plum, 1988) to refer to one of several types of stories that English speakers can select to use. It will also be recalled that an anecdote unfolds some event(s) leading to a crisis, or at least some very unexpected incident. In speech, it is the storyteller's emotional reaction that gives "point" to the tale, its presence often acknowledged by the responses of interlocutors, either in a laugh of pleasure or a gasp of shared horror. The anecdote is, in fact, a very familiar genre in the Australian culture (it may be in other cultures as well), and it was a matter of some interest to me that the same spoken genre emerged among students of different ages and living in different cities. Both the younger students whose anecdote was discussed in Chapter 2 and David, whose work will be discussed below, demonstrated a shared understanding of a quite important genre in the oral discourse of Australia: one that allows the construction and communication of values and ideas of an amusing and entertaining kind.

The text is set out with the elements labeled: The Orientation introduces the storyteller in a setting and the Events, Crisis, and Reaction are so brief in this case that they are displayed together. The grammar of the text is congruent. The marked themes are shown in bold and the text is displayed as David spoke it. Ellipses indicate short pauses in the text.

Text 3.1 David's story of being Superman.

Orientation	***When I was younger, I'm not sure how old***, *I just saw Superman for the first time . . . and* ≪***after I'd seen it***≫, *I thought I could fly*
Events/ Crisis/ Reaction	*so I climbed up to the top of my mezzanine, jumped off and landed on my brother and he had to . . . he got injured, but I came out all right but he had to go to hospital.* [The last clause said on a high rising note, and David grins as he speaks it. Loud laughter from the other members of the class.]

David has stood to face the class with pleasure, smiling as he talks, and the concluding burst of laughter from the class reveals that the other students have understood and shared his sense of the rather naughty thing he has done. It is in this shared sense of pleasure in the story that the emotional reactions of David and his audience are expressed. In fact, an oral anecdote depends for its success very much on the implicit nature of the attitudes involved. Though very brief, the little text successfully creates its Orientation, using two marked themes, strategically placed, to establish the context and the experiential information having to do with the film of Superman and his response to it:

> ***When I was younger, I'm not sure how old***, *I just saw Superman for the first time . . . and* ≪***after I'd seen it***≫ *I thought I could fly.*

The start of the next element is signaled with the conjunction of consequence, *so*:

> *so I climbed up to the top of my mezzanine, jumped off and landed on my brother.*

David's emotional reaction to events commences when he says:

> *he got injured*

and he uses a contrastive conjunction to help establish his own well-being:

> ***but*** *I came out all right*

and going on immediately to use a second such conjunction to introduce the clause that offers the "punch line":

> ***but*** *he had to go to hospital*

for he is here acknowledging the problem he caused. The contrast between David's own state of good health and that of his brother provokes the shared mirth.

The text is lexically quite thin, and we can demonstrate this by setting it out clause by clause, revealing the lexical or content words in each clause, much as Halliday (1985) suggests one can do. Even among adults, such casual conversation is lexically thin, and the grammar is congruent. (Lexical words are shaded.)

When I was younger
I'm not sure how old
I just saw *Superman* for the first time
and ≪after I'd seen it≫ I thought
I could fly
so I climbed up to the top of my mezzanine
jumped off
and landed on my brother
and he had to ... he got injured
but I came out all right
but he had to go to hospital.

The written version, Text 3.2, is another anecdote (though it could have been some other story genre, such as a narrative), and its elements are generally longer than in Text 3.1. Experientially, the text is more detailed, fleshing out aspects of what is narrated in a number of ways. This is in part a condition of the difference in mode: in speech one has the advantages of face-to-face interaction, with all the benefits of facial expression, tone of voice, and gesture, whereas in writing one needs to provide detail, including in particular attitudinal detail. In fact, it is the quite rich attitudinal detail that most marks the differences between Texts 3.1 and 3.2.

Text 3.2 The written version of David's story.

Orientation	**A few years ago, ≪when I was three or four years old≫**, my brother brought home a video of Superman, and said, 'No one can watch, it's for my eyes only'. **So typically ≪as soon as Timmy had gone out≫**, I put it in the VCR and started to watch it. It was the most amazing movie [[I had ever seen]].
Events	**After the movie** I had nothing much to do, so I decided to test MY super powers. We had a mezzanine floor in our house. I climbed to the very top and it took me a while [[to get psyched]].
Crisis	**For the few seconds [[that I was in the air]]**, I realized something. The door was open, my brother was in the room, but **by then** it was too late. Not even my super powers could save

| | him. Crash! I clobbered my poor innocent brother and brought him to the ground. My super powers were enough [[to break my fall]], but unfortunately my brother had to go to the local hospital for a week. |
| Reaction | And I've never had to use my super powers since. |

David's attitudinal response to the events in the tale and his efforts to communicate these to his interlocutors are evident in several ways. We can note, for example, that he expresses some affect (or feeling) concerning his brother, some appreciation (or evaluation) of the film, and some judgment of the propriety of his own actions (Martin & White, 2005). Thus, offering judgment of his own behavior he notes that *typically* he put on the VCR:

as soon as Timmy had gone out

and he then offers appreciation of the movie:

it was the most amazing movie I had ever seen

while he also alludes ironically to his own capacities:

I decided to test MY super powers

He later expresses some feeling of remorse:

I clobbered my poor innocent brother

and again:

unfortunately my brother had to go to the local hospital for a week.

Emotional and attitudinal expression are much more evident in the written text than in the spoken text, and that is a consequence of the shift in the mode here. All the advantages in speech of face-to-face interaction, body movement, and facial expression as well as gesture are removed for the purposes of writing.

Turning to the linguistic organization of the text, we can see that, like Text 3.1, Text 3.2 relies on several marked themes of time to help unfold the story:

A few years ago, ≪when I was three or four years old≫, my brother brought home a video of Superman
So typically ≪as soon as Timmy had gone out≫, I put it in the VCR

In an unmarked way these would read:

> *A few years ago, when I was three or four years old, my brother brought*
> *home a video of Superman*
> *so typically I put it in the VCR as soon as Timmy had gone out*

As noted in Chapter 1, this capacity to use enclosed dependent clauses in marked theme position is a relatively late development in children's writing, typically emerging in late childhood to early adolescence. It reveals developing confidence in playing with what can be made thematic and developing skill in handling the grammatical organization of written discourse. The presence of such a phenomenon here is one measure of the fact that the writer is older than those whose texts were considered in Chapter 2.

The text has greater lexical density than Text 3.1. According to Halliday (1985), lexical density can be established by counting the lexical items in a text and dividing them by the number of ranking clauses (embedded clauses are thus not included, as they operate within the clauses). He writes, "a typical average lexical density for spoken English is between 1.5 and 2, whereas the figure for written English settles down somewhere between 3 and 6, depending on the level of formality in the writing" (Halliday, 1985, p. 80). The density in Text 3.1 is about 1.5, whereas that in Text 3.2 is about 2.75.[1]

The text is displayed thus:

a few years ago when I was three or four years old
my brother brought home a video of *Superman*
and said
"No one can watch
it's for my eyes only."
so typically I put it in the VCR
as soon as Timmy had gone out
and started to watch it.
it was the most amazing movie [[I had ever seen]]
after the movie I had nothing much to do,
so I decided to test MY super powers
We had a mezzanine floor in our house.
I climbed to the very top
and it took me a while [[to get psyched]]
for the few seconds [[that I was in the air]], I realized something.
the door was open,
my brother was in the room
but by then it was too late

not even my super powers could save him
Crash!
I clobbered my poor innocent brother
and brought him to the ground.
my super powers were enough [[to break my fall]]
but unfortunately my brother had to go to the local hospital for a week
and I've never had to use my super powers since.

Text 3.2 is grammatically different from Text 3.1, revealing some of the characteristics of written language, even though its grammar is congruent, its field of knowledge remains the same, and its tenor is quite informal. Students can be usefully engaged in exploring the differences between spoken and written texts like these. In the example used here, for example, they might

- o Discuss the schematic structure in each text, considering the function of each. For example, they could examine the Orientations in both cases and consider why the writer found it necessary to tell his readers his age at the time of the events; in the Events, they might consider why the writer told of the fact that he "had nothing much to do," and why in the Crisis he told his readers that "for the few seconds that I was in the air I realized something." They might also consider why David told his readers "and I've never had to use my super powers since." They could also consider the effect if the Reaction were left out altogether: what difference does it make and what is its purpose?
- o Discuss why the written mode requires the provision of rather more contextual information than the spoken, and consider what this tells us of the functions of writing rather than of speech
- o Identify all the language items where attitude is expressed in both texts and then consider their significance. What happens in the case of the written text if we remove most, or all, of the attitudinal language from the text?
- o Discuss the humor in the two texts: Why are they funny?
- o Discuss why the activity of writing about a topic tends to produce a distancing effect. What does this tell us of the relative advantages and disadvantages of writing and of speech?

Finally, as a further activity, students could be involved in their own activities of telling stories of their own experiences, using these for subsequent writing activities as well.

All such discussion and related talk and writing of stories can encourage a developing understanding that language is a resource or tool to be manipulated, rewarding in its potential for making meaning in different modes. Its patterns are to be comprehended but also played with in order to explore and expand its meanings.

3.2.1 A Summary of Matters Discussed in This Section
I have sought to establish that

- √ speech is dynamic, unfolding in a series of interconnected clauses;
- √ writing is static and dense, compressing its meanings particularly in its lexis;
- √ written language tends to create meanings that are distanced from activity;
- √ speech allows a great deal of expressive meaning in tone of voice, facial expression, and gesture. Written language, on the other hand, at least for the purposes of storytelling, often requires use of attitudinal language that gives color to the story, and the written mode frequently requires more explicit expression of attitude than does the oral mode.

These broad understandings about the grammatical differences between speech and writing having been established, I now turn to the first of the texts to be considered here as part of studying the processes by which in late childhood to early adolescence young people need to achieve a growing mastery of the grammar of writing.

3.3 Writing Social Studies in Late Childhood

Texts 3.1 and 3.2 were both experientially very simple, drawing on familiar or commonsense experience. The challenge in producing either of them was not primarily one of selecting a field of knowledge, but rather one of crafting the text in each case for pleasure and entertainment. Creation of both was an exercise in verbal art, and the English teacher used them to develop some awareness of the nature of stories and their purpose. A great deal of schooling, however, involves students in working with researched or unfamiliar knowledge, or both, to some of which we now turn.

Text 3.3 is a recount genre written by Tom, age nine, a native speaker of English. At the time he wrote the text, he was in Year 4 of primary school. This is one of a number of texts written by Tom that I have collected since he was 8 years old, following his school career over the primary and secondary years, so that at the time of writing this chapter he was in the last year of his secondary school education. I collected his first texts as part of the database I amassed in preparing a study of children's writing development with Derewianka (Christie & Derewianka, 2008), and I have continued to collect texts to add to that database. We examine another text of his in Chapter 4.

We have already seen a recount of personal experience written by a young child of six in Chapter 2. A recount genre is one of the several types of story genres described by SFL theorists (e.g., Martin & Rose, 2008), its most distinctive characteristic being that it unfolds a series of events in time, so that temporal sequence is important. Tom's recount records details of a class visit made to two sites of historical interest in Sydney, known as "The Rocks" and "Hyde Park Barracks." The former is famous because English people settled there early in the days of the then penal colony in the late 18th century, and it retains a number of its oldest buildings. The barracks were convict built in the early 19th century, and they are preserved today as part of Australian colonial history. Class visits to such places are part of learning about Australia's social history. The text is of interest for a number of reasons, including the fact that two fields of experience are recreated. One concerns the details of family and class activity, where Tom draws on commonsense experience having to do with home and school, whereas the other concerns the uncommonsense history of the sites visited and some reflection on matters observed and learned. In his meaning making, Tom shows himself moving easily between the two fields, and it is of some interest that his conclusion—really a Coda—shows him reflecting on the historical information he had gained.

An older student might well have been invited to write another genre, perhaps a *site study* (Christie & Derewianka, 2008, p. 106), in which the details of family and class would not be considered and in which attitudinal expression—if any—would be of a different kind. As it is, the recount genre here, and its register values, create a transitional text, one in which the student is moving toward capacity to build the uncommonsense knowledge of a subject specialism—history—while also drawing on personal or commonsense fields of experience to write the text.

Text 3.3 has several other features worthy of comment. Like the earlier texts, its grammar is congruent, and Tom shows himself able to exploit the resources of noun group structure and prepositional phrase to flesh out the experiential information he creates. Textually, the text is well organized, its thematic progression confident. Interpersonally, the text creates strong attitudinal values, mainly those of affect, expressing Tom's feelings, though some involve evaluation of matters seen or learned. Logically, the clauses are linked by various conjunctive relationships, showing some grammatical intricacy (Halliday, 1985; Halliday & Matthiessen, 2004) in sequencing and linking different clause types. Marked topical themes are displayed in bold and embedded clauses are also noted. Where clauses occur within embeddings, these are also noted (//) in order to reveal one of the ways in which experiential information gets packed into the text. It contributes to the density that is a feature of written language.

Text 3.3 Hyde Park Barracks.

Orientation	I woke up excited, for **today** we were going to The Rocks and Hyde Park Barracks. I immediately rocketed out of the bedroom and into the living room where I bolted down breakfast, then zoomed out the door and leaped into the car.
Record	**At school** Mrs. Brown* made sure everyone was here and **almost instantly** we had piled into the bus and were speeding off towards the Rocks. We weren't on the bus very long but it seemed like it for there wasn't any air conditioning. **When we arrived at The Rocks** we were split into two groups and walked off with the tour guide who showed us the convicts' houses [[where the bakery was]] and a map of Sydney Cove which had a name of a place, and its Aboriginal translation. **At the end of the tiring tour** we climbed onto a train which took us to Hyde Park barracks.

As we walked off the platform I started to chew on lollies. I visualized what the barracks would look like. **Almost immediately** I found out what it did look like. It was lots of tiny offices [[surrounding a humungous convict jail // which is now a museum]]. **In the past** the convicts would stumble out of the giant building and slump towards the main officers' window to collect their tools, so they could start working on the buildings. **In the building** we walked into a room which stored the convicts' tools and the things [[the officers and the people in charge used.]]

Secondly we piled into a room where the convicts were kept and the guide told us that the convicts used to keep their possessions under the floorboards, but the problem with this was the rats. The rats would take the possession and drag it to their den.**If you put something thin on the floorboards** the pests would slide it through the cracks on the floor.

Another pest is ants as everyone knows. The barracks were swarming with them, so the convicts made nit combs out of chicken bones. Convicts' beds were just uncomfortable, unsafe old hammocks. The convicts even slept with rats in their beds and with their filthy clothes on. **Later**, the building was turned into a place for refugees.

| Reorientation | We soon left the barracks to drive back to school. **At home** I fell onto my bed exhausted from a day at Hyde Park Barracks and The Rocks. |
| Coda | The most interesting thing [[I learned]] was [[that the convicts weren't always kept in jails]]. |

*Not her real name

The Orientation element is entirely devoted to personal commonsense experience, as Tom writes of his actions before going to school. Here the interpersonal character of the text is evident. Writing in the first person, Tom adopts a friendly tenor, as of one who assumes his readers know him and his classmates. He creates a strong sense of pleasure or positive affect, apparent in the opening relational attributive process and the associated clause of reason:

> *I woke up **excited** // for today we were going to The Rocks and Hyde Park barracks*

though attitude is also apparent in Tom's various lexical verbs (and one adverbial expression, *immediately*), all of them realizing material processes, yet doing so in ways that add attitudinal color:

> *I **immediately rocketed** out of the bedroom*
> *I **bolted** down breakfast*
> *then **zoomed** out the door*
> *and **leaped** into the car*

Intensity is often achieved in English through use of adverbs such as *very* or *so*, as in *he was very excited*. In discussing ways speakers and writers of English intensify their meanings through lexical choices, Martin and White (2005, pp. 143–148) suggest such intensity is often "infused" in the lexical verbs chosen. Tom makes good use of such infusion of meaning. Consider the changes to his meanings had he written:

> *"I immediately went out of the bedroom"*
> *"I ate breakfast fast"*
> *"I went out the door"*
> *"I got into the car"*

All the verbs substituted here realize material processes, though they do not realize the same meanings, for the writer's excitement is completely lost. The intensity and excitement achieved in the lexis heightens or "scales up" the attitudinal meanings (Martin & White, 2005, p. 136).

In fact, attitudinal meanings function prosodically throughout the whole text, so that they are interwoven with the experiential meanings, as in these examples from the Record, where the two processes are again material, also creating attitudinal color, and one modal adjunct (*almost instantly*) adds to the intensity of the meanings, when Tom again builds commonsense experience, this time having to do with the bus travel of the class:

> **almost instantly we had piled** *into the bus*
> *and **were speeding** off towards the Rocks*

In these two instances, it is of interest to note that the tenses selected represent more than the simple past tense found in texts by younger children of the kind discussed in Chapter 2, for the writer uses past perfect (*we had piled*) and present continuous (*were speeding off*; Halliday & Matthiessen, 2004). Developing confidence in control of the written language expresses itself, among other matters, in emergent control of the various English tense choices. Halliday (personal communication) has observed that the English tense system is more complex than that of any other language known to him. It is certainly difficult for second language users, but, at least for the purposes of learning to write, I have found it remains problematic for many native speakers throughout the years of a secondary education. Even some university students continue to have difficulties.

Attitudinal expression is sometimes achieved in ways other than in lexis. Consider, for example, how this clause provides a simple assertion of what was the case:

> *we weren't on the bus very long*

where ths is immediately challenged by a clause with a contrastive conjunction indicating attitudinal response To events:

> **but** *it seemed like it*

and a reason is then offered:

> **for** *there wasn't any air conditioning*

In the Record both fields—personal and historical—come into play. Tom tells us, for example, when approaching the barracks:

> *I visualized what the barracks would look like. Almost immediately I found out what it did look like*

and then he goes on to construct aspects of what he observed, where experiential and attitudinal values are both expressed, partly with intensity (**lots** *of tiny offices*), which scales up the attitude, and partly in colorful lexis (*humungous*):

> It was lots of tiny offices surrounding a humungous convict jail which is now a museum.

Subsequent processes create both experiential and attitudinal values:

> in the past the convicts **would stumble** out of the giant building (material process)
> and **slump** towards the main officers' window (material process).

Experiential meanings are, of course, expressed in other transitivity resources. Consider, for example, these participants expressed in noun groups with clause embeddings, building aspects of the historical field:

> the convicts' houses [[where the bakery was]]
> the things [[the officers and the people in charge used]]

In addition, the Coda—already alluded to above—employs a relational identifying process involving embeddings, capturing quite a lot of information, while also asserting a sense of Tom's evaluation of an aspect of the historical knowledge he has learned:

> The most interesting thing [[I learned]] was [[that the convicts weren't always kept in jails]].

All such resources serve to expand both the experiential information and the evaluative meanings in the text, giving it the enhanced lexical density that is the mark of a text by a somewhat older writer.

Circumstantial information expressed in prepositional phrases also contributes to the relative lexical density of the text, some having to do with the commonsense field:

> **today** (time) *we were going* **to The Rocks** (place) **and Hyde Park Barracks** (place)

but others having to do with historical field:

> **in the past** (time) *the convicts would stumble* **out of the giant buildings** (place) *and slump* **towards the main officers'** *window* (place).

Two others are of accompaniment:

> *(we) walked off* **with the tour guide**
> *The convicts even slept* **with rats in their beds and with their filthy clothes on.**

Circumstances of time and place tend to emerge first, as noted in Chapter 2, though among successful students by age nine, other types of circumstances will appear. In fact, all the circumstantial information in Text 3.2 is of time, place, or accompaniment, and this reflects the two fields of interest, for time, place, and accompanying activities are at issue.

It is easy to underestimate the importance of prepositional phrases building circumstantial information, for among native speakers they emerge readily, typically developing from those of time and place to such circumstances as accompaniment (*with*), matter (*about*), reason (*because of*), condition (*in case of*), and angle (*according to*), to name some common ones. Among second-language users, English prepositional phrases often prove very difficult, as I have found over many years of teaching international students at the postgraduate level. Such students, themselves teachers of English as a foreign language from Asian and South East Asian countries, told me that the differences between English prepositions are often perceived as elusive, and because of this the experiential information expressed in the prepositional phrases is often hard to understand. A great deal of deconstructing texts in which prepositional phrases appear is required, as well as modeling of ways of creating experiential information using prepositional phrases.

Above I suggested that Text 3.2 was marked by greater clause intricacy than texts by younger writers in that a more varied range of clause types emerges. Consider the following, where the first clause is a dependent one, followed by several that are linked in different ways:

> *when we arrived at The Rocks* (clause of time)
> *we were split into two groups*
> *and walked off with the tour guide* (two equal clauses)
> *who showed us the convicts' houses where the bakery was and a map of Sydney Cove* (nondefining relative clause)
> *which had a name of a place, and its Aboriginal translation.* (nondefining relative clause)

and here, where the first two clauses are equal and there are two subsequent clauses of purpose:

> *In the past the convicts would stumble out of the giant building*
>   *and slump towards the main officers' window* (two equal clauses)
> *to collect their tools* (clause of purpose)
> *so they could start working on the buildings* (clause of purpose)

Children inevitably progress at different rates and in different ways, so not all children show the facility shown by Tom in Text 3.3. As a general principle, however, we can say that by about age 9 or 10, successful children should be displaying facility in control of grammatically intricate written texts, where these involve the ability to deploy a range of different clause types (Christie & Derewianka, 2008). In fact, dependent clauses of time:

when we arrived at The Rocks *we were split into two groups,*

reason:

I woke up excited, for today we were going to The Rocks and Hyde Park Barracks,

purpose:

we soon left the barracks to drive back to school

and place:

secondly we piled into a room where the convicts were kept

tend to appear first, normally by age 7 or 8. Other clauses, though in no particular order, tend to appear later, such as those of condition:[2]

If you put something thin on the floorboards *the pests would slide it through the cracks on the floor*

result:

The barracks were swarming with them, so the convicts made nit combs out of chicken bones

manner:

As promised, he was awarded the prize (this is a made up example)

or concession:

Nelson believed that although the white population oppressed them, both races should live equally and in harmony (see below)

as well as various nondefining relative clauses:

(we) walked off with the tour guide who showed us the convicts' houses where the bakery was and a map of Sydney Cove which had a name of a place, and its Aboriginal translation

and clauses of projection:

Nelson believed . . . that both races should live equally and in harmony (see below).

It should be stressed that the appearance of any clause type depends very considerably on the field of knowledge being dealt with and the kind of genre that is being created. Recounts, for example, recreating past experience, make frequent use of clauses of time, whereas clauses of reason, indicating why characters behave as they do, can appear in early narratives. What is of interest developmentally is the fact that once the range of clause types is mastered, grammatically linked clauses of the type we are discussing will often tend to disappear, as the resources of grammatical metaphor are better mastered and understood by children and as the meanings are eventually expressed in other ways. However, the take up of these matters is very uneven among different children and adolescents, for the challenge of handling dense written language is considerable. I return to these matters below and more fully in Chapter 4.

Text 3.3 was written by a native speaker of English. An analysis of the kind I have provided for this text serves to illuminate the linguistic tools young writers need by the upper primary years, while it also serves as a guide for considering ways to teach children experiencing difficulties in their writing. As an example, using a functional grammar, Schleppegrell and Go (2007) discuss the writing needs of Chinese and Vietnamese children of the upper primary years in American schools, also writing about class events. They outline suggestions for analysis of children's texts and for subsequent guidance of students, helping them, for example, to play with and expand their noun groups and prepositional phrases in order to extend the range of meanings they can make, and they also outline ways to introduce and extend attitudinal meanings. These things need to be explicitly modeled for such children learning English, and a functional analysis provides a strong basis from which to do this.

3.4 An Instance of Oral Language for Performance in Subject English in the Late Childhood to Early Adolescent Years

At this point we turn our attention to an instance of an oral presentation by a 12-year-old girl, in her first year of a secondary education, whose name is Amy. She is, in fact, a sister of Tom's, and, as in the case of Tom, I have collected her written texts from the primary school into the secondary years. I have selected Amy's text at this point because it is an example of a text by an older child whose genre and register values are quite different from those considered in Text 3.2. Analysis of the text reveals something of the developmental changes that take place in children as they mature in late childhood to early adolescence, extending our understanding of the processes of ontogenesis. Amy had been asked by her English teacher to research a topic of interest and prepare an oral presentation on it. This is an important point of difference from Text 3.3 above, whose field involved historical experience, researched as part of a class visit. Here, the field is to be researched by reference to books and perhaps other sources such as the Internet, for it involves seeking out an esoteric, or at least unfamiliar, field of information. Amy chose the field of "heroism," and, more specifically, she chose to research the life of Nelson Mandela as an example of a hero. Interpersonally, she adopted a rather formal role as lecturer to her class. Experientially, the text deals largely with abstract information, though in this case this is not because of use of grammatical metaphor. Rather, the abstract nature of the text is evident, partly in such abstract nouns as *hero*, *heroism*, and *injustice* and partly in the patterns of evaluative discourse in which she deploys such words. For example, she defines:

> *Heroes are people who help others, who put themselves in danger to save other people.*

and she describes how heroic people behave:

> *Heroes try to make things right and fight injustice where it can be found.*

Hence, she makes clear that her text is very much concerned with judgment about ethical behaviors.

Textually, the talk shows some features of the spoken mode—for example, Amy commences with a rhetorical question and she uses both opening and closing salutations—whereas elsewhere the text has features of written language, as in its various sentence structures. The text was, in fact, written to be read out loud, and it is a persuasive genre, in which Amy proposes a thesis about heroes and then argues her case, both about the values of heroism and about Mandela as an example of a hero. We may display its schematic structure thus:

Issue/Thesis ^ Argument ^ Restatement of Thesis.

Marked topical themes, two expressed in enclosed clauses, are shown in bold, and clause embeddings (and any clauses within these) are also indicated.

Text 3.4 Nelson Mandela.

Issue/Thesis   What are heroes? Heroes are people [[who help others]] [[who put themselves in danger //to save other people]]]]. They fight for [[what is right]] even if their own life could be taken away.

A hero can also be someone [[who helps us reflect on ourselves// and how we interact with other people// so that we may better ourselves// and help each other.]]

Good afternoon 7C, I am going to talk about my hero, Nelson Mandela.

Argument

Heroes try to make things right, and fight injustice where it can be found, which is [[why I look at Nelson Mandela as my hero]]. Nelson Mandela was a freedom fighter in South Africa, who struggled to relieve the people of apartheid. This was [[where the races of the country were separated // and forced to live in different areas]], although it was worse, as white people were always given the upper hand, and were ruling over the South African people.

Nelson Mandela saw this injustice and spoke out against it. **In other parts of Africa,** peoplewere fighting against their oppressors violently, taking back the land and killing many. Nelson believed that ≪**although the white population oppressed them**≫ both races should live equally and in harmony.*

He is a hero, because he fought to destroy the injustice [[that was occurring]], he even sacrificed his freedom to save others. He was sent to prison, but during his trial he said, "During my lifetime I have dedicated myself to the struggle of the African people. I have fought against white domination, andI have fought against black domination. I have cherished the ideal of a democratic and free society in which all persons live together in harmony and with equal opportunities. It is an ideal which I hope to live for and to achieve. But if needs be, it is an ideal for which I am prepared to die."

This is a great example of Heroism, because in it is shown that Nelson Mandela is trying to stop injustice in South Africa, and he says he is willing to give his life so others could live freely, and equally.

Restatement of Thesis

A Hero ≪while being someone who helps people≫ doesn't, however, have to be recognized for his or her achievements, so they could even be a volunteer at a charity, or a member of the Salvation Army. **Whatever little they can do for others,** they will do. This is [[what makes them a Hero, their willingness and eagerness [[to help others.]]]]

Heroes vary from the very strong, to the very weak, rich or poor. Anyone [[who strives to help others in their struggle]] can be recognized as a hero. Nelson Mandela is a hero, because he sacrificed his own freedom to help the people around him, he was brave, as he was willing to die for his beliefs, and he was determined not to give up, and determined to abolish apartheid, so that all the people could live equally.

He is my hero, because he saved so many from the apartheid, and he can help us all to reflect on ourselves, and in our own way, help against injustice too.

Thank you.

*This sentence is a little awkwardly expressed, as the referent of "them" is not clear. It should have read: *Nelson believed that ≪although the white population oppressed blacks≫, both races should live equally and in harmony.*

The text foregrounds the issues having to do with heroism and Mandela: that is to say, Amy's personal identity, although evident in her occasional use of the pronouns *I* or *my*, is generally absent, for she has taken up abstract realms of discussion and opinion. Interpersonally, the text is marked by strong attitudinal expression. Here the contrast with Text 3.3 is of some interest, although very different genres are involved, having different social purposes. However, the contrast is also a factor of age. Whereas Text 3.3 showed the writer's response to events in terms of affect or feeling, with a concluding sense of his evaluation of matters learned, Text 3.4 expresses judgment about heroes, where ethical values having to do with the social esteem attaching to people are involved. The capacity to express judgment is one measure of the fact that this text is by an older writer than the writer of Text 3.3, for it involves evaluative meanings not readily available to younger children, not, at least, in their writing. Consider for example the judgments involved here:

Heroes vary from the very strong, to the very weak, rich or poor.
Anyone [[who strives to help others in their struggle]] can be recognized as a hero.

Of the various resources in which attitude is expressed, several instances are realized in adverbial groups creating evaluation or appreciation:

*people were fighting against their oppressors **violently***
*both races should live **equally and in harmony***
*he says he is willing to give his life so others could live **freely and equally***

All such instances realize circumstances of manner, and they are of interest because, as noted in Chapter 1, younger children do not typically use adverbs of manner. Circumstantial information among younger writers is typically expressed in prepositional phrases, and the adverbs that are generally used are those of intensity (*very, so*). Adverbs expressive of evaluation, judgment, or opinion are more typically a phenomenon of adolescence and beyond (Christie & Derewianka, 2008). Their presence here is a further measure of the fact that the writer of Text 3.4 has developed considerably. She is capable of using linguistic resources that give particular attitudinal values to her language in a manner not yet available to many younger writers, such as Tom, who was younger when he wrote Text 3.3. (It will be recalled that David, who wrote Text 3.2, made use of one modal adjunct *unfortunately* in an interpersonal theme position.) In that sense, her language is beginning to display some of the mature expression of opinion and judgment that adult life will ideally expect of her, apparent also in her uses of modality:

> *a hero **can** also be someone who helps us reflect on ourselves*
> *so that we **may** better ourselves*
> *he **was determined** not to give up, and **determined** to abolish apartheid*
> *both races **should** live freely and equally*

One further developmental matter of interest in Text 3.4 lies in some of its theme choices. Like David in Text 3.2 above, Amy has twice used an enclosed clause in theme position, selected to foreground the information in a rhetorically interesting way. The first instance is

> *Nelson believed that ≪**although the white population oppressed them**≫ both races should live equally and in harmony.*

In an unmarked way this would be written

> *Nelson believed that both races should live equally and in harmony, although the white population oppressed them (i.e., the blacks)*

The second is

> *A Hero ≪**while being someone who helps people**≫ doesn't, however, have to be recognized for his or her achievements*

In an unmarked way this would be written

> *While being someone who helps people, a hero doesn't . . . have to be recognized . . .*

As I have already noted above, capacity to play with the position of dependent clauses in this manner, placing them in an enclosed position in theme, is another developmental feature of an older writer, for it adds to the rhetorical force of what is said. Such expressions are not commonly found in younger writers.

3.4.1 A Short Summary

To summarize the discussion to this point, I note that Texts 3.3 and 3.4 each show evidence of growth in control of literacy, the former in late childhood, the latter in early adolescence, suggestive of some of the developmental changes of late childhood to early adolescence. Table 3.1 summarizes the developmental changes with respect to the four metafunctions.

Table 3.1 A summary of developmental changes across the four metafunctions, evident in control of written language displayed in Texts 3.3 and 3.4

Textual meanings	Emergent capacity is apparent in ability to control overall thematic progression, selecting relevant marked or unmarked topical themes, where the latter reveal growing facility in playing with various dependent clauses and/or circumstances, placed in theme position:
	when we arrived at the Rocks we were split into two groups *in other parts of Africa* people were fighting *a hero* ≪*while being someone who helps people*≫ *doesn't however, have to be recognized for his or her achievements*
Experiential meanings	Both texts reveal developing capacity to express experiential meanings, evident, for example, in expanding control of noun group structures to create participants:
	lots of tiny offices [[surrounding a humungous convict jail // which is now a museum]] *heroes are people [[who help others]] [[who put themselves in danger // to save other people]]]]*
	and in a growing number of prepositional phrases creating circumstantial information:
	*the convicts used to keep their possessions **under the floorboards*** *the convicts even slept **with rats in their** beds*

(Continued)

Table 3.1 Continued

	*while people were ruling **over the South African people** Nelson Mandela saw this injustice and spoke out **against it***
Interpersonal/ attitudinal meanings	Both show developing attitudinal meanings, evident in various lexical choices, including lexical verbs:
	*the convicts **would stumble** out of the giant building and **slump** towards the main officers' window Nelson Mandela was a freedom fighter . . . who **struggled to relieve** the people of apartheid,*
	as well as adverbial expressions involving interpretation of behaviors:
	*people were fighting against their oppressors **violently** both races should live **equally and in harmony***
	and an associated capacity to use modality:
	*a hero **can** also be someone who helps us both races **should** live equally*
Logical meanings	Emergent capacity is also evident in selected clause types and their relationships, involving a range of clause dependencies, achieving different kinds of logical connectedness:
	when we arrived at the Rocks // we were split into two groups // and walked off with the tour guide // who showed us the convicts' houses; this is a great example of Heroism // because it is shown // that Nelson Mandela is trying to stop injustice in South Africa // and he says // he is willing to give his life // so others could live freely, and equally)

Finally, as a consequence of achieving mastery in all these areas, children and young adolescents show developing ability to create abstract meanings in their written discourse:

Heroes try to make things right, and fight injustice where it can be found

and to adopt evaluative positions:

The most interesting thing I learned was that convicts weren't always kept in jails.
What are heroes? Heroes are people who help others, who put themselves on danger to save other people.

3.5 Writing Science in Early Adolescence

Texts 3.3 and 3.4 each dealt with attitudinal expression, among other things, though in rather different ways, the former in terms of affect, the latter in terms of judgment about desirable social values and practices. I have suggested that though the attitudinal differences were in part a feature of the different genres, they were also in part a feature of the different ages of the young people concerned. Development of capacity to express evaluation is an important matter. As we saw in Chapter 2, young children can be encouraged to offer simple evaluation, though the language resources required for more mature evaluation emerge more fully later, apparent by late childhood, and requiring further development and refinement in later years. Equally, however, one significant aspect of developing control of evaluative and attitudinal resources generally lies in recognizing when attitude is restrained. This is true of scientific knowledge, which we now turn to while developing this account of the ontogenesis of language in the late childhood to early adolescent years.

The technical language of subject specialisms like science is often unfamiliar and difficult, though it is misleading to suppose that students' difficulties in speaking, reading, or writing about science are primarily a matter of unfamiliar vocabulary, if by that we mean learning the meaning of words like "photosynthesis," "velocity," "peristalsis," or "atom." The issue is more complex, and here once again a functional grammar is helpful. The issue is one of the total pattern of discourse in which technical language is deployed and specialist meanings are made, creating texts that are dense, abstract, and seemingly remote from lived experience as children know it. The abstractions are often built using grammatical metaphor. Consider for example, the scientific field of the human digestive system, commonly taught to young adolescents in Australia in the first or second year of a secondary education. We begin by taking a brief look at some extracts from a textbook dealing with the topic, and though it is not the textbook actually used by the teacher whose student's work I shall refer to, its language is at least similar.[3]

The relevant section of the textbook (Campbell et al., 2009, p. 898) has a heading, remarkable in itself because of its two dense noun group structures involving grammatical metaphor:

> *Organs [[specialized for sequential stages of food processing]] form the mammalian digestive system*

This dense structure creates one clause involving a relational identifying process, where the verb *form* realizes the process. It means

The mammalian digestive system consists of (is formed by/ is made up of)
organs specialized for sequential stages of food processing.

If we reexpress this as speech, perhaps as a teacher might explain the matters involved to the class, it becomes something like this:

"Mammals digest their food
and they do this in a series of stages in a sequence
by using a number of different organs
and each organ has a special role
in order to process the food."

One written clause has become five in speech. Furthermore, several words are reexpressed as different classes of words: the adjective *digestive* has reappeared as the verb *digest*; the noun group *sequential stages of food processing* has become a simpler noun group, *a series of stages in a sequence*, and the latter part of the noun group *food processing* has changed to become *to process food*. Finally, note that the verb *form* has disappeared. This is because the relations between the newly separate clauses created in speech obviate the need for the verb and the process it realizes. In writing, such separate clauses often disappear, their meanings collapsed within dense noun groups, and often, as in this case, reexpressed differently in a verb realizing a relational process.

In much scientific endeavor, as a general principle, the actions of life and activities of many kinds (typically expressed in verbs) become abstract phenomena (typically expressed in nouns and noun groups) around which discussions and explanations can be developed for the purposes of building written knowledge (Halliday & Martin, 1993). Reading such dense scientific language is a considerable challenge for young readers, and research has shown that many students of science in the secondary years hardly read their textbooks at all, so alienating is their language (Fang & Schleppegrell, 2008). It is essential, where this occurs, for teachers to devote a great deal of time in class talk to deconstructing the grammatical complexity as a necessary part of building comprehension while also building confidence and capacity to attempt writing of similar language.

I shall say a little more of the language of the science textbook in order to capture a sense of the ways in which the scientific knowledge is constructed. Experientially, it will be noted that the scientific phenomena are foregrounded, so that despite the fact that it is human digestion that is at issue, there is little sense of any human agency involved. Interpersonally, the tenor is formal, as of an expert informing the reader, and there is no attitudinal expression. Textually, the text unfolds using largely unmarked themes that identify the phenomena being described, for the object is to explain a process, and that requires frequent naming, either of the phenomenon or of some aspect of it. Most notably, the text is very dense, its lexis often abstract and difficult, and at least some of its terms are potentially confusing. I refer, for example, to the expression "mechanical digestion," a term used to name the processes by which food is broken down into smaller pieces for its digestion. For the average student, familiar with the notions of things "mechanical" as having to do with machinery, the term invites some misunderstanding, so that time would need to be devoted to exploring the differing meanings of the word "mechanical" in order to clarify it and also to distinguish it from "chemical digestion," which occurs a little later in the text extract.

---

*Ingestion and the initial steps of digestion occur in the mouth or **oral cavity**. Mechanical digestion begins as teeth of various shapes cut, smash, and grind food, making the food easier to swallow and increasing its surface. Meanwhile the presence of food stimulates a nervous reflex that causes the **salivary glands** to deliver saliva through ducts to the oral cavity. . . . . . .Saliva initiates chemical digestion while also protecting the oral cavity.*

. . . . .

*Much as a doorman screens and assists people entering a building, the tongue aids digestive processes by evaluating ingested food and then enabling its further passage. . . . . . .Tongue movements manipulate the food, helping shape it into a ball, called a **bolus**. . . . . .*

*The pharynx, or throat region, opens to two passageways: the oesophagus and the trachea (windpipe). The **oesophagus** connects to the stomach whereas the trachea leads to the lungs. . . . .*

Having explained that most mammals, including humans, have "alimentary canals," the science writers go on to describe the human digestive system via the alimentary canal by a process called "peristalsis" (Campbell et al., 2009, pp. 898–899). (The technical items shown in bold are displayed as they are in the book while rows of dots indicate that text is omitted.)

Expressions such as *ingestion and the initial steps of digestion* are abstract and would need to be broken down into more commonplace language, and expressions like *the presence of food stimulates a nervous reflex* would also need explanation. On the whole the language of the textbook is well away from the way people normally talk, so that children in late childhood to early adolescence need assistance in grappling with the meanings involved. This will be, in particular, the case where they are reluctant or indifferent readers, when the sound of the teacher's voice reading the text will assist comprehension and frequent discussion of the meanings of the text will be important.

3.5.1 Writing about the Human Digestive System

Text 3.5, to be examined below, was written as part of a genre-based study I initiated in a secondary school in a poor area of Melbourne, where a group of about 20 English teachers worked with me and my colleague Anne Soosai. Over a period of 3 years we studied functional grammar and instituted genre teaching across all the junior secondary school years. One of these teachers taught secondary science as well as English, and she chose to implement genre pedagogy in her science program as well as her English program. Concerned that her students did not always understand or write good explanations, she chose to introduce explanation genres in a major unit of work dealing with several human systems: the respiratory and digestive systems and the system of blood circulation. The class involved was in Year 8, the second year of junior secondary school, and the students were 13 to 14 years old.

The work on the digestive system commenced with reading the class text-book, and this led to class discussion of the system, where the teacher took time to discuss the technical terms involved. They also considered the nature of the human body and the apparent sequence involved in eating and digest-ing food and also eliminating waste. After class discussion over two lessons, as a further step toward clarifying the class understanding of the system, the students were encouraged to draw flow charts showing the various steps in-volved, which caused them to see the sequence of steps in an ordered way. They could discuss them and explain in talk why the steps occurred as they did.

In a subsequent lesson, with teacher-guided discussion, the students exam-ined a model example of an explanation genre that Soosai and I had used in workshops with the teacher and her colleagues concerning how cyclones are caused. An explanation genre typically explains why or how some phenomenon occurs.[4] Its elements of structure may be displayed thus:

Phenomenon Identification ^ Explanation Sequence.

As the labels suggest, the Phenomenon Identification introduces the phe-nomenon to be explained, and the Explanation Sequence provides the sequence of steps that occur to create the Phenomenon.

Using a projector to visibly display the model genre, the teacher reads through the text with her class, stopping to discuss any unfamiliar terms while also drawing attention to the two major elements of schematic structure, their names and meanings. She asks the children to comment on how the model explanation genre compares with, and also contrasts with, a report genre, examples of which the children had read and written earlier in the year in their science program.[5] This is a useful first step toward establishing the purpose of an explanation: It compares with a report in that it deals with factual, often scientific information, stating some entity or phenomenon of interest. However, where the report goes on to describe an entity or phenomenon, the explanation seeks to explain why or how some phenomenon occurs. Discussion of these matters leads to some consideration of the tense choice for explanation genre writing, for in this it is also like a report genre, which typically (though in fact not always) uses the present tense.

Discussion of other language items in reports and explanation leads to talk of the conjunctions chosen, and it is noted that several having to do with time sequence typically appear in an explanation genre unfolding a sequences of steps. Here the earlier production of flow charts assists an understanding of the selected conjunctions of time (*as*, *when*). Thematic progression in the model genre is also discussed, and it is noted that although many sentences start with conjunctions (*as*, *when*) signaling the sequence of steps, the topical themes expressing content tend to identify the phenomenon under discussion. Thus is new information introduced into one sentence and then reinstated in a later sentence to build unity of meaning. Discussion of these matters leads to the recognition of a need to repeat the phenomenon or aspects of that phenomenon in building the explanation. In a subsequent lesson the students go on to write their own explanation genres.

Text 3.5 was written by Samantha. The language of this text, unlike those we examined above, is now grammatically metaphorical. Marked themes and embedded clauses are again shown, and where clauses appear within embeddings they are again noted, principally to draw attention to the manner in which information is packed into the language. This constructs dense discourse.

Text 3.5 The human digestive system.

Phenomenon Identification	The digestive system is a system [[that helps break down food // absorb the nutrients from food // as well as eliminate waste.]] The nutrients [[that are absorbed from your food]] are used for growth and tissue maintenance, or burnt off as energy. The main parts of the digestive system

are the mouth, esophagus, stomach and the two intestines (small and large).

Explanation Sequence

The first part of mechanical digestion happens in the mouth, where teeth grind the food with the help of the tongue, which flips the food around. **To help chew and swallow food**, saliva spurts from the walls in your mouth, this makes your mouth stay moist so you don't get a dry throat.

Saliva contains an enzyme [[called amylase]] which breaks down the starch in your food and turns it to sugar. We need this as fuel to burn as it travels around the body.

When it is time to swallow the tongue tosses the food to the back of the mouth (top of the throat) and **when you gulp,** the food slides down the oesophagus. **As you swallow,** the muscles [[that the food has just passed]] contract, and the muscles in front of the food relax, to make the food travel down the oesophagus easily, this is called peristalsis.

Once the food is in the stomach ≪ after traveling down the oesophagus // which takes approximately seven seconds≫ the second step of mechanical digestion takes place. The muscles in the walls of the stomach squeeze the food to make it smaller to help with the chemical digestion in the stomach. Chemicals (enzymes) in the stomach contain hydrochloric acid, which once again breaks down the food even further. **So that the walls of the stomach don't get burnt by the hydrochloric acid,** the stomach is lined with a layer of mucus to protect it.

The next step of digestion takes place in the small intestine. **As the food is travelling towards the large intestine,** enzymes from the small intestine break the food down for the last time.

At the end of the small intestine is the large intestine. The left over food remnants travel through the large intestine and portions of the food get hardened. The last step in the process happens as the food remnants move out of the large intestine and out of the anal hole into the toilet.

The most distinctive feature of Text 3.5 is its very dense abstract meanings. Consider the grammatically metaphorical nature of this single clause sentence:

> *The nutrients [[that are absorbed from your food]] are used for growth and tissue maintenance, or burnt off as energy.*

As speech, this would probably be expressed thus, creating six clauses:

> *"When you eat food*
> *your body absorbs the nutrients in the food*
> *and it uses these*
> *to help your body grow*
> *and to maintain the tissues in your body*
> *or it burns the nutrients to create energy."*

This example serves to illustrate the point made above: namely, that with the emergence of grammatical metaphor, the practice of creating meanings by using a series of logically interconnected clauses often disappears, the separate clause relations buried within the new structures in which nominalization plays an important role.

There are a large number of abstract noun groups in the text: *digestive system, tissue maintenance, mechanical digestion, chemical digestion.* Other noun groups compress relevant information in different ways, sometimes with embedded clauses:

> *the nutrients [[that are absorbed from your food]]*
> *saliva contains an enzyme [[called amylase]]*

and sometimes with embedded phrases:

> *the walls [in your mouth]*
> *the muscles [in front of the food]*
> *the muscles [in the walls of the stomach]*

This is language to be read, rather than spoken, and the lexical density is largely responsible for that. Its tenor is formal, as of an expert explaining a phenomenon to one who needs to be informed. Its overall organization, clearly established by a glance at its thematic progression, is well directed, so that the opening phenomenon having been established, the explanation develops an account of the various stages and steps involved in the process of digestion. A great deal of the organization of this sequence of activities is captured and directed in eight marked topical themes, all but one of which, *at the end of the small intestine*, are realized in dependent clauses. One such marked theme involves three clauses, two of them enclosed:

> ***Once the food is in the stomach*** ≪ ***after travelling down the oesophagus // which takes approximately seven seconds***≫ *the second step of mechanical digestion takes place.*

Thus does this young writer compress relevant information in order to advance the direction in which her written text will take place.

Overall, Text 3.5 represents further evidence of growth in control of literacy. It displays many of the features of written as opposed to spoken language, and it makes extensive use of grammatically metaphorical expressions in order to build its abstract meanings.

In reading about such scientific fields of knowledge, and in preparing to write about them, students can usefully be involved in discussion of the meanings made in science, bringing to consciousness how such texts are constructed and also reflecting on the ways in which knowledge in the sciences is created. They could, for example

o identify the large noun groups or naming groups and the meanings they express;

o deconstruct them with teacher guidance into several clauses, noting the conjunctive relations that appear between clauses and any other changes in the grammar;

o discuss the meanings made in the spoken version and consider why the written version is formed as it is, and reflect on why it is useful to compress information in writing;

o explore other resources such as prepositional phrases and the information they provide (a particularly useful activity for second-language users);

o discuss what comes first in a series of clauses, developing some understanding of the ways thematic choices work to shape and direct written text; and

o use all these understandings to write scientific texts themselves in groups, enjoying the benefits of collaboration and collective effort.

3.6 Conclusion

This chapter has sought to consider language and literacy development in the transitional years from late childhood to adolescence, when children pass from primary to secondary school. It is in these years that the distinctive subject specialisms of secondary schooling become more apparent, involving abstraction of various kinds. The nature of the language changes in order to deal with the often complex meanings of school subjects. Although talk remains important for school learning, written discourse becomes very important as the principal mode in which performance is assessed in writing and as the principal mode in which information is accessed in reading. The grammatical organization of written language is different from that of speech, and the literacy skills of young people are particularly challenged in the movement to a new kind of schooling. Written language is more dense than speech, its meanings expressed in dense noun groups creating participants, verbal groups expressing a range of process types, prepositional phrases building often dense circumstantial information, and adverbial groups expressing attitude appearing more frequently. Series of interconnected clauses, creating grammatical intricacy, build longer passages of written discourse to sustain and develop meanings. However, their nature and their frequency always depend on the register and genre values involved. Grammatical metaphor appears, helping to contribute to density and abstraction, because what would otherwise be meanings expressed in interconnected clauses are reexpressed in the resources of noun groups in particular. Abstract meanings are also expressed in uses of abstract nouns, revealing that as they mature, young people must learn to handle abstract qualities and values of many kinds.

In all, teachers need a considerable knowledge of oral language and literacy in order to guide and direct the learning of their students. This is an issue to which I return in the next chapter.

Notes

1 These measures are by their nature a little imprecise, not least because what constitutes a lexical item as distinct from a grammatical item is not always clear and might well be the subject of disagreement. Halliday's advice is that frequently used lexical items like *go* or *get* can be counted as grammatical, as they express very little experiential content, and I have followed this advice here.

2 I note an example did appear in the written text about chickens in Chapter 2, which had also appeared in a child's speech first before the teacher used a similar one in the written text. The children were not themselves independent readers and writers.

3 Unfortunately, when the student's text displayed and discussed below was collected, no record was kept of the textbook the student had relied on, and it has proved impossible to locate it.

4 Several types of explanation are recognized in the SFL genre literature (Christie & Derewianka, 2008; Martin & Rose, 2008); the one selected here is a common one.

5 Report genres differ to some extent depending on the field. However, they typically start with a General Statement—sometimes a General Classification of some phenomenon—and then they describe it. The two elements are thus *General Statement* ^ *Description* (Christie & Derewianka, 2008; Martin & Rose, 2008).

Language Learning   ISSN 0023-8333

CHAPTER 4

The Years of Midadolescence: Dealing With Abstract Knowledge

4.1 Introduction

The various school subjects have distinctive methods of inquiry, distinctive modes of knowledge building, and distinctive "styles of reasoning" (Muller, 2000, p. 88), all of which are expressed in a range of semiotic modes, including the "subject-specific literacies" that I discussed in Chapter 3. Achieving some control of the various subjects or areas of knowledge and the discourse patterns in which they are expressed is an important challenge of schooling, and, as we have seen, the work of achieving such control commences early. It commences with the entry to school in early childhood, when the initial work is done in learning patterns of talk characteristic of schooling as well as patterns of written language in learning to read and write. In the early years, much of the knowledge learned is common sense in that it draws on relatively simple experience, though with the passage of time the learning becomes more demanding, and the developmental tasks in handling written discourse in reading and writing become more challenging. After some years of expanding and consolidating what is learned, as we have seen, children move to late childhood and early adolescence, and as they do so, they move away from the immediacies of relatively simple experience toward the more complex uncommonsense experiences of new knowledge and ideas. They also move into the secondary school, where the distinctive knowledge features of the school subjects become more marked, and there is a challenge to master the changing nature of language, literacy in particular, because it is in literate language that so much of the knowledge is expressed. Above all, the movement into the literate language of adolescence requires the ability to handle abstract experience and information as a necessary part of interpreting and building the knowledge of the secondary years. The language students must read and write becomes dense, its grammatical organization more noncongruent, increasingly unlike the more familiar congruent expressions in which much early commonsense experience is expressed. Although many young people enjoy the challenge of engaging with the discourse patterns in which uncommonsense experience and knowledge are expressed, others find this difficult, apparent in the fact that with the entry to the junior secondary school, many children drop behind, their reading and writing skills not adequate to the tasks they confront. By the time such young people reach midadolescence—the principal concern of this chapter—they are often in difficulties.

Evidence for recent concern about issues having to do with adolescent literacy is apparent in several countries. In England, for example, the government commissioned a 2-year study (2003–2005) devoted to identifying ways to improve children's school performance at Key Stage 3, when children are aged 11–14 years, and covering the years of their entry to secondary school. The study was particularly concerned with reading and writing, and it subsequently led to a program called *Assessing Pupils' Progress* (APP), providing advice and guidelines to teachers on ways to enhance young people's reading and writing. The program has been more recently extended to cover all core subjects in the National Curriculum, and both the primary and secondary years (Qualifications and Curriculum Development Authority, 2010). The Australian government sponsored a National Inquiry into the Teaching of Literacy (2005), which, despite its preoccupation with reading and its rather cursory treatment of writing, stressed that teaching reading in particular should continue beyond the primary school and into the adolescent years. In the United States, Strickland and Alvermann (2004) referred to the literacy achievement gap in late childhood to early adolescence, though they discussed the problems primarily in terms of reading performance, rather than reading and writing (see Fang & Schleppegrell, 2008, for a related discussion). The National Commission on Writing (2003, 2006) identified problems in young people's writing performance, referring to what it termed "the neglected 'R'" (p. 9). Snow and Biancarosa (2003) produced a research report sponsored by the Carnegie Corporation addressing what was known of adolescent literacy. This then led to a major program of research on literacy in the adolescent years, whose final reports (Carnegie Council on Advancing Adolescent Literacy, 2010a, 2010b) provide strong evidence of the concern in the United States to address the apparent decline in literacy performance beyond fourth grade.

Many factors are said to be responsible for the emergence of adolescent literacy problems: early reading programs that focus on the years up to third grade, with the apparent assumption that after that time, literacy performance will be adequate, not requiring further teaching, when in fact such teaching should be ongoing; the changing school demands met by young people in the transition to secondary school; the nature of adolescence and the pressures felt in growing up; "a lack of capacity, time and will for middle and high school teachers to teach literacy within their content areas";[1] and "few strategies provided pupils at the end of their third grade for dealing with a rapid shift from narrative to expository text" (Carnegie Council on Advancing Adolescent Literacy, 2010b, p. 8). The problems particular to students learning English as a second language are also noted, becoming more apparent in the United States because of the significant increase in students in this group over the last decade.

All such factors no doubt are responsible, though it is a matter of some interest that the changing nature of the discourses students are learning to handle in the transition from primary to secondary school is not foregrounded. Reference is made in the Carnegie Report, as I have noted, to the need for teachers in the middle and high schools to teach literacy within their subjects— what is sometimes referred to as teaching the language of content areas (see also Mohan, 1986). Furthermore, though the report also references a shift from narrative to expository text as children move up in school, such a distinction hardly provides a sufficient basis from which teachers might proceed, both because it is too general in character and because it hardly does justice to the linguistic features of the variety of factual and story genres potentially read and written by children. Moreover, the commitment to teaching content as a necessary aspect of teaching language and literacy, although laudable in itself, often becomes no more than an interest in teaching the relevant vocabulary of the content, rather than the discourse patterns in which it is expressed. A functional grammar of the kind proposed in this book provides a tool for analyzing the nature of the written discourses students must read and write, allowing them to penetrate and interpret the many text types or genres students need to learn in handling knowledge in the various content areas.

As in earlier chapters, I examine a selection of texts drawn from history, English and science, seeking to demonstrate how the knowledge and associated subject-specific literacy in each subject are constructed. Although there are obvious connections across the various school subjects, in that they all draw on the same linguistic system to build their meanings, they nonetheless all construct knowledge in different ways. History and subject English both belong to the group of studies loosely referred to as the humanities. Where history explores the past, seeking to explain how and why events in different societies occurred, subject English studies the language itself, as well as the many texts, literary and otherwise, and their meanings and values. Science deals with the natural world, seeking to examine its many phenomena and building an ever-expanding knowledge about them. Learning how to handle the differences between the subjects, marshalling relevant information, interpreting and evaluating various phenomena, is a particular challenge of secondary schooling, putting pressure on the linguistic resources of young people, even the most able of them. In particular, it calls for the capacity to handle abstract phenomena and fields of information, all of them aspects of the various disciplines studied and taught primarily in universities and whose impact on the school curriculum is considerable. Notions of disciplines and of disciplinarity (Christie & Maton, 2011) will be referred to again in Chapter 5.

4.2 The Challenges of Writing History in Adolescence

The first historical genres children read and produce in childhood are recounts, in which they learn some of the skills required to recreate aspects of the past in an ordered way. Text 3.3 by Tom in Chapter 3 was one such early genre, in which he constructed personal and researched fields of experience, though the main object was to recreate some aspects of Australian history. By adolescence, history is about more than retelling events from the past. Rather, it involves interpreting past events and evaluating them for their significance, taking readers and writers into more abstract fields of knowledge. The facts, for example, that people fought battles and conquered others, or that other people were dispossessed of their land, or that some were transported as convicts to an unknown land, or that some Act was passed in order to regulate the activities of people, no doubt need to be known. However, history seeks to explain why such actions took place, what their impact was on future human activities, and, in some instances, to argue about their significance, persuading the reader of a particular interpretation of events.

The range of genres potentially available to write history is considerable: Coffin (2006), Martin (2003), Schleppegrell (2004, 2005), and Christie and Derewianka (2008) offer detailed discussions. Here, in the interests of space, I consider only one history genre students need to master by midadolescence: a *consequential explanation*, a term taken from Coffin (2006). Such a genre identifies some event or phenomenon in history of importance and then offers an explanation of its impact or consequences. An example of an essay question requiring a consequential explanation, taken from data collected in Australian schools (Christie & Derewianka, 2007), identified the introduction of conscription in Australia in World War II as a significant phenomenon and asked students to discuss its impact on the Australian people. Discussion of the impact or consequences included, for example, the movement of women into jobs hitherto filled by men, though other social changes were also discussed.

History essays of this kind require capacities in using language that take students beyond simple re-creation of past time, though such capacities remain relevant. Indeed, the skills acquired in reading about and constructing past events, as in historical recounts, need to be maintained and extended for the purposes of handling both historical explanation and argument. Such skills include the ability to capture long sequences of events in time and to compress them, achieving some control over ways to express these in an economic and ordered way. For that reason, I briefly review some of the resources in which the passage of time is captured, going on to say a little of problems having to do with increasing abstraction that emerge as young people go further into their historical studies. The emergence of metaphor, both lexical and grammatical, is important to the emergence of the capacity to handle abstraction. These matters having been briefly outlined, I then consider an example of a consequential explanation written by an adolescent writer in which he displays many of the features I have outlined.

4.2.1 Time, Abstraction, Metaphor, and Agency in History

The most common way to express the passage of time is to use preposi-tional phrases that create circumstances of time. For example, Tom, writer of Text 3.3, made use of one such circumstance, carrying a rather general sense of time:

> *In the past the convicts would stumble out of the giant building and slump towards the main officers' window to collect their tools, so they could start working on the buildings.*

Other instances of a less general nature, found among older writers by mid-adolescence include

> *Soldiers were conscripted **during World War II** as the Australian government recognized this was necessary to win the war against Japan.*
> ***At the beginning of World War II**, people were paranoid, especially the government, about critical information concerning the Australian Defense Forces leaking out to the enemy.*

In other contexts time is expressed using a dependent clause of time:

> ***Ever since Australia was colonized,** Aborigines have been treated extremely poorly.*
> ***After Japan surrendered in August 1945**, the nationalist leader, Sukarno, declared that Indonesia was independent and he was appointed president.*

All such resources are important in breaking up sequences of events into manageable bits so that the writer can capture these, achieving some control and some sense of direction in dealing with events. With growing maturity, students of history learn to handle a range of linguistic resources to mark the passage of time, organizing it into manageable pieces. One professional historian (Macintyre, 2004), writing of early European settlement in Australia, captures events over some centuries in a matter of a few sentences:

After several centuries of European voyaging in the southern oceans, the English naval lieutenant James Cook sailed the eastern coast in 1770, named it New South Wales and claimed possession in the name of his monarch. Within twenty years the British government dispatched an expedition to settle New South Wales. On 26th January 1788 its commander, Arthur Phillip, assumed government over the eastern half of the country. The thousand officers, troops, civilian officials and convicted felons who came ashore from the eleven vessels of the First Fleet anchored in Sydney Harbour prepared the way for later immigrants, bond and free, who spread over the continent and settled, possessed and subdued it. (p. 1)

Note, for example, Macintyre's use of nominalization (itself an example of grammatical metaphor), in his opening circumstance of time:

*After several centuries of **European voyaging** in the southern seas*

his other circumstances of time:

in 1770
within twenty years
on 26th January 1788

and the manner in which he captures a sense of shifts in time, and also in space, apparent in several of the lexical verbs he selects to express his processes:

*the British government **dispatched** an expedition*
*the thousand officers ... who **came ashore** ... **prepared the way** for later immigrants ... who **spread over the continent and settled, possessed and subdued it***

By adolescence, successful students need to achieve some control of ways to compress historical sequences in such a manner. Among other resources, that of grammatical metaphor enables the student of history to turn activities into phenomena—actually grammatical participants—about which subsequent explanation and interpretation can be developed. Consider Table 4.1, where

Table 4.1 Congruent and noncongruent expressions

Congruent expression	Noncongruent expression
(1) Austronesian people, who form the majority of the modern population, were originally from Taiwan and they arrived in Indonesia around 2000 BCE.	*(1a) The Austronesian occupation of Indonesia by Taiwanese people occurred in about 2000 BCE.*
(2) Ever since Australia was colonized, Aborigines have been treated extremely poorly.	*(2a) Ever since the colonization of Australia, Aborigines have been treated extremely poorly.*
(3) After Japan surrendered in August 1945, the nationalist leader, Sukarno, declared that Indonesia was independent and he was appointed president.	*(3a) The Japanese surrender in August 1945 led to the declaration of independence of Indonesia and the appointment of Sukarno as the first president.*

congruent clause complexes, all drawn from students' writing, are displayed to the left, and those to the right represent noncongruent versions that I have created, using the resource of grammatical metaphor. It will be observed that

- in (1) there are three clauses, one of which is an enclosed nondefining clause:

  Austronesian people, ≪who form the majority of the modern population≫ were originally from Taiwan // and they arrived in Indonesia around 2000 BCE

  whereas the noncongruent expression collapses these clauses into one clause (1a);

- in (2) there are two clauses:

  Ever since Australia was colonized // Aborigines have been treated extremely poorly

  whereas the noncongruent version creates one clause (2a);

- and in (3) there are four clauses, which are also collapsed into one clause (3a), using the resource of grammatical metaphor:

  After Japan surrendered in August 1945 // the nationalist leader, Sukarno, declared // that Indonesia was independent // and he was appointed president

Are the meanings to the right "the same" as those to the left? Not entirely, because the noncongruent versions construe or interpret the experiential information a little differently from the congruent versions. Are the expressions to the right "better" than those to the left? No, they are not. Rather, they represent alternative ways to express meanings, often found in writing history, and for that reason they are important to learn about; the abstractions they create can become matters for class discussion, explanation, analysis, and interpretation. Such matters can be usefully deconstructed for students in early to midadolescence, when they are learning to handle written historical discourse, enabling them to see how information can be constructed and then developed and extended. For example, instance (1a) could be redeveloped thus, where a causative process (*led to*) is used to develop the experiential information expressed:

> *The Austronesian occupation of Indonesia by Taiwanese people, which occurred in about 2000 BCE, **led to** the emergence of several later civilizations, which were, in order, Hindu, Buddhist and finally Moslem.*

In contrast, in the following two cases, the new information found toward the end of each clause has been reinstated as an abstraction in theme position in the subsequent clause, thereby building some unity in the unfolding of the text.

> *Ever since the colonization of Australia Aborigines have been treated extremely poorly.*
>
> *Such treatment has included forcible eviction of Aborigines from their land, murdering Aborigines who resisted and more recently, denial of good health services to Aborigines living in remote areas of Australia. After the Japanese surrender in August 1945, the nationalist leader, Sukarno, declared independence and was appointed president.*
>
> *During Sukarno's presidency, Indonesia resisted attempts by the Dutch to re-establish rule, and Sukarno went on to develop a constitution for Indonesia.*

In each case the abstraction helps to "package" information in a manner that is useful to the historian (Martin, 2003, p. 27). Such abstractions can often prove elusive for students to understand, especially if they are reluctant readers[2] and writers or learners of English as a second language or both. The packaging will often need to be unpacked, and the potentially mysterious ways in which many abstract entities can achieve agency, or capacity to act in the world, will often need to be explored (Schleppegrell, 2011). The notion, for example, that *the Austronesian occupation of Indonesia . . . led to the emergence of several civilizations* carries a sense that *the occupation* had agency. This is potentially confusing, though very characteristic of a great deal of historical interpretation and explanation. Indeed, history typically packages events in many ways, as in the following, rather different example, using lexical metaphor, where the First World War becomes an entity given metaphorical status as something that can "see":

> **The First World War** *saw many young Australian and New Zealand men enlist in the services in search of adventure.* (written by a student aged 15)

or in the following, drawn from an essay, where *events* achieve a metaphorical status, again in a lexical sense, in which they can *aid*:

> **Domestic events in Germany and other global events** *aided Hitler in his quest for power.* (written by a student aged 17)

A great deal of writing in history relies heavily on such abstractions to create its experiential meanings, where metaphor in both senses will be involved.

4.2.2 A Consequential Explanation in History

Text 4.1 was written by Steven, about 15 years old, when he was in Year 10 of a secondary school in the state of New South Wales. His text was one of a very large sample of texts collected by Christie and Derewianka (2007) investigating writing development in English, history, and science across the years of schooling. Texts were collected in several high schools, both public and private, over the years, and they were analyzed using the functional grammar. Christie and Derewianka (2008) provide a detailed discussion of the results of the study. The question Steven had been given by his teacher read: "Explain how, why and in what areas the Federal Government introduced censorship during World War II."

The wording of the question makes clear that the function of the text to be written is quite different from that of Text 3.3, written in childhood, though it was also about history. Where Text 3.3 sought to retell the details of a class visit to historical sites in the manner of a simple recount, Text 4.1 is intended to explain history, accounting for "how, why and in what areas the Federal Government introduced censorship." As I have suggested, Steven writes a Consequential Explanation (Coffin, 2006, pp. 69–73), though the text departs in some ways from the examples Coffin gives. Coffin identifies the schematic structure thus:

Input ^ *Consequences* ^ *(Reinforcement of consequences).*
According to Coffin, such a genre has two obligatory elements and one optional element. The obligatory elements are the Input, which identifies the historical phenomenon that has led to some change, and the Consequence element(s), which detail the consequences of the phenomenon. Because more than one consequence will normally be involved, there will generally be more than one Consequence element. The optional element is a final one, termed the Reinforcement of Consequences, which emphasizes the consequences, often evaluating them. Steven provides both an Input and a Consequence, and also provides a Reasons element, for the terms of the question required it. Finally, he writes a Reinforcement of Consequences element, whose function is very much one of evaluation of the impact of the consequences discussed.

The field for Text 4.1 is that of Australian federal government actions in the Second World War, where this needs to be researched from books, websites, and any other relevant sources. The terms of the field and the genre require a very formal tenor, where the identity of the writer is not revealed. The mode of the text is constitutive of the meanings, requiring a written text of reasonable length in order to do justice to some complex social issues.

As in earlier chapters, marked topical themes are bolded in Text 4.1, and embedded and enclosed clauses within these are also noted.

Text 4.1 Explain how, why and in what areas the Federal Government introduced censorship during World War II.

Input	**At the beginning of World War II**, people were paranoid, especially the government, about critical information [[concerning the Australian Defense Forces leaking out to the enemy]]. So, **in an attempt to remedy this fear**, the Federal Government set up the Department of Information, which was responsible for hiding any dangerous information from the public. The government also introduced certain censorship laws in the form of the *National Security Act* which was passed on the 7th September in 1939.
Consequence	The *National Security Act* allowed the Federal Government to censor any material [[that they thought could be counter-productive to the allies' cause in the war]]. This included censoring information [[given to the public via radio, telegraph, telephone, newspapers and magazines]]. However, this was not the only way [[the authorities hid information from the enemies and at the

same time the public]]. The Department of Information would also censor letters from Servicemen and women to their families. Letters were not allowed to contain any information on the whereabouts of troops and/or details of [[where and when ships were sailing]]. Servicemen and women were also forbidden to keep a personal diary for fear of it [[falling into the wrong hands]], and [[being used against them]].

When Australia or any of the allied countries achieved a victory, it was widely publicized and they were celebrated. However ≪**if the allies suffered a loss≫**, it was only briefly mentioned and quite often numbers of deaths and injuries were covered up or made to sound much more insignificant [[than they really were]].

Reasons   There were many reasons for [[the government taking the steps [[that they did // to hide information]]]]. The first and foremost was [[to prevent any important or critical information from falling into the wrong hands, i.e.; the enemy's]]. This was definitely a competent move on the Federal government's part as this approach did give the allies an advantage when it came to the element of surprise. The other main reason for censorship was [[to keep Australia's morale high]], for ≪ **if the public of Australia believed // that the allies had had too many major losses≫,** they would have begun to question the government and the war itself, and in some cases they may have even refused to support the war altogether. This would not have been in the government's best interests and so censorship was introduced.

Reinforcement of   In retrospect, the censorship laws were definitely useful
Consequences   in many ways. Especially to keep allied movements a secret.* It was also logical to keep certain information from the public, as there were more than likely enemy spies [[situated in Australia]] during the war, and it would have been very difficult if not impossible [[to locate and identify each and every one of them]]. Therefore censorship seems to have been a useful tactic during WWII.

*This is not a complete sentence. The whole sentence should have read *"In retrospect, the censorship laws were definitely useful in many ways, especially to keep allied movements a secret."*

Despite some awkward expressions, Text 4.1 has a reasonably clear structure, its various elements signaled with opening generalizations, which are then elaborated. (Figure 4.1 reveals its structure.) The wording of the opening sentence of the Input is somewhat clumsy, in that a more mature writer would probably not write:

> At the beginning of World War II, people were paranoid, especially the government, about critical information concerning the Australian Defense Forces leaking out to the enemy.

Making *people* and *the government* apparently synonymous terms is not really acceptable, and the attribute in the relational attributive process (*people were* ***paranoid***) seems rather excessive in such a context. This is an instance of the tendency to overwrite often found in adolescents as they develop some control of their language for writing, remarked by both Myhill (2008, 2009) and Christie and Derewianka (2008). A more mature writer would probably adopt an expression such as:

> "At the beginning of World War II, the government was very concerned that information about the Australian Defense Forces might leak out to the enemy."

Students of history, like writers of other school subjects, need to learn their craft, and in other ways Steven makes a reasonable attempt at his opening element, evident if we display its thematic progression a little more closely as follows. The themes are mainly topical, though one instance of a textual theme expressed in the conjunction *so* is used, to help build an unfolding sense of consequence:

> **At the beginning of World War II** , people were paranoid, especially the government, about critical information concerning the Australian Defense Forces leaking out to the enemy.
> So, **in an attempt to remedy this fear**, the Federal Government set up the Department of Information,
> which was responsible for hiding any dangerous information from the public.
> The government also introduced certain censorship laws in the form of the National Security Act
> which was passed on the 7th September in 1939.

Two marked themes, the first expressed in a circumstance of time, the second in one of manner, help shape the directions the discourse takes, though

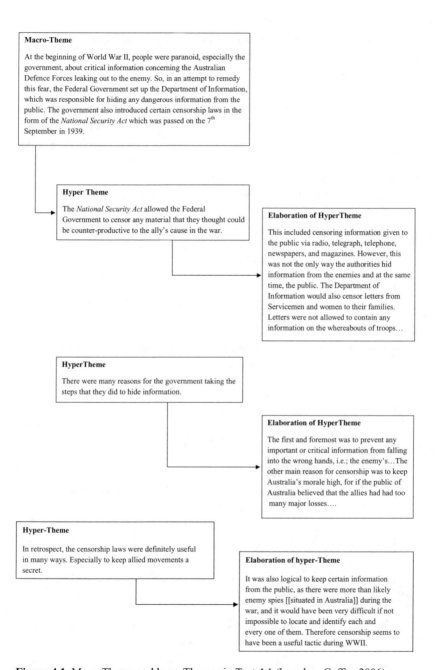

Macro-Theme

At the beginning of World War II, people were paranoid, especially the government, about critical information concerning the Australian Defence Forces leaking out to the enemy. So, in an attempt to remedy this fear, the Federal Government set up the Department of Information, which was responsible for hiding any dangerous information from the public. The government also introduced certain censorship laws in the form of the *National Security Act* which was passed on the 7th September in 1939.

Hyper Theme

The *National Security Act* allowed the Federal Government to censor any material that they thought could be counter-productive to the ally's cause in the war.

Elaboration of HyperTheme

This included censoring information given to the public via radio, telegraph, telephone, newspapers, and magazines. However, this was not the only way the authorities hid information from the enemies and at the same time, the public. The Department of Information would also censor letters from Servicemen and women to their families. Letters were not allowed to contain any information on the whereabouts of troops...

HyperTheme

There were many reasons for the government taking the steps that they did to hide information.

Elaboration of HyperTheme

The first and foremost was to prevent any important or critical information from falling into the wrong hands, i.e.; the enemy's...The other main reason for censorship was to keep Australia's morale high, for if the public of Australia believed that the allies had had too many major losses....

Hyper-Theme

In retrospect, the censorship laws were definitely useful in many ways. Especially to keep allied movements a secret.

Elaboration of hyper-Theme

It was also logical to keep certain information from the public, as there were more than likely enemy spies [[situated in Australia]] during the war, and it would have been very difficult if not impossible to locate and identify each and every one of them. Therefore censorship seems to have been a useful tactic during WWII.

Figure 4.1 MacroTheme and hyperThemes in Text 4.1 (based on Coffin, 2006).

the lexis of the historical field is also obvious: *the Australian Defense Forces*, *the Department of Information*, and *the National Security Act*, as well as in other noun groups expressing abstract notions, such as *critical information*, *dangerous information*, and *censorship laws*.

The second element is built confidently, and this depends in large measure on the success with which the topical themes develop the direction of the discourse, allowing the discourse to flow in a coherent way, much as we have just seen is true of the first element. The opening sentence builds with the reference to the *National Security Act*, which was introduced in the last sentence of the previous element (where it was new information); this is placed in topical theme position (where it is now given information), while later topical themes continue the pattern of picking up what has been introduced and then reinstating it, and a contrastive conjunction (*however*) creates a textual theme, also helping to shape the logic of the explanation:

> *The National Security Act allowed the Federal Government to censor any material that they thought could be counter-productive to the allies' cause in the war.*
>
> *This included censoring information [[given to the public via radio, telegraph, telephone, newspapers and magazines]].*
>
> *However, this was not the only way [[the authorities hid information from the enemies and at the same time the public]].*
>
> *The Department of Information would also censor letters from Servicemen and women to their families.*
>
> *Letters were not allowed to contain any information on the whereabouts of troops and/or details of [[where and when ships were sailing]].*
>
> *Servicemen and women were also forbidden to keep a personal diary for fear of it [[falling into the wrong hands]], and [[being used against them]].*

A new phase within this element is signaled with a marked topical theme, with which Steven also commences a new paragraph:

> **When Australia or any of the allied countries achieved a victory,** *it was widely publicized and they were celebrated.*

A contrastive conjunction signals a change of direction, whereas a dependent clause of condition in marked topical theme pursues the experiential information involved in the change:

However ≪*if the allies suffered a loss*≫, *it was only briefly mentioned and quite often numbers of deaths and injuries were covered up or made to sound much more insignificant [[than they really were]].*

Abstraction abounds in the element. The notion of something being *counterproductive* is itself an abstraction, as is the notion of *the allies' cause.* Moreover, although it will be noted that people are mentioned in the element, it is not for their status as individuals, but rather as members of generic or generalized groups: *the enemies, the public, Servicemen and women, troops.*

History of this kind, dealing with the broadly understood results of social actions and movements, does not typically deal with individuals. Furthermore, agency or capacity to act in the world, as already noted above, is often attributed in history to Acts of Parliament (as here) or to organizations such as governments (also as here) and sometimes even to ideas or movements (such as democracy or justice). Writing of the many problems adolescents encounter in reading history textbooks, Schleppegrell (2011) has noted the difficulties students can have in dealing with the abstract entities that cause, or are affected by, actions of many kinds. It is in practice important for teachers to guide discussion of the passages of written history, deconstructing it into oral language, so that the nature of the abstractions involved is uncovered.

The second element involves some nominalizing of an aspect of the question, for in explaining *why* events occurred, Steven commences this element by introducing the noun *reasons*, creating an associated dense circumstance of purpose:

*There were many reasons **for [[the government taking the steps [[that they did // to hide information]]]].***

This enables him later to create two subsequent relational identifying processes with quite dense noun groups:

*The first and foremost was [[to prevent any important or critical information from falling into the wrong hands, i.e.; the enemy's]]
The other main reason for censorship was [[to keep Australia's morale high]]*

Coffin (2006) notes that in explanation genres "dense nominal groups are frequently placed in relationship with each other" (p. 72). They compress information in a manner that a more congruent realization would not necessarily achieve. For example, Steven could have written

"The government took steps to hide information // because it wanted to stop important or critical information falling into the enemy's hands"

and

"The government introduced censorship because it wanted to keep Australia's moral high"

but these two sentences would not have allowed him to proceed so easily with the subsequent discussion.

In the Reasons element Steven introduces evaluative language, offering some assessment of the practices and consequences of censorship. Thus, he offers judgment about the wisdom or value of government actions:

*[prevention of important or critical information from falling into the wrong hands] was **definitely a competent move** on the Federal government's part;*
*this approach did give the allies **an advantage when it came to the element of surprise;***
*if the public of Australia believed that the allies had had too many major losses, they **would have begun to question the government and the war itself**, and in some cases they **may have even refused to support the war altogether;***
*this **would not have been in the government's best interest***

In the final element Steven evaluates the consequences of the government actions in introducing censorship, and again he offers judgment:

*In retrospect, the censorship laws **were definitely useful in many ways**. It was **also logical to keep certain information from the public**, as there **were more than likely enemy spies** [[situated in Australia]] during the war, and it **would have been very difficult if not impossible to locate and identify each and every one of them**. Therefore censorship **seems to have been a useful tactic** during WWII.*

Evaluation is a necessary aspect of most historical discourse, involving capacity both to marshal the relevant experiential information and to weigh up and assess its significance. It involves a rich range of language resources for its expression including

o relevant lexis that often infuses experiential information and attitude (*critical information, dangerous information, if the allies suffered a loss*);

o intensity to scale up the values attaching to experience *(the **first and fore-most** (reason) was to prevent, the **other main reason**, the censorship laws were **definitely useful**)*;

o various modal adjuncts to help intrude judgment *(servicemen and women were **also** forbidden, it was **only briefly** mentioned)*; and

o modal verbs also to intrude judgment *(they **may** have even refused to support the war altogether)*.

None of these items is sufficient or even significant in itself. Rather, it is the total pattern of discourse in which they are deployed that builds the historical evaluation required. It takes some years of reading, writing, and discussion about historical events, and purposes for studying them, in order to build a sense of the reasons for valuing in history and the methods for expressing it. In consulting the various textbooks, videos, and websites available to read and research history, students need questions to pursue in order to guide their learning. Students need to be encouraged to consider, for example,

o What is this topic in history and why do we study it? (This helps to establish experiential information by getting at "actors" in history, be they persons, movements, phenomena, and so forth, as well as some sense of causes.)

o How is the written passage organized? (This helps to establish textual organization by looking at how the discourse unfolds, moving from one theme to another to construct its meanings.)

o What actions, persons, events are valued, either as good or bad? (This helps to establish interpersonal/attitudinal information by looking at evaluation and when it occurs.)

Figure 4.1 sets out the structure of Text 4.1, showing how the logic of the text is constructed and unfolded. Here I introduce two terms not so far used in this book: *macroTheme* and *hyperTheme* (Martin & Rose, 2007b). There is a relationship here to the traditional term "topic sentence," familiar in teaching rhetoric. The terms are used metaphorically, in that the notion of theme, familiar in the functional grammar for its relevance in the organization of the clause, is borrowed for use in discussing the larger unity of the written text. The macroTheme is the overall theme, "main point," or idea for the whole text. It is sometimes expressed in one sentence, though it often is expressed in a paragraph, and in some cases it might be more than one. HyperThemes, on the other hand, create the opening "main points" (often generalizations) of the subsequent elements in the text, all of which both look back to what has come before, and look ahead to what is to come in terms of elaboration of the hyperTheme. The overall pattern of theme choices within clauses, and of macroTheme and hyperThemes across a text, directs the discourse in waves of information, giving *periodicity* to the information flow. A successful text in history, as in many other disciplinary discourses, has a coherent structure, achieved both through its broad patterns of theme in clauses within the text and across the overall schematic structure.

Figure 4.1 displays how the opening establishes the macroTheme for the text, and subsequent elements commence with hyperThemes that look back, on the one hand, while also looking forward to elaboration of the information within each element. The organization of the text, as I have discussed it above, is thus exposed. Such a structure, mapping the progress of the text, could be displayed for students learning to write a Consequential Explanation in history, providing a model for deconstruction.

4.2.3 A Summary of Matters Discussed in This Section

By midadolescence history discourse is expressed in a range of potential genres, where the discourse

- √ experientially constructs meanings about events, people, and social movements that are normally remote from the lived experience of those who read or write it. In this sense the knowledge constructed is uncommonsense;
- √ is typically concerned to explain why or how events occurred, to argue the importance or consequences of such events, or both;
- √ tends to use a noncongruent grammar;
- √ employs language to compress long periods of time and events in human affairs, packaging such information in manageable ways;
- √ uses both lexical and grammatical metaphor, where grammatical metaphor has a role in contributing to the compression, often causing otherwise independently linked clauses to collapse and disappear, though some logical relationships remain between clauses expressed through the conjunction system;
- √ creates abstract meanings, turning phenomena such as wars, Acts of parliament, or ideas (like "democracy" or "justice") into entities that are said to act on human affairs in various ways;
- √ tends to deal with generic groups and movements rather than individuals (though this differs according to the field of knowledge involved);
- √ interpersonally removes the identity of the writer from the discourse;
- √ nonetheless expresses evaluation of phenomena and events considered, where such evaluation is often expressed as judgment about the propriety of events or actions;

√ generally requires reading and writing of longer texts than those found in childhood, so that the texts need to be well organized textually, their discourses shaped and ordered through patterns of thematic progression.

4.3 Subject English in Midadolescence

By midadolescence, subject English involves young people in studying various literary texts. Here, as in history, well-directed class discussion is essential to development of the necessary understandings and language capacities in dealing with literature. Sometimes students will be involved in discussion of themes developed from a reading of texts or a viewing of films. Themes of courage or injustice can be explored from a reading of *To Kill a Mockingbird*, for example, as well as other themes for reflection and interpretation, both in talk and in writing. Just as in history, the range of potential genres that students can write in English is considerable (see Christie & Derewianka, 2008, pp. 30–85), though I shall consider only one—a *thematic interpretation*. Like other examples of *response genres* (a term proposed by Rothery, 1994), the thematic interpretation is a genre written to respond to and interpret a literary text, though its principal function, unlike a book review for example, is to identify a major theme in the piece and explore that.

One of the several tasks of adolescent study of English is learning to respond to, interpret, and evaluate other texts. As they learn to respond, subject English involves young people in going beyond the immediate and the familiar in their reading and writing to interpret experience in more abstract and unfamiliar ways. What are some of the linguistic resources needed to construct the necessary discourses involved in writing thematic interpretations?

4.3.1 Interpreting and Responding to Other Texts

Although it is clear that students must learn to offer interpretations and responses, one important aspect of the challenges in writing all response genres lies in avoiding extensive reference to self, as in this made up example: "I like *To Kill a Mockingbird* because it is about children growing up in an American community."[3] Instead, the student must learn to stand back from the text and to generalize about its themes, thereby achieving some sense of detachment, while foregrounding the matters to be considered. An example, drawn from the opening of an essay written by a girl aged about 15, reads

Life is about growing up, learning new things, meeting different people, and the book "To Kill a Mockingbird" is about all these things.

The use of the abstract noun *life* to start the text signals to the reader immediately that it is abstract experience that is at issue, and the student goes on to discuss how the text "shows" or reveals this, again using an abstraction in the expression *many situations*:

> *Many situations throughout the book show the children's reactions and emotions.*

The writer who begins thus positions herself to go on developing the discussion by building other abstractions about the novel and about life as interpreted through its pages.

In fact, writers learn to shift constantly between the general statement about experience and the less general statement about the specific experience or incident of the novel that symbolizes or reveals what is involved. Tom, author of Text 3.3, here reappears as the author of Text 4.3, now aged 14 years, and he writes:

> *Throughout the book, Harper Lee uses the mockingbird as a symbol of innocence, as mockingbirds don't do anything but sing all day.*

A notable feature of texts written by successful students in adolescence discussing and responding to literary texts appears in their frequent use of a range of lexical verbs having to do with "showing." Although these appear in other subjects, including history and science, they have a particular role in response genres of all kinds (Christie & Cléirigh, 2008). Examples include

> *Through this character study of Antonio I **have shown** how Antonio changes through the play.*
> *Biographical details and anecdotes effectively **illustrate** how Archimedes' methods and ideas "set the world on a course"*
> *This quote [from the novel, The Catcher in the Rye] **shows** that Holden is not taking this advice seriously.*

Other lexical verbs used for similar purposes to those displayed include *reveal*, *suggest*, and *indicate*. Teachers can usefully guide students to use such verbs for writing response genres by, for example, asking what an incident *reveals*, *demonstrates*, or *shows*.

In building the symbolic meanings of subject English, adolescents are required to evaluate the texts they read, where this can involve evaluation of characters:

*Felix is an adventurous person who does not entertain himself but others
entertain him. He takes life as it comes and does not enjoy the idea of
settling down,*

evaluation of main ideas or themes:

*Harper Lee's use of a mockingbird as her central symbol of innocence in
the story is very effective*

or evaluation of verbal techniques:

*Paton uses different uses of language and descriptions to illustrate that
mankind shapes the land they live on, which in turn shapes the humans.
By using personification, imagery, and parallel structure, Paton subtly
conveys ideas and connections that explain the different interactions
between the land and the humans who live on it.*

The challenges of writing literary response genres of all kinds are considerable, made harder for those students who are in any case reluctant readers
themselves or those for whom English is a second language, or both. For them,
the immediate and often overwhelming challenge is to read and understand the
novel (or the play or poem) while they must in addition learn to stand back
from it and interpret its themes and ideas. Moreover, it is quite hard to understand that requests to write "personal opinions" about texts are often seriously
misleading, though English teachers often tell their students they are to write
their own ideas or their own opinions. In fact, the request to write personal
opinion is to be interpreted against the often invisible requirement that it be
expressed using a formal tenor, when personal identity has little or no role,
and where generalization about themes and human experience is rewarded.
Christie and Macken-Horarik (2007, 2011) discuss these matters in some
detail.

4.3.2 Talk about To Kill a Mockingbird

Here I display texts from two different Australian classrooms of 14- to 15-year-
olds in which *To Kill a Mockingbird* is being studied. Text 4.2 is an extract from
much longer oral text, revealing students in a Melbourne high school in class
discussion, reflecting on the motives of people in an incident in the novel in
discussion with their teacher. This involves not only recalling the incident—a
relatively easy thing to do—but interpreting it for its significance, which is,
of course, much harder. Here the values of teacher-guided talk are apparent,
as students learn language for reflection on experience. Text 4.3 is drawn

from ongoing research in Sydney (Christie, 2011) in which Tom discusses the symbolism in the novel. Both texts in their different ways suggest the challenges met by students in midadolescence in discussing literary texts and responding to English literature.

In Text 4.2 the students have been asked by their teacher to discuss the incident when the lynch mob disperses outside the jail, and explain why the mob moved away peacefully. The teacher has advised the students to talk among themselves in small groups before participating in whole class discussion. After some 15 minutes of group talk, Kim, invited by her teacher, starts to talk to the whole class. (A row of dots indicates a short pause.)

Text 4.2 (extract only) Why the lynch mob dispersed.

Kim: *Well. Tom Robinson's in the jail and Atticus is sitting out the front in a chair. Then the lynch mob turns up and they're there to get Tom Robinson and to hang him right there and then, so. . . because they don't like him, and because they don't believe he's right and they think he's lying. And Scout and her two little friends, whoever they are, turned up and, then, isn't there? . . . and Scout starts talking to the lynch mob as if they're completely rational and it's just everyday conversation and they realize what they're doing is wrong and then they just leave.*

Teacher: *Right. OK, ah, take, ah, that's perfect, ah, take thirty seconds to explain to the person next to you why it is that they do it.* [Group discussions go on for several minutes, too hard to record]

Teacher: *Thanks, Kirstin.* [he nods to her]

Kirstin: *OK, um, I'm not sure, but it might have had something to do with the fact that Scout was just, as Kim said, was talking to them rationally and made them for a moment, exactly what they were doing. And so they just had doubts about it or something along those lines anyway . . . and that's it.*

Teacher: *Anybody want to add anything to that? . . . OK, fine.*

Kim reconstructs the events using a congruent grammar, in the manner of much talk, using simple additive and temporal connectedness to build the sequence, for here she does not interpret but, importantly, she tells:

> *Tom Robinson's in the jail*
> **and** *Atticus is sitting out the front in a chair.*
> **Then** *the lynch mob turns up*
> **and** *they're there to get Tom Robinson*

and some conjunctions of reason, building connectedness in a different sense:

because *they don't like him*
and because *they don't believe he's right and he's lying.*

At this point Kim offers her interpretation of the behavior involved and the discourse changes. Thus, her two relational processes of attribution take her beyond simple reconstruction:

*and Scout starts talking to the lynch mob as if **they're completely rational** and **it's just everyday conversation**,*

after which she goes on to interpret the thoughts of those she describes using a mental process:

*and they **realize** what they're doing is wrong and then they just leave.*

The shift in the spoken discourse is quite noticeable: it is a shift from common-sense reconstruction of the event to more abstract reflection on the significance of the event. Notably, the teacher has provoked the response, for a teacher's role in such discourse construction is essential.

Kirstin's contribution, after several minutes of talk, shows tentativeness, including some use of modality, suggesting she is aware that human behavior is often difficult to interpret:

*Ok, um, I'm not sure, but it **might** have had something to do with the fact that Scout was just, as Kim said, was talking to them rationally and made them think for a moment, exactly what they were doing.*

Such classroom talk, carefully orchestrated by the teacher, allows adolescents to explore the fields of human experience as encountered in novels and other literature and to develop a language for talking about them. This is to go beyond the immediate details of the novel and into abstract areas of interpretation of behavior and ideas. Good classroom talk leads in time to writing about the novels or other literary texts studied, as did Tom, writing about the symbolism in *To Kill a Mockingbird*.

4.3.3 Writing a Thematic Interpretation about *To Kill a Mockingbird*

Above I noted that Text 4.3, a thematic interpretation genre, was written by Tom, who was at the time in Year 9 of secondary school. He is one of several students in Sydney whose progress I currently continue to follow as part of an ongoing research interest in the teaching of subject English (Christie, 2011). Tom, who had enjoyed reading the novel, had been asked by his teacher to write an essay discussing the symbolism in *To Kill a Mockingbird*. He constructs an appropriate schematic structure for his text, where macroTheme and hyperThemes are established. Despite that, his text is not entirely successful, though it displays several strengths. For example, experientially, Tom demonstrates familiarity with the field, evident in the lexis he uses and in the details of the story he constructs. Interpersonally, he also understands that the goal is to offer interpretation of that field, so that his uses of evaluative language, at least in some parts of the text, are good, though this is not consistently the case. Organizationally, the text reveals a good control of grammatical intricacy, in that Tom is able to produce series of interconnected clauses that help build the fabric of the text well in several places. Textually, Tom shows a reasonable grasp of thematic progression, more evident in some phases of the text than in others. The problems he has are most apparent in the third element or stage of his text, where he seems to lose control of the ordering of his experiential information. The difficulty may be due to the fact that he does not use grammatical metaphor, a resource that might well have assisted him in capturing and ordering his experiential and evaluative information more satisfactorily. All these matters are of some developmental significance, and I return to them below.

The schematic structure of a thematic interpretation may be displayed thus:

Thematic Interpretation/Preview of Elements ⌒ *Element Evaluation* ⌒ *Reiteration of Theme.*

The Thematic Interpretation/Preview of Elements establishes the main theme taken from the literary work and elements selected from that work for discussion in light of the theme. The subsequent elements develop and elaborate on the theme (Elements 1, 2, and so on). A final element, the Reiteration of Theme, restates what has been argued. Christie and Derewianka (2008, pp. 76–83) discuss such genres in some detail.

Text 4.3 is set out with marked topical themes bolded as before, and embedded and enclosed clauses are also shown. MacroTheme and hyperThemes are shaded.

Text 4.3 Symbolism in *To Kill a Mockingbird.*

Theme Identification/ Preview of elements	"You can shoot at all the popinjays you like, but it's a sin to kill a mockingbird." These are the instructions [[Atticus gives to his children]] when he gives them their first air rifles in "To Kill a Mockingbird." Throughout the book, Harper Lee uses the symbol of the mockingbird as a symbol of innocence as mockingbirds don't do anything but sing all

day. They aren't a pest to anyone. She says that it would be a
sin to kill one, as they hadn't done anything wrong. She uses
the innocent mockingbird symbol to describe two characters in
her book, their names are Tom Robinson and Boo Radley.

Element 1   **In the case on Tom Robinson** a black man is accused of rape
by Bob and Mayella Ewell, two white people [[who have been
known to be untrustworthy on many other accounts]]. He is
sent to court, where Atticus defends him against a biased jury
who will almost certainly convict him regardless of [[whether
it is proved // he did it]]. **Throughout the court scene**, it
becomes more and more obvious [[that not only did he not do
it, // but he couldn't have done it without great personal strain
//as his left hand had been severely damaged // when he was a
child // and the person [[who beat Mayella Ewell up]] was
obviously left-handed]]]]. This even seems to point to Bob
Ewell as the primary suspect in the case after it was proved he
had a motive and he was definitely left-handed. **Against all the
evidence,** the jury (although not without consideration)
convicts Tom and his case is to be taken to the high court.
Before it can be dealt with though, Tom makes a desperate
rush to freedom from the jail [[he is imprisoned in]]. The
fictional witnesses say he "ran like a crazy man" and was
sprinting as fast as he could and leapt over the fence, but ≪just
as he was going over ≫he was shot. The prison warden shot to
wound him and bring him back to jail, but instead shot and
killed him. Atticus describes this as senseless killing.

He says that ≪ **although Tom was innocent of the crimes
[[he was accused of]]** ≫ he was dead from the start. He didn't
have a chance in the world of winning his case, so he ran for it.
He was innocent and would've died anyway, by gun, or by
electric chair. He is like a mockingbird because he is innocent
of [[what he is accused of]] and he is killed regardless.

Element 2   The other person [[Harper Lee uses the metaphor of the
mockingbird to describe]] is Boo Radley, the child of Arthur
Radley who has been cooped up in his house for as long as
[[the children in the story can remember]]. **In Boo's case** the
innocence varies because, **instead of being convicted**, he is
only confused and is innocent in the way [[that he has never
had much experience with other people]]. He was only trying
to save Jem and Scout, but he ended up killing Bob Ewell.
When Bob Ewell attacks the children after a Halloween

pageant, he knocks Jem out and breaks his arm and starts to go after Scout. Boo runs down to them from his porch to save them and just as Bob is suffocating Scout, he steals his knife and stabs him in the heart, killing him. **Afterwards at the Finches' house,** Heck Tate the Sheriff of Maycomb County has to decide [[what to do]], relying on Scout's explanation of [[what happened]]. **According to her explanation** it could've been either Jem or Boo who killed him and Atticus reckoned it was Jem. **Later in the conversation though,** they realize it must've been Boo [[who did it]] and start to think about [[what to do about it]]. **Eventually** Heck decides not to convict him as more than anything he had saved the lives of two young children. He didn't know exactly [[what he was doing]] and he had to kill Bob to save them. Heck says "taking the one man who's done you and this town a service an' dragging' him with his shy ways into the limelight – to me, that's a sin".

Reiteration of Theme   In all, I think Harper Lee's use of a mockingbird as her central symbol of innocence in the story is very effective because it gives the characters [[it symbolizes]] more depth and makes a strong point about [[what is innocence and sin]].

The opening element makes confident use of a quote from the novel, already cited above, establishing that a symbolic reading of the novel is involved, and signaled in part in the marked topical theme:

Throughout the novel Harper Lee uses the symbol of the mockingbird as a symbol of innocence as mockingbirds don't do anything but sing all day.

This enables Tom to go on to elaborate:

She says that it would be a sin to kill one, as they hadn't done anything wrong. She uses the innocent mockingbird symbol to describe two characters in her book, their names are Tom Robinson and Boo Radley.

Element 1 begins with its hyperTheme referring to what has been established, its presence signaled with another marked theme:

In the case on Tom Robinson a black man is accused of rape by Bob and Mayella Ewell, two white people who have been known to be untrustworthy on many other accounts.

Tom then elaborates on this, selecting and ordering sufficient specific events to illustrate what has been said, while also intruding some judgment about the probability of the events described:

> *He is sent to court, where Atticus defends him against a **biased jury** who will **almost certainly** convict him regardless of whether it is proved he did it.*

A pattern emerges by which experiential and evaluative information are interwoven, hence building interpretation.

One reason the elaborating information in this element works well is that Tom has good control of the textual resources employed to build the discourse. He uses four more marked themes at strategically useful points in the unfolding of the discourse, helping to shape the ordering of his account of events:

> ***Throughout the court scene**, it becomes more and more obvious that not only did he not do it, but he couldn't have done it*
> ***Against all the evidence**, the jury . . . convicts Tom*
> ***Before it can be dealt with though**, Tom makes a desperate rush to freedom*
> *He says that **although Tom was innocent of the crimes he was accused of** he was dead from the start.*

Interconnected series of clauses also help to build the unity of the discourse:

> *He is sent to court* (initiating clause)
> *where Atticus defends him against a biased jury* (dependent clause of place)
> *who will almost certainly convict him regardless of [[whether it is proved he did it]]* (non-defining relative clause with embedding)

and

> *The fictional witnesses say he "ran like a crazy man"* (initiating clause)
> *and was sprinting [[as fast as he could]]* (an equal, additive clause with embedding)
> *and leapt over the fence* (an equal, additive clause)
> *but ≪just as he was going over≫ he was shot.* (an equal though contrastive clause, in which is enclosed a dependent clause of time)

In Chapter 3, I noted that by late childhood to adolescence control of grammatical intricacy enables young writers to achieve control of quite long passages of written language, building meanings in sustained coherent ways, though their nature always depends on the register and genre values that apply. Such control involves mastery of the conjunction system and some awareness of the range of meanings that can be expressed by deploying different clause types in sustained sequences. Where young people in midadolescence show limited capacity to exploit different clause types, they need to be shown how to do so. This will involve for example, such activities as

o reading passages of well constructed written language, identifying conjunctions and discussing their role in meaning making;
o playing with different conjunctions and the connections in meaning they create; and
o joint construction of passages of written language, examining different conjunctive relations in text construction.

In general, Tom demonstrates good control of grammatical intricacy, though he does not use grammatical metaphor, which, I also noted, tends to be a development that emerges after achieving some control of grammatical intricacy.

Turning to other matters having to do with Element 1, I have already noted that experiential information is interwoven with evaluation, so that interpretation of events is offered and sustained throughout this element. Several relational processes are used, among others, helping to build description, and evaluative language is frequently deployed:

> *it becomes **more and more obvious that not only did he not do it but he couldn't have** done it **without great personal strain***
> *the person who beat Mayella Ewell up was **obviously left-handed***
> *he was **definitely left-handed***
> *Tom makes a **desperate rush to freedom***
> *Atticus describes this as **a senseless killing***

The element is brought to a close with a summarizing judgment about Tom Robinson, using a clause of reason:

> *He is like a mockingbird // **because he is innocent of what he is accused of** // and he is killed regardless.*

Element 2 is not as well constructed as Element 1. It commences with its statement of hyperTheme, but the sentence involved, although in one sense dealing with accurate experiential information, is very awkwardly expressed:

> *The other person Harper Lee uses the metaphor of the mockingbird to describe is Boo Radley, the child of Arthur Radley who has been cooped up in his house for as long as the children in the story can remember.*

In the effort to elaborate on this, Tom writes, a little confusingly:

> *In Boo's case the innocence varies because, instead of being convicted, he is only confused and is innocent in the way that he has never had much experience with people.*

The meaning is not clear here, for Tom confuses issues of innocence and of Tom Robinson's conviction in a court of law. Tom may have meant to write something like this:

> *"Boo is also innocent, although in a different way from Tom Robinson. Boo is innocent of the ways of the world because he has had very little experience with people."*

As it is, the opening two sentences of Element 2 are not successful. It is possible that if Tom had used grammatical metaphor he might have created a more satisfactory opening to the element. He might, for example, have written something like the following, hence positioning himself to proceed more confidently with the relevant experiential details:

> *"The symbolism of the mockingbird illuminates Boo Radley's actions in the novel. An innocent, shy man, he lives an isolated life cooped up in his house. He behaves metaphorically a little like the mockingbird, causing no harm to anyone. His decision to leave his house one night to rescue Scout and Jem from Bob Ewell's attack demonstrates his kindness and bravery."*

However, such expression is not, on the evidence, available to Tom at the time of writing his essay here. The rest of the element unfolds using several marked themes:

> **When Bob Ewell attacks the children after a Halloween pageant,** he knocks Jem out
> **Afterwards at the Finches' house,** Heck Tate the Sheriff of Maycomb County has to decide what to do
> **According to her explanation** it could've been either Jem or Boo who killed him
> **Later in the conversation though,** they realize it must've been Boo
> **Eventually** Heck decides not to convict him.

Evaluative language is used more sparingly in this element than in the previous one, as in

> *(Boo) is **only confused and is innocent***
> *he was **only trying to save** Jem and Scout*

The general significance of the events is established in the last sentence:

> *Heck says "taking the one man who's done you and this town a service an'*
> *dragging' him with his shy ways into the limelight—to me, that's a sin."*

At times, in fact, rather more evaluative language might well have been introduced in order to enhance the reconstruction of experiential information, adding to the evaluation involved. For example, the following reconstruction of events has a very limited sense of evaluation and therefore of interpretation:

> *When Bob Ewell attacks the children after a Halloween pageant, he*
> *knocks Jem out and breaks his arm and starts to go after Scout. Boo runs*
> *down to them from his porch to save them and just as Bob is suffocating*
> *Scout, he steals his knife and stabs him in the heart, killing him.*

The relative absence of evaluative language in a section of the text whose experiential information is not always well controlled may indicate a more general uncertainty in handling the experiential information. That is because interpretation in constructing such a field ideally involves capacity to blend experiential and attitudinal information.

In the final element Tom restates his overall theme having to do with the symbolic reading of the novel. It is here that he uses the first person, for in offering his final judgment about the novel it is appropriate to do so:

> *In all, I think Harper Lee's use of a mockingbird as her central symbol of*
> *innocence in the story is very effective because it gives the characters it*
> *symbolizes more depth and makes a strong point about what is innocence*
> *and sin.*

One final point I shall make about Tom's text: he shifts confusingly from the present to the past tense. This is very common among adolescents learning to control discussion and critique about other texts, among both L1 and L2 students. Teachers should take time to teach and discuss the English tense system, exploring its meanings and the manner in which it is used in different contexts and different texts. The convention that the present tense is normally adopted for review and discussion of novels, plays, and films, for example, should be explained, and opportunity to practice using it should be developed.

4.3.4 A Summary of Matters Discussed in This Section
By midadolescence subject English is expressed in a number of potential genres, where the written discourse

√ constructs its experiential meanings about other discourses or texts, often though not always, literary;

√ is typically concerned to identify and foreground themes, values, and attitudes expressed in the selected texts. In this sense the knowledge constructed is uncommonsense;

√ interpersonally seeks to achieve some detachment from themes discussed by making limited reference to the identity of the writer;

√ nonetheless interprets and evaluates actions and characters in the light of the theme(s), building symbolic meanings, and using attitudinally rich language to do so;

√ employs language to move between specific details of actions or events and symbolic generalizations about experience, where they "show" the significance of these things;

√ tends to use noncongruent grammar (though Tom did not);

√ can make good use of clause intricacy, linking series of interconnected clauses to organize meaning;

√ is often metaphorical in both the lexical and grammatical senses, where, as in history, grammatical metaphor tends to bury otherwise overt conjunctive relations; and

√ creates longer texts than those found in childhood, so that texts need to be well organized and their symbolic meanings introduced, developed, and elaborated in quite long passages of written language.

Learning to use language in all these ways is demanding, not least because it requires a degree of "cultural capital," to use Bourdieu's term, not possessed by many adolescents, who find it difficult to elaborate on the meanings and themes of literary texts they are asked to read. Active involvement of students is needed in building knowledge of the necessary language and values involved.[4] Hammond and Gibbons (2005), for example, provide an account of scaffolding in classrooms with second phase[5] secondary English as a second landguage (ESL) students in Australia, learning to discuss character and motivation in *Romeo and Juliet*. The teacher involves the students, among other matters, in talk of what the characters are thinking as a means of getting at motivation by generating constructive talk about the text. Such strategies are as relevant for L1 students as they are for L2 students, allowing them to develop some facility in mastering the necessary language for literary interpretation. In a parallel fashion, Land, Anselmi, and AuBuchon (2010) offer a detailed account of strategies they developed to teach what they call interpretive essays about theme, specifically for use with L2 learners of English, where these involve deliberate structuring of ways to design "theme statements" and developing subsequent elaborations of these.

4.4 Science in Midadolescence

In the opening section of this chapter, I alluded to some differences between history and English on the one hand and science on the other. Whereas the humanities deal with phenomena of human affairs—human and social activities, attitudes and values of many kinds—the sciences deal with observation, experimentation, and documentation of the phenomena of the natural world. Unlike the humanities subjects, the sciences build their knowledge hierarchically (Bernstein, 1990): that is, they build their data and theory through careful experimentation and observation, revising what is known in the light of new observations, while subsuming the new information into ever increasing and coherent bodies of knowledge. It does not follow, of course, that scientists all agree about many matters. On the contrary, discussion and critique of the findings of scientific research are very much part of the processes of science building. However, it does follow that many scientific principles and procedures for addressing scientific phenomena are well established, and some fundamental understandings about phenomena and procedures for identifying them are held in common by scientists as they advance their work. Physics is generally identified as the paradigm case for building hierarchically, though other sciences such as the biological sciences similarly build their knowledge. Christie and Derewianka (2008, pp. 149–152) discuss these matters, and Bazerman (1988) and Halliday and Martin (1993) discuss the origins of much scientific endeavor and the language in which it is expressed. O'Halloran (2007) also discusses knowledge in science and mathematics, reflecting on aspects of the emergence of hierarchical structures in science.

School science is different from the science of universities and other research sites in that it is not directly involved in research (though school students sometimes do original experiments), for it primarily seeks to apprentice the young into some understanding both of the scientific information now known and of the scientific procedures by which that information is gained. In this sense, as Bernstein (1990) suggests, scientific knowledge is taken from the university setting and "relocated" for the purposes of pedagogy. School science generates a number of genres (see, e.g., Christie & Derewianka, 2008; Martin & Rose, 2008; Unsworth, 2000; Veel, 1997). Here I select only one science text written by a student in midadolescence, a report on hemophilia. First I comment briefly on some of the challenges in reading and writing science.

4.4.1 The Language of Science: Abstraction, Technicality, Multimodality, and Absence of Human Agency

By early to midadolescence, science deals with abstractions, and to this extent its meaning making compares with that of history and English. However, where the abstractions of history and English literary studies are built primarily using grammatical metaphor, the abstractions of science are created for the most part using a technical language, though grammatical metaphor is also often involved. It is the technicality in scientific language that students find arcane and intimidating. Consider, for example, two sentences that appear in a student's report on rubber and its uses:

> Rubber occurs as a milky emulsion (known as latex) in hundreds of
> different plants, such as dandelions and figs. Its chemical name is isoprene
> and it has the formula C_5H_8 in its pure form.

Two technical terms appear here—*latex* and *isoprene*—the former as a participant in a mental process:

> rubber occurs as a milky emulsion (**known** as latex)

the latter as a participant in a relational identifying process:

> Its chemical name **is** isoprene

whereas the second sentence uses a relational possessive process to introduce the chemical formula:

> it **has** the formula C_5H_8 in its pure form

In the space of two sentences, the example here moves the reader from the relatively commonplace notion of *rubber* to the introduction of some technical terms, and from there to presentation of a chemical formula, establishing a very uncommonsense form of knowledge.

Scientific language of the kind discussed here makes considerable use of relational identifying processes and relational attributive processes to introduce technical language.

Technicality is quite fundamentally a part of building the knowledge of science. Consider another example, this time from a report on Down Syndrome (from Christie & Derewianka, 2008, p. 190), written by a student, about 15 years old and in Year 10, where the opening sentence uses a relational attributive process to define:

> Down Syndrome **is** a chromosomal disorder [[that affects the genetic
> makeup of human beings]]

whereas the second sentence uses another, rather different, relational attributive process to express causation:

> Its cause **is** directly **related** to a mutation or abnormality of chromosome 21

Technicality in these two sentences compresses a great deal of information. A number of terms are used, each of which might well need explanation for the student struggling to make sense of this: *chromosomal disorder*, *genetic makeup of human beings*, *mutation or abnormality of chromosome 21*. Even the notion of a cause *being directly related to* something else probably needs explanation. Expressed less cryptically, the sentence means:

> "A mutation or abnormality of chromosome 21 causes (leads to) the chromosomal disorder called Down Syndrome."

In my observation, science teachers attach considerable importance to accurate use of technical language. Some years ago I was asked to participate in a study led by Cumming and Wyatt-Smith (2001) in which the language and literacy demands of Years 11 and 12 were examined by a team of researchers, each working with different passages of discourse recorded in senior classrooms in the city of Brisbane. Among other data I examined, I was asked to consider texts from classes studying agricultural science and biological science. Both teachers were insistent about accurate use of language, even demanding a repeat of an answer where needed. For example, the agricultural science teacher, who was teaching about the reproductive cycles of cows and horses, asked a question at one point about the best time for a horse to mate.

A student: *About three days.*
Teacher: *"Three days?" That's a very technical answer.* [said sarcastically]
Another student: *As close as possible to ovulation.*
Teacher: *"As close as possible to ovulation." Well done. Excellent answer.*

This was not an isolated instance, as this particular teacher frequently challenged his students to use language that was "technically accurate." The biological science teacher was similarly insistent on accuracy.

The requirement for accuracy in use of scientific language is part of the process of apprenticing students into an appreciation of science and its methods. To speak, write, and think scientifically is to use the necessary language with precision. Individual self-expression, valued, ostensibly at least, in much work in subject English, is not an aspect of learning science. On the contrary, success in learning scientific language depends on grasping the uncommonsense meanings of science, where these are expressed in well-defined discourse patterns whose technicality is employed in an exacting manner. Furthermore, much of the language of science, as, for example, in research articles or accounts of experiments, tends to follow clearly prescribed methods in constructing its discourse, and students are trained to use these patterns.

In the contemporary world, scientific texts are increasingly multimodal, adding some sources of potential complexity to the study of science. Both Lemke (2001, 2002) and O'Halloran (2007, 2011) have argued that science has always been multimodal in that it has made use of images, diagrams, graphs, and so on. But in the multimodal world, they point out, a variety of semiotic resources will be used simultaneously in many science texts, so that students need to develop skills in processing the messages involved and in producing multimodal texts of their own. Text 4.4, discussed below, has one figure displaying scientific information, and in Chapter 5, I introduce a multimodal text in science.

Overt expression of opinion is discouraged in science, though judgment about scientific probability or likelihood may appear. The interest is in foregrounding the phenomena of concern. Hence it is of some interest that at a time in their development when adolescents are required to master a language for evaluation of events in history and for evaluation of character and themes in literature, they are required to suppress a great deal of evaluative language for building scientific meanings. Where judgments occur, they typically involve modality, and personal opinion is not an issue here:

*Diagnosis of the disease **usually** occurs before birth*
***Generally** women are not affected by this particular disease*
*People with hemophilia do **not often** bleed to death*
*Most cases of hemophilia **can** be, and are, diagnosed at an early age*

Moreover, human agency generally finds little expression in science writing. No doubt, for example, medical scientists in more than one part of the world have contributed to the body of knowledge now possessed about either Down Syndrome or hemophilia, but their identity finds no acknowledgement in most science texts that deal with these topics. Where humans are mentioned in a science text, they are referred to only with general referents: *people with hemophilia, people with Down Syndrome, about 1 in 8000 babies.*

Many adolescents are reluctant readers of science, and for this reason alone a great deal of classroom talk is needed to unpack the dense language, rendering its meanings accessible to students. Fang and Schleppegrell (2008) offer a very useful discussion of the nature of scientific language and of strategies for teachers to guide students' reading of it. Consider, for example, the opening definition in Text 4.4, containing a dense noun group:

> Hemophilia is *a genetically linked blood disease [[that mostly affects males]]*.

While the term *hemophilia* is itself difficult for some to pronounce, let alone spell, the dense noun group structure accompanying it is also difficult. If we unpack the grammatical metaphor that is involved we find something like the following (though more than one unpacking might be proposed):

> *"Hemophilia is a disease of the blood // which people inherit // because it is genetic // and it is mostly inherited by males."*

The original sentence containing one clause (albeit with one embedded clause within it) has become four clauses when turned into speech.

In learning to read and understand science texts as in textbooks or website, students can be assisted by considering such questions as these, which are similar to those I suggested above for history

o What is this topic in science, and why do we study it? (This helps to establish experiential information by getting at the phenomena of the field, also assisting identification of difficult technical terms.);

o How is the written passage organized? (This helps to establish textual organization by looking at how the discourse unfolds, tracing thematic development, also considering the role of images, diagrams, and graphs that express information in ways other than in the verbal text.);

o Where, if at all, is evaluation expressed in the text? (This helps to establish interpersonal and attitudinal values, leading to discussion of the reasonably limited evaluation normally found in the text and its function.)

4.4.2 Writing a Report about Hemophilia

In the SFL genre tradition reports are various, and they are found extensively both in the social sciences and the natural sciences. Their schematic structures differ a little, though they typically introduce or classify some phenomenon, or both, and then describe it. Christie and Derewianka (2008) and Martin and Rose (2008) discuss them in some detail. The schematic structure for a report in science is typically displayed thus:

General Statement ∧ Description ∧ (References).

The General Statement establishes the phenomenon of interest, and the Description element describes it. The References element is optional but in fact, reasonably common in science genres, because students are expected to identify the sources from which they gained their information.

Text 4.4, the report on hemophilia, was written in Year 10 by Steven (who also wrote Text 4.1, considered above). This was one of a number of genetically derived illnesses that the Year 10 students were asked to research and report on. The text on Down Syndrome, referred to above, was another.

The field of hemophilia requires research because its information is quite esoteric, and Steven is expected to provide a set of references from which he has gained his information. The experiential information is evident in the lexis and in the discourse patterns in which he deploys that lexis. Moreover, part of the experiential information is displayed in a diagram.

Interpersonally, Steven adopts a very formal tenor to develop his report, so that his own identity is not apparent in the text. Furthermore, attitude in the report is confined to matters such as expression of the likelihood or probability of babies being born with hemophilia. Textually, the text is set out following a formula for preparing and writing such a Report suggested by his teacher; the presence of the diagram reveals that this is a multimodal text.

Marked topical themes are noted again, as are clause embeddings. MacroTheme and hyperThemes are shaded, revealing the manner in which the information flows across the text. (A list of references Steven had used is not displayed.)

Text 4.4 Hemophilia.

General	Hemophilia
Statement	Hemophilia is a genetically linked blood disease [[that mostly affects males]]. **Generally** women are not affected by this particular disease, though it is possible for them to be carriers. Hemophilia is [[when a person's body cannot clot properly]], and it affects approximately 6 in every 10,000 males.
Description	Symptoms
	Seeing as hemophilia is a disease [[in which the blood does not clot as well as a normal person (or at all, depending on the severity of the disease)]] the symptoms include severe bruising and internal bleeding. People with hemophilia do not often bleed to death, because of external cuts or scratches, the

most danger comes from the event of internal bleeding. Hemophiliacs are especially vulnerable to internal bleeding and spontaneous hemorrhaging (where the hemorrhaging occurs for no apparent reason) because of the nature of their disease. They generally have repeated bleeding in the joints, especially the knees, as they are weight bearing and are continuously used. **When this happens** the area swells and puts pressure on the nerves and can result in numbness, pain, or inability to move the limb. This is true more so when bleeding occurs in the forearm, calf, or groin. In old age, hemophiliacs are more prone to arthritis and chronic pain.

Diagnosis

Most cases of hemophilia can be, and are, diagnosed at an early age. **With the exception of circumcision** the disease is detected generally when a child first starts to squirm and attempts to crawl and walk, or at about 9 months of age. It is usually fairly easy to detect, as the child will bruise very easily and severely. The bruises are commonly larger [[than would be normal for a normal child]] and they turn yellow, green and purple. A blood sample will be taken to determine whether the child in question has the disease or not.

Causes

Hemophilia is a hereditary disease [[in which there is a defective gene [[that causes the owner of this gene to be unable to clot efficiently]]]]. The deficiency can be carried by both the X and the Y (female and male) chromosome, but it only seems to affect the Y or male chromosome. There are 13 main proteins or factors, concerned with creating a blood clot. **When even one of these is missing**, the "chain" is broken and therefore the body is unable to create clots. Hemophilia occurs when there is a defect in one or more of the blood coagulation protein factors which results in low levels of fibrin, which in turn, prevents the body from creating strong blood clots.

Incidence in the Population

Hemophilia occurs mostly in males, though it does not discriminate between races. It occurs in approximately 6 out of every 10,000 men; about 1500 men in Australia are affected by Hemophilia. Probability of a child having hemophilia is demonstrated in this diagram:

When the mother carries the haemophilia gene and the father is unaffected

There is a 50% chance at each birth that a son will have haemophilia. There is a 50% chance at each birth that a daughter will carry the haemophilia gene

When the father has haemophilia and the mother is unaffected

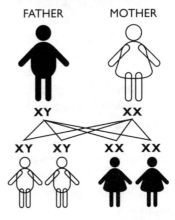

None of the sons will have haemophilia All of the daughters wil carry the haemophilia gene

Figure 4.2 Hemophilia and heredity.
(*Source*: Haemophilia Foundation Australia. Haemophilia inheritance [diagram]. HFA, Melbourne, 2009.)

Treatment and control

So far, there is no *cure* as such for Hemophilia, though there are many treatments available. Gene replacement therapy is thought to one day be the cure, but at present, it is only being trialed. People [[who have tried gene replacement therapy]] have had promising results although some have had side effects, though for most, the occurrence of bleeds have dropped considerably. Injections of certain blood products are usually needed to prevent cases of internal bleeding; these infusions or injections can cure the clotting defect for a short period of time, though ≪ if the same treatment is used over a long period≫ the subject can develop an immunity to it. People with mild cases of hemophilia sometimes use desmopressin (also called DDAVP), which is a synthetic hormone [[that forces the production and release of certain factors in the blood // to aid clotting for a short period of time]].

The opening element, which also establishes the macroTheme for the text, identifies the field by defining the disease in a manner I have already referred to above. The word *hemophilia* appears twice in unmarked topical theme positions in the first and third sentences in this opening element, and this is characteristic of much report writing: The phenomenon of concern is often thematized, and though marked themes appear in later parts of the text, they are not extensively employed. That is because the primary object in such a genre is to identify and describe.

The nature of the description provided in the second element always depends on the phenomenon, and in this case the items were actually suggested by the teacher, so that Steven follows the model provided in setting out his subheadings. In the first Description, he starts with his hyperTheme, which looks back to the opening while also looking forward to what is to come in terms of elaboration of the overall concern with *Symptoms*. Two themes are marked, the first to open the descriptive element:

> **Seeing as hemophilia is a disease [[in which the blood does not clot as well as a normal person (or at all, depending on the severity of the disease)]]** *the symptoms include severe bruising and internal bleeding*

and the later marked theme is part of elaborating on information within the element:

> **When this happens** *the area swells*

Thematic progression has mainly to do with elaborating the information about *symptoms*.

A similar pattern applies in the next descriptive element, devoted to *Diagnosis*, though this starts with a unmarked theme, which establishes the main concern for this element:

> *Most cases of hemophilia can be, and are diagnosed at an early age.*

One marked theme follows, expressed in a circumstance of concession (Halliday & Matthiessen, 2004):

> **With the exception of circumcision** *the disease is detected*

The object in this element is again primarily to describe.

The element devoted to *Causes* unfolds similarly, its opening theme unmarked:

> *Hemophilia is a hereditary disease*

and later themes essentially identify more aspects of the cause, with the exception of one marked theme:

When even one of these is missing the *"chain" is broken*

The measured thematic progression, in this as in the other elements, accounts for the very ordered way in which the text unfolds, elaborating on matters broadly indicated in the opening element, or macroTheme.

The next element, having to do with *Incidence in the population*, is relatively brief in terms of its verbal text, though it is here that the diagram appears, lengthening it but also providing information in a visual rather than a verbal way. The diagram is one Steven has taken from the website of the Hemophilia Foundation of Australia, which is one of the sources he has consulted in researching the field. As he states, he uses the diagram to demonstrate the *probability of a child having hemophilia*, though he could also have noted that it visually reinforces the information in his verbal text regarding the distribution of X and Y chromosomes in men and women. To that extent, Steven does not use the diagram as well as he might have done, though its placement in the report where it appears makes clear its general relevance.

The final element concerning *Treatment and control* again has an opening hyperTheme that links back to earlier matters while carrying the discourse into a new if related area. It uses a marked theme:

So far, there is no cure as such for hemophilia

and the rest of the element elaborates on this general point, using one marked theme to foreground some relevant information:

though ≪*if the same treatment is used over a long period*≫ *the subject can develop an immunity*

The text abounds in dense noun group structures, many of which Steven has taken from the sources he has consulted, and many created using grammatical metaphor, for this is instrumental in building the technical language of the scientific field:

severe bruising
internal bleeding
blood coagulation protein factors
genre replacement therapy
injections of certain blood products

Such scientific language is hard to read and write. Writing of science, Halliday and Martin (1993) have suggested "if a text is hard is to read the difficulty is bound to be in some sense linguistic" (p. 124); they might well have added that it will be difficult to write as well. Extensive review and discussions should be a necessary feature of classrooms in which texts such as Text 4.4 are to emerge.

Interpersonally, Steven distances himself from the field and from the potential reader, so that no sense of his identity appears in the text. Such evaluative language as appears has to do with the field and with expression of judgments about features of the disease, its appearance or its treatment:

> *They* (i.e., hemophiliacs) ***generally*** *have repeated bleedings in the joints*
> *The disease is detected **generally** when a child first starts to squirm*
> *It is **usually** fairly easy to detect*

The presence of the diagram ensures that Steve's text can be considered multimodal, though its meaning are primarily constructed in the verbal text so that the diagram, although useful, has a rather ancillary role in the overall meaning making. The text to be examined in Chapter 5 is more genuinely multimodal, in that its meanings are created in its images as well as the verbal text.

4.4.3 A Summary of Matters Discussed in This Section

By midadolescence science is expressed in a number of potential genres, where the written discourse

- √ constructs its experiential meanings about various phenomena of the natural world and creates a technical language to deploy in its discourse;
- √ is concerned to apprentice students into control of this technical discourse in which the uncommonsense knowledge of science is expressed;
- √ requires an interpersonal tenor that is formal and detached from the phenomena observed and reported on, so that the identity of any writer is removed or at least not foregrounded;
- √ removes human agency in many instances in the interests of foregrounding the natural phenomena of concern;
- √ uses little evaluative language and, where it does, tends to make observations about the likelihood or probability of aspects of the phenomena, hence making considerable use of modality;
- √ often uses noncongruent grammar;
- √ is characterized by considerable lexical density, making it difficult to read at times;

√ frequently expresses its meanings in semiotic resources other than verbal text, for instance, images, tables, figures, and graphs;

√ often uses chemical formulae and statistics to express its meanings as well.

4.5 Conclusion

I began this chapter with some reflection on the nature of knowledge and on the various literacies in which the knowledge valued in English speaking is expressed. The school subjects deal with phenomena in distinctive ways, reflecting the different "styles of reasoning" (Muller, 2000, p. 88) each represents. Although some sense of the differences is apparent in the discourses of schooling even in the primary years, the differences become more marked by midadolescence. By this stage, an understanding of the distinctive characters of the various school subjects should be well established if young people are to handle the language of learning well. Each of the subjects represents a different way of proposing and answering questions about experience. Each expresses itself in distinctive patterns of discourse. Each makes use of abstraction, generalization, and dense written language to build its meanings. However, by midadolescence, so the evidence suggests, many young people drop behind in their schooling because the challenges of the changing discourses of school become too great. Grammatical metaphor, dense lexis, and many abstract meanings are hard to handle for many young people because they lack the necessary language resources. It is important, then, that teachers have a thorough understanding of the various discourses in which their subjects are expressed, the better to intervene in and enhance their students' learning.

Notes

1 One anonymous reviewer who responded to a draft of this manuscript suggested it is worth pointing out that teaching problems of the kind mentioned are more often related to systemic, rather than personal issues.

2 Readers are reluctant for many reasons, some of them already alluded to in Chapter 2 when I considered the differential preparedness of children for schooling. For reasons having to do with social location, including social class, ethnicity, and gender, children are sometimes reluctant readers because they are alienated from the discourses of schooling, resentful of, or confused by, what these seem to offer. In the Australian context Rose (2007) who has worked extensively with disadvantaged Aboriginal children, argues that reading failure is responsible for school failure generally, and he has thus devised his *Reading to Learn Program*, intended, in

particular, to address the needs of struggling readers. His website is available at http://www.readingtolearn.com.au/.

3 Although the example I have used is made up, it is not unusual to encounter students who continue to write like this in adolescence.

4 One of the anonymous reviewers who responded to the first draft of this manuscript suggested that there may be a problem in such activities as responding to literary texts in that young adolescents do not always share the values expressed in the literary texts selected and are reluctant to engage with them. This is not always an easy issue for the teacher to address, though where it occurs I suggest it needs to be brought out into open discussion in order to examine how students' values might differ from those found in a literary text. I also think it important that the students be asked to consider why in an English-speaking society the various values involved might be upheld. Even where some continuing disagreement with any values is acknowledged, the exercise both respects young people's ideas and potentially allows fruitful discussion of values.

5 The term refers to ESL students who have a degree of oral language proficiency adequate for joining the mainstream classroom, but who lack an appropriate grasp of the demands of academic English of the kind needed for secondary schooling.

Language Learning   ISSN 0023-8333

CHAPTER 5

Late Adolescence to Adulthood: Engaging With Theoretical Knowledge

5.1 Introduction

The knowledge dealt with in all school subjects in the last years of schooling is uncommonsense in that each deals with abstract phenomena and ideas. Each subject has a distinctive method of inquiry and knowledge creation, generally drawn from university disciplines, for it is in universities and related research institutions that new knowledge is normally generated. Access to the various traditions of knowledge in the sciences and the humanities, among other fields of knowledge, according to Wheelahan (2010), enables students to enter with some understanding into "society's conversations" about theoretical knowledge. Wheelahan is one of a number of sociologists of knowledge who argue the importance of teaching a strong grasp of theoretical knowledge as a matter of social justice (see also Maton & Moore, 2010; Moore, 2008; Muller, 2000). Writing in a manner that owes much to Bernstein (2000), Wheelahan (2010) writes:

> Access to theoretical knowledge is an issue of distributional justice because society uses it to conduct its conversation about what it should be like. Society uses theoretical knowledge to think the unthinkable and the not-yet-thought, and this makes such knowledge socially powerful and endows it with the capacity to disrupt existing social relations. It plays this role because it is society's collective representations about the social and natural worlds, and we use it to access these worlds to understand how they are constructed, their processes of development and how they can be changed. Knowledge is continually revised as we engage with the world using knowledge that others have created before us, and in that process we change it and often change the world, or some aspect of it. (p. 145)

A very strong argument for access to theoretical knowledge on grounds of social justice can indeed be mounted, as Wheelahan and others maintain, though for reasons argued in this book, achieving such access to theoretical knowledge depends on attaining a mastery of the discourse patterns in which it is expressed. Preparation for mastery of the theoretical knowledge and its discourse patterns starts early, as we have seen, and continues over the years of schooling. By midadolescence, successful students will achieve a great deal of the necessary language for dealing with abstraction, generalization, evaluation, and argument. They will, in that sense, have some access to many of society's conversations. However, even the talented students continue to need assistance for the remaining years of school, for there is more to be learned, and the evidence already discussed in Chapter 4 suggests that many adolescents encounter continuing difficulties in their grasp of literacy learning.

This chapter concerns language and literacy learning in the last years of school, when young people are 16 to 17 or even 18 years old. Ideally, the last years of schooling serve to extend, strengthen, and consolidate the language capacities established in earlier years, preparing young people for entry either to work or further study. This applies, even though in the years beyond school they will continue to learn new oral language and literacy in many situations, whether personal, occupational, or communal, for language learning is life-long. Indeed, in the contemporary world, such is the pace of change—including changes in knowledge—that oral language and literacy are constantly subject to pressures in dealing with and constructing new experience, ideas, and informa-tion. One important implication of this is that young people should finish their school years confident in their grasp of the language system, able to face new contexts and challenges with some facility in their oral language and literacy. Confidence will be expressed in many ways, depending on the fields of knowl-edge involved in the school subjects studied and purposes in constructing those fields. All will require facility in offering observation, description, generaliza-tion, and abstraction, and these depend on considerable skill in manipulating oral language and literacy.

I develop this chapter by looking at selected texts drawn from history, sci-ence, and English studies, with a view to providing an account of the language capacities required by students if they are to deal adequately with the knowledge of the last years of schooling. All the school subjects considered involve capac-ity for interpretation, analysis, and evaluation of phenomena, whether human or social, as in the humanities, or physical or biological, as in the sciences. As we shall see, interpretation is very differently expressed in the different subjects, and considerable skill is required in mastering and deploying the necessary language resources for negotiating the differences.

I have already referred in Chapter 4 to Bernstein's work on knowledge structures, and in particular the manner in which he argued that the sciences have hierarchical knowledge structures (Bernstein, 1990, 2000). This was because, he argued, the sciences amass knowledge and understandings through a variety of established research procedures, and they tend to integrate these into reasonably coherent knowledge structures, as in physics, astronomy, or the biological sciences. The range of studies found in the humanities, on the other hand, he argued, are said to have *horizontal knowledge structures*, in that they build their knowledge by creating "a series of specialized languages with specialized modes of interrogation and criteria for the construction and circulation of texts" (Bernstein, 2000, p. 161). In this context, one thinks, for example, of the variety of literary theories that have been proposed from time to time in order to discuss and critique works of English literature, and history and philosophy similarly expand by proposing new theoretical lines of inquiry. (For further discussion, see Christie & Martin, 2007; Christie & Maton, 2011; Moore, 2011; Muller, 2001; Young, 2008.)

Bernstein wrote of knowledge structures in their original sites of production, namely universities, and he observed that such structures were "recontextualized" to other sites, including schools. Our concern in this chapter is with the recontextualized studies that are school English literary studies, history, and science. I commence with some discussion of history, examining initially some of the resources in which historical interpretation is constructed. I go on to examine science, selected next with a view to sharpening the contrast with history. Finally, I conclude with some consideration of English literary study, considering how it differs from the other two subjects in its knowledge structures and hence in its meaning making.

5.2 Constructing and Interpreting Historical Fields in Late Adolescence to Adulthood

Talking, writing, and reading about history at the senior levels are all very much about interpretation of events. Historical scholarship requires the capacity to construct knowledge of the historical field (experiential information), to offer some interpretation of its significance (interpersonal and attitudinal information), and to organize the information so that it creates a coherent argument (textual information).

Consider how 17-year-old Alice proposed an opening thesis for her expository genre in which she had been asked to consider factors responsible for Hitler's rise to power and, in particular, whether the weakness of the Weimar government was a factor. Thus, she constructs experiential information about the Weimar republic and Hitler's rise while also offering interpretation of events, and she arranges all this in a manner that builds direction and development:

> *The weakness of the Weimar Government was not the only reason [[Hitler was able to take control of Germany]]. Other causal factors influenced his rise to power. The signing of the Versailles Treaty, the Great Depression and tactics [[used to gain popularity by Hitler and the Nazis]] all contributed to this. Although there were many weaknesses to the Weimar government there were also evident strengths, which shows it was a true attempt at [[forming a democratic nation]].*

Interpretation depends in part on the negative polarity:

> *The weakness of the Weimar Government was **not** the only reason [[Hitler was able to take control of Germany]]*

and a subsequent abstract noun group encapsulates and compresses information:

> ***other causal factors** influenced his rise to power*

allowing Alice to go on to unpack the compression and elaborate on the meanings:

> *The signing of the Versailles Treaty, the Great Depression and tactics [[used to gain popularity by Hitler and the Nazis]] all contributed to this.*

Finally, having briefly reviewed reasons for Hitler's rise to power, Alice concludes her statement of thesis, partly by using a dependent clause of concession in theme position, conceding a point worth making for her argument:

> *Although there were many weaknesses to the Weimar government*

and partly by using another two clauses, in one of which she employs one of the processes of "showing" I referred to in Chapter 4:

> *there are also evident strengths, which **shows** it was a true attempt at [[forming a democratic nation]]*

I have already referred to verbs of "showing" in Chapter 4 because use of such terms may emerge in the phase of development discussed there. Where verbs of "showing" or "revealing" appear in a text in the manner identified, the writer or speaker is moving away from the events referred to in order to offer some abstract reflection on them. Verbs of "showing" do not normally occur in childhood, though they can appear among successful students by early to midadolescence (Christie & Cléirigh, 2008; Christie & Derewianka, 2008); their appearance is one measure of capacity to handle abstract experience.

Elle, 16 or 17 years old and studying the history of ancient Egypt, also offers interpretation while drawing on quite a different field of historical information. While studying ancient history, she had been asked by her teacher to "explain the political and religious significance of changing burial complexes from Dynasty III to Dynasty VI" in old Egypt. She wrote:

> *Architectural changes in royal burial complexes Dynasty III to Dynasty VI reflect many of the political and religious changes in Egyptian society. These changes include a realignment in religious beliefs, a varied status of the pharaoh as a god-king and the decentralization of power within the society. All of these factors can be examined in relation to each other, as seen in the construction of burial complexes and religious monuments throughout Old Kingdom Egypt.*

Interpretation here commences with the opening clause, in which two participants are expressed in very large noun groups that are linked using an abstract material process:

> *Architectural changes in royal burial complexes from Dynasty III to Dynasty VI **reflect** many of the political and religious changes in Egyptian society*

Elle then picks up a noun group just used (*changes*) and reinstates it in theme position, much as does Alice with her expression *causal factors*, to suggest compression of items, which enables her to go on to elaborate on those items, using a relational identifying process:

> *These changes **include** a realignment in religious beliefs, a varied status of the pharaoh as a god-king and the decentralization of power within the society*

The language is here very dense, apparent in particular in the series of abstract noun groups identifying the *changes* of concern, some involving grammatical metaphor, such as *a realignment in religious beliefs and the decentralization of power within the society*. Expressions such as these are so metaphorical that it takes some effort to deconstruct them as more congruent expressions, though a good way to do that is to think of what the teacher might say by way of explanation and the manner in which the overt causal connection between matters would therefore be expressed. Thus, in the case of a realignment in religious beliefs, the teacher might say:

> *"People held different religious beliefs about members of the royal family **and as a result** there were changes in the way members of the royal family were buried."*

In the case of "the decentralization of power within the society," the teacher might say:

> *"As religious beliefs changed, the pharaohs (or kings) became god-kings **and so** the way power was distributed also changed."*

In each case a causal connection is made evident, though this is otherwise buried within the noun group structures found within clauses. Martin (2003) refers to this kind of phenomenon as building causality in history "within rather than between clauses" (p. 32).

In the final sentence, the first clause encapsulates the *changes* in the noun group *all these factors*, which is placed in theme position, and another abstract material process identifies what can be done with the changes:

> *All of these factors **can be examined** in relation to each other*

and the second, dependent clause (in this case one of manner) brings this to a close:

> *as seen in the construction of burial complexes and religious monuments throughout Old Kingdom Egypt.*

Where Alice's text is reasonably abstract, Elle's is even more so, partly because it deals with a more remote period of history, about which less is known, so that the sources of information are different, and partly because its manner of building causal connection using grammatical metaphor is more marked. One notes, furthermore, the absence of human agency in what Elle writes and the relative absence of value judgment. Nonetheless, what Alice and Elle have in common is a sense that they are constructing aspects of historical fields, interpreting the significance of these aspects, and using the interpretations to commence building arguments about causal connections between phenomena or events. Linguistically, their interpretations depend on such factors as the capacity to

- o compress relevant historical information, often using the resource of expanded noun group structure to do so;
- o employ grammatical metaphor, often turning the actions of life into the phenomena of historical concern and eliding meanings that are otherwise expressed in conjunctively linked clauses;
- o elide meanings related to agency, so that human actions and interventions are sometimes rendered invisible;
- o employ abstract material processes to link the phenomena dealt with; and
- o construct and sequence the information in such a way that an argument having to do with the interpretation and explanation unfolds, where this depends in particular on well-structured thematic progression.

It will be useful now to turn to an instance of a sustained text about history in which we can follow the development of interpretation and causal explanation, noting in particular the ways in which judgment about the accuracy and merit of historical sources used is constructed.

5.2.1 Developing a Sustained Factorial Explanation Genre About Ancient History

Text 5.1 is by Elle, the author of one of the history texts examined above. Elle attended a high school in New South Wales, and she produced the text in Year 12, when she was 16 to 17 years old. Elle's texts in English and history are among a number I have collected as part of the body of data for a large study (Christie & Derewianka, 2007). I continue to add to that body of texts (Christie, 2011). Text 5.1 was written to be delivered as a talk. As part of work in ancient history, Elle was studying "Spartan society to the battle of Leuetra 371 BC." She had been asked by her teacher to produce a talk explaining "the religious role of kings, funerary customs and rituals" in Sparta. She was also asked to produce a one-page summary of points for distribution to other class members as she addressed them. (See Figure 5.1 below.) The written advice she received from her teacher specified that she should note "any areas of controversy/debate" and "sources of evidence" while offering "analysis rather than description"; she should also indicate "aspects of Spartan society" that the analysis illuminated. Elle prepared three drafts of the talk to show her teacher before the latter deemed it ready to be presented. Her teacher was particularly concerned that she demonstrate appropriate use of the references she consulted.

The field of Spartan history is a specialist one, and like other aspects of ancient history, much of it is not well documented. The field is thus, on the one hand, one which requires considerable research to develop an account, and, on the other hand, one which is by its nature open to speculation and differing points of view. Elle's task then, experientially, is to construct the field with some sense of accuracy about detail and, interpersonally, to do so in such a way that she reveals she knows she is offering interpretation and hence taking a stance toward the material as well as toward her audience. She needs to identify sources of information providing evidence about her given topic and to offer some assessment of the value of such evidence. She has set out the talk under a series of headings that I have preserved, though because I would argue that this is an instance of a *factorial explanation*, I also display the elements of structure of such a genre.

According to Coffin (2006), whose analysis I draw on here, a factorial explanation differs from a consequential explanation of the kind examined in Chapter 4. Where the consequential explanation takes a historical phenomenon and explains its consequences or effects, factorial explanations explain "the reasons or factors that contributed to a particular event or outcome and are typically multi-layered" (Coffin, 2006, p. 68) in the sense that several elements or factors need to be offered in order to develop adequate explanation. Both kinds of genres involve more than a simple reconstruction of time; in fact, time is not primarily foregrounded, as causal connection between events and phenomena is at issue. The elements of schematic structure may be displayed thus:

Outcome ^ Factors ^ (Reinforcement of Factors).

The Outcome (that phenomenon that is to be explained) opens the genre, and subsequent elements are the Factors, all said to be responsible for the Outcome. An optional final element is the Reinforcement of Factors, in which the factors involved are reinforced and some evaluation of these is offered.

From the outset, Elle makes clear that she is engaged in construction of a dialogic text in the sense that she is at some pains to establish the various authorities whose work she has consulted in developing her explanation, for this is part of establishing her own credentials as a scholar, able to offer interpretation of historical phenomena. According to Martin and White (2005, p. 36), her text is thus "heteroglossic" in that speakers and writers other than herself are acknowledged.[1] Text 5.1 is quite rich in the resources it uses to acknowledge and indeed invoke the authority of other sources, as in

> *Herodotus, an ancient Athenian writer, provides an anecdote* which is
> evidence of the influence of religion in Spartan society.

Elsewhere, authority is invoked in more tentative ways, as in

> *It is believed* that the kings passed messages down from the oracles down
> to the rest of society

and occasionally it is not identified at all:

> *It appears* that in contrast to those surrounding the death of the king, the
> death and burial practices of other Spartans were subdued.

Considerable skill is involved in determining both where to use such expressions and how strongly "graded" or "scaled" (Martin & White, 2005) the expressions need to be. When is it appropriate, for example, to assert that something is so, as in

> "In summary, religion occupied an important place in Spartan life"

and when is it appropriate to write:

> "It appears that religion occupied an important place in Spartan life"?

Developing facility in invoking the authority of others is quite challenging, requiring that teachers both explain social purposes for making use of references to other sources and draw attention to the necessary discourse patterns in which they are expressed.

I have identified (in SMALL CAPS) the many points where Elle acknowledges some source of information as part of building her explanation (HERODOTUS AN ANCIENT ATHENIAN WRITER, PROVIDES AN ANECDOTE), and those where (underlined) references to what is "known" are expressed in less categorical terms (it can be assumed that; we already know that). In some cases, the processes selected are verbal (*state, suggest*), others are mental (*believe*), and others are material (*provides an anecdote*). I also identify points (double underlines) at which Elle asserts that there is reliable evidence, because these have an important role in the unfolding of her explanation and the amassing of information to support her claims. Finally, I indicate topical theme choices and embedded clauses and macroTheme and hyperThemes. As the text is a long one, I break it up, intruding some discussion on its development as I do so, though in the interests of space I do not discuss all elements in equal detail.

Text 5.1 Spartan society: Religion, death, and burial.
Religious role of kings, funerary customs and rituals

Outcome   **Importance of Religion**

HERODOTUS, AN ANCIENT ATHENIAN WRITER, PROVIDES AN ANECDOTE [[which is evidence of the influence of religion in Spartan society]]. HE RECOUNTS an incident [[in which an Athenian runner is sent to Sparta // to request help in the battle of Marathon]]:
The Spartans, though moved by the appeal, and willing to send help to Athens, were unable to send it promptly because they did not wish to break their law. It was the ninth day of the month, and they said they could not take the field until the moon was full.
HERODOTUS PROVIDES ACCOUNTS OF OTHER SIMILAR EVENTS, **which** almost certainly led to mockery by other states but in **a society [[so dominated by military success as Sparta]],** the importance of religion in the community is often overlooked or taken for granted.

It HAS BEEN SUGGESTED BY SOME ANCIENT SCHOLARS that religious temples, gods and sacrifices were common to both Sparta and Greece in general. However we know FROM THE MORE RIGOROUS AND RECENT STUDY OF SPARTA that there were obviously very different cults, festivals and rituals celebrated. **In particular**, the way [[in which non-secular life both served and drove important military moments, as well as life and death rituals]], was considered unique. **This connection between religion, military and social life** can be demonstrated by investigating the life and death of Kings and others in Spartan life.

The Outcome establishes Elle's claims to offer interpretation and evidence in support of it. She makes use of three references to one authoritative writer:

Herodotus, an Athenian writer, provides an anecdote which is evidence of the influence of religion in Spartan society
He recounts an incident
Herodotus provides accounts of other similar events

and she then alludes to other authoritative writers:

*It has been suggested **by some ancient scholars** that religious temples, gods and sacrifices were common to both Sparta and Greece in general.*

She goes on to build her interpretation, using a contrastive conjunction that helps to counter the claim:

However, we know from the more rigorous and recent study of Sparta that there were obviously very different cults, festivals and rituals celebrated

and then uses a marked theme that carries emphasis:

In particular, the way in which non-secular life both served and drove important military movements, as well as life and death rituals, was considered unique.

All this enables Elle to make a principal claim that she intends to explain and elaborate in the rest of the text:

This connection between religion, military and social life can be demonstrated by investigating the life and death of kings and others in Spartan life.

Here the noun group *this connection between religion, military and social life* alludes to, and summarizes, what has been written, and the use of the "showing" verb *can be demonstrated* (realizing a verbal process) helps reveal her intention in *investigating the life and death of kings and others in Spartan life.* Abstract information is very much at issue here.

In general, and in a manner consistent with her teacher's advice, Elle provides overall analysis, not description, though descriptive language is used at times. The tenor is authoritative, in that Elle addresses her audience formally, demonstrating an understanding that she must amass information in such a way that she builds explanation while weighing the value of the evidence used.

Factor 1 is set out here, the hyperTheme for this element shaded.

Factor 1   **Religious role of kings**
Spirituality and violence went hand in hand in Spartan society. XENOPHON STATES, "A king, by virtue of his divine descent, should perform all the public sacrifices on the city's behalf and should lead the army wherever the city dispatches it . . . ."

Despite Sparta's unique government (which combined elements of monarchy, oligarchy and democracy), EARNING IT THE TITLE OF A 'MIXED CONSTITUTION' (PLATO), its kings had two main roles: they were important religious figures as well as leaders of the military.

ACCORDING TO HERODOTUS, Spartans worshipped their kings as Gods. **This** IS ASSOCIATED WITH SUGGESTIONS [[that the practice of 'dual kingship' arose from the sons of Zeus, the Dioscuri]].

We already <u>know</u> of their strict obedience and dedication to the gods, so **it <u>can be assumed</u>** that **the Spartans** would see the kings as means of divine communication. **<u>It is believed</u>** that **the kings** passed messages down from the oracles to the rest of society, **in a sense** elevating the king's position to one close to that of the gods.

The king served as chief priest, although ACCORDING TO H.W PARKER, there must have been other priests as well. It is also worth noting [[that **all political units of Sparta** had religious duties [[to perform]] as part of their functions]]]]. **The king's main religious function** was to do with sacrificial duties. **These** included sacrifices to their respective gods Zeus Uranios and Zeus Lacedaemon on behalf of the people of the city on the 1st and 7th days of the month. **They** also made sacrifices as part of the important annual festivals and at funerals. **Of most importance** were the sacrifices made to the gods of war. XENOPHON PROVIDES DETAIL on these practices:

The king first sacrifices while still at home to Zeus . . . If he gets a good omen here, the fire carrier takes fire from the altar and leads the way to the borders of the land. The king sacrifices there too.. When the sacrifices . . . produce good omens he crosses the borders of the land. And the fire from these sacrifices leads the way and is never put out, and all kinds of animals follow.

Particular events were seen to have religious significance in times of war. For example, XENOPHON ALSO TELLS THE STORY of a Spartan king [[leading an army into battle // interpreting an earthquake as a sign of encouragement from Poseidon // prompting a sacrificial offering to the god]].

It <u>can be argued</u> [[that religious authority equated to political power in Sparta]]. **An example of such power** IS PROVIDED IN AN ACCOUNT of an incident [[in which King Cleomenes refused to go into battle (which was a criminal offence)]], but got off trial by saying that the omens were bad so he could not fight. **If a Spartan King had a reasonable religious excuse** he could be forgiven for losing battles and refusing battles. Thus, <u>it</u> can be <u>argued</u> [[that for kings at least, religion also had a higher status than the legal system]].

Such religious connection was important in gaining loyalty and obedience in the political arena, for the **divine status of the Kings** was a sign of military elitism. **Spartan society** ACCORDING TO XENOPHON depended on the king and was loyal to the King, even

believing **that if an untitled person occupied the royal seat**
military disaster and famine would ensue.

The opening statement about spirituality and violence is immediately supported by reference to an authority:

Xenophon states "A king, by virtue of his divine descent, should perform all the public sacrifices on the city's behalf and should lead the army where the city dispatches it"

The rest of the element builds its elaboration of matters that support the claim made, as, for example, in the reference to Plato, who saw Sparta as having *a mixed constitution*, and Herodotus is cited once more:

According to Herodotus, Spartans worshipped their kings as gods

Elle intrudes reference to herself and others of the scholarly community she claims to be part of, building causal connection in what she says:

We already know *of their strict obedience and dedication to the gods,* ***so*** *it can be assumed that the Spartans would see the kings as means of divine communication.*

As the element unfolds, the evidence to elaborate on and support the general explanation builds. Authorities are again cited (*H.W. Parker* and *Xenophon*), and Elle goes on to say:

Thus, it can be argued that for kings at least, religion also had a higher status than the legal system.

Here and elsewhere, Elle introduces language that expresses strong judgment about matters discussed, realized in lexis that "grades up" the force of the judgments (Hood, 2010, p. 76; Martin & White, 2005):

*religious authority **equated** to political power*
*such religious connection was **important** in gaining loyalty and obedience*

Factor 2 takes the explanation into different though related areas, when it turns to the *funeral customs for kings*.

Factor 2   **Funeral customs for kings**
Due to the significant place [[that the kings traditionally held]] and in keeping with their divine origins and religious significance, their funerals were a considerably elaborate and widely acknowledged event. ACCORDING TO SOURCES SUCH AS H.W. PARKER, these funerary customs and rituals give further weight to the evidence of kings being treated as "demi-gods."

HERODOTUS PROVIDES US WITH A DETAILED ACCOUNT of the
customs before and after the burial of a king:
Horsemen proclaim their death throughout all Laconia, and
women go about through the city beating a cauldron . . . . two free
people from each house are required to put on the signs of
defilement [go into mourning]; failure to comply incurs heavy
penalties . . . after the burial there is no meeting for market or
judgment for the ten days following, these days being a period of
mourning.
The kings were buried outside the city because **it** was thought
safer if the spirit of the dead king was removed from close
association with the living. **Other sources (both ancient and
modern) add that Helots as well as Spartans** gather and "smite"
their foreheads and lament loudly.

If the king has died in battle, the town creates an image of him
and carries it on a bier or wooden frame. THIS DESCRIPTION IS
ACCOUNTED FOR in many other sources, providing reliable
evidence on the extent of the king's power and their popularity
amongst the populous.

A strong evaluative quality is maintained in this element, apparent where
evidence is assessed and given particular force, and authorities are invoked to
reinforce what is said

Due to **the significant place** that kings traditionally held
According to sources such as H.W. Parker, these funerary customs and
rituals give **further weight to the evidence** of kings being 'demi-gods'.

A later description is said to provide

reliable evidence on the extent of the king's power.

Factor 3 turns to the funeral customs for others, where the tentative nature
of many observations is made evident.

Factor 3 **Funeral customs for others**

**The information on the death and burial practices for other
members of Spartan society** is relatively scarce, as **writers at the
time** wouldn't have been as exposed to the rituals and customs, as
they were not as central to society to the extent that the king's
funerals were. **It** appears [[that <<in contrast to those [[surrounding
the death of a king]] >> the death and burial practices of other
Spartans were subdued]]. Nevertheless, **religious beliefs and
military practices** were still influential.

ACCORDING TO PLUTARCH, as one of Lycurgus' reforms, only men [[who died in battle]] or women [[who died in childbirth]] were permitted to be buried in marked graves. **This** is further evidence of the central role of war in Spartan society and similarly of the role of the women in the production of strong Spartan warriors. **These warriors [[who fell on the battle field]]** were often buried at that site in simple pit or tile graves. **Spartan soldiers** were simply to be wrapped in their red cloaks and olive leaves placed around them.

FROM PLUTARCH WE ALSO LEARN that Lycurgus aimed to "remove all superstition by not placing any ban on the burial of the dead within the city or on siting tombs close to temples." **The Spartans** were encouraged to view death as "familiar and normal" and were not afraid to touch a corpse or walk between gravestones. LYCURGUS ALSO STATED that attendants were not to place grave goods with the dead. **For those who died within Sparta**, the deceased female relatives generally conducted the funerary rituals; laying out the body, the funeral procession and the burial itself. **It** is suggested [[that a strict period of eleven days was set for mourning]], although **this** is questioned, because **this** is a longer period of time [[than was set for the mourning of the kings]]. **The twelfth day** was then marked by a sacrifice to Demeter, the goddess of grain and fertility and the preserver of marriage and the sacred law. **This sacrificial practice** strengthens the link between Spartan religion, health and family structure.

Despite the religion undertones of these more ordinary rituals the difference in status of the monarch and the people is obvious. **In this way**, Sparta is similar to many other societies throughout history and around the world.

Elle is aware not only that she should acknowledge the sources of her evidence but that she should also indicate some reservations about the certainty of some sources:

> ***It is suggested*** *that a period of eleven days was set for mourning,* ***although this is questioned****, because this is a longer period of time than was set for the mourning of kings.*

The Reinforcement of Factors brings the Factorial Explanation to a close.

Reinforcement of Factors	**Impact of religion (and the king's role) on Sparta, what is revealed?**
	An important issue for research such as this is the relative absence of primary sources of Spartan life. **There** is quite a deal of material available on Sparta, however, judging its credibility is difficult, K.H. KELLY IN SPARTA: SOME MYTHS ANCIENT AND MODERN DESCRIBES THE SITUATION: . . . in ancient times hardly any writer interested in Sparta seems to have been depressed by lack of information and . . . generation after generation of Greeks cheerfully discussed, described and criticized Sparta . . . (Kelly in Lumb)
	Sparta was said to be a secretive state, **what little [[is available]]** tends to be that [[RECORDED BY HERODOTUS]], itself quite sparse and [[written from the perspective of an Athenian]]. **ACCORDING TO LUMB**, the "cloud of mystery" around Sparta has meant that a good deal of writing is "creative," building cumulatively on myths. **HE ALSO POINTS OUT** that writers' interests influence what they select to write about, eg Xenophon was interested in the military, hence he focuses on that aspect of life. **For these reasons**, it is quite difficult to locate a variety of sources about this topic, **the few [[that exist]]** are used by a number of different commentators.
	In summary, **religion** occupied an important place in Spartan life. **In particular** the Spartan kings were seen as "quasi-gods," that is almost as significant as the gods, and with divine powers. **The kings** performed many of the duties of high priests and drew on religious beliefs and practices to support their military campaigns, often allowing religious beliefs to drive military decisions. **Their deaths** were observed with much ritual, in contrast to those of ordinary people.

The element commences with a reasonably lengthy assessment of the reliability of the sources consulted, for Elle notes:

*An important issue for research such as this is **the relative absence of primary sources** of Spartan life*

Having reviewed several potentially insufficient sources she writes, using a circumstance of reason to commence:

For these reasons, it is quite difficult to locate a variety of sources about this topic, the few that exist are used by a number of different commentators.

Nonetheless, and despite earlier reservations expressed, Elle's final paragraph offers a concluding judgment about the importance of religion in Sparta, where the language of evaluation is marked by a sense of certainty, because Elle's task now, despite acknowledged reservations, is to offer a conclusion in the light of the evidence:

> *In summary, religion occupied **an important place in Spartan life**. In particular the Spartan kings were seen as "quasi-gods," that is **almost as significant as the gods**, and with divine powers. **The kings performed many of the duties of high priests** and drew on religious beliefs and practices to support their military campaigns, often allowing religious beliefs to drive military decisions. **Their deaths were observed with much ritual, in contrast to those of ordinary people.***

Figure 5.1 displays the handout Elle has prepared for distribution to the class while she is talking. This is prepared as part of the overall assignment given her by her teacher. It will be seen that although it covers the same field of historical information, the handout often uses different language, because its function is to compress her talk, reducing much that is said to points for ease of following the more detailed account provided in her talk.

Text 5.1 and its construction have revealed considerable linguistic complexities. Elle needed to research and read widely in the first place, employing considerable skills in interpretation of what she read. Then she turned to construction of an interpretive text of her own, in which she needed to construct both experiential and evaluative information, marshaling and organizing this information in a well-focused and directed text. The language of analysis, evaluation, and interpretation was of quite a high order as she dealt with challenging abstract information.

The language of analysis, interpretation, and evaluation is very different if we turn to the sciences in the latter years of schooling, for here the demands on young people's language are of a very different order from those in the humanities. In order to sharpen our sense of how considerable are the differences between the horizontal knowledge structures of history and the hierarchical knowledge structures of the sciences, I now turn to some consideration of aspects of scientific discourse.

Figure 5.1 Spartan religion handout.

5.3 Constructing and Interpreting Scientific Fields in Late Adolescence to Adulthood

The sciences concern exploration of all things having to do with the natural world, whether physical or biological, and they build their knowledge by careful investigation of phenomena, constructing explanation and interpretation out of the observations that are made. The young children who were learning about the life cycle of chickens in Chapter 2 were being inducted into aspects of scientific method and its language when they kept chickens in their classrooms and observed their incubation and eventual hatching. The students who, in Chapter 3, learned about the human digestive system, and in Chapter 4, studied the genetic disease of hemophilia needed to research the results of others' investigations into these phenomena and to construct appropriate scientific genres. These students (apart from the very young ones in Chapter 2) composed their texts themselves, though they relied heavily on the results of others' research efforts to do so. It is this overt attention to the results of research by others that is one of the distinctive marks of the scientific discourses that children and adolescents need to master. In this sense, as I noted much earlier, the knowledge of the sciences is built hierarchically (Bernstein, 2000) in that what is investigated and learned is understood as part of an emerging body of ideas with established procedures and principles. Many of the activities pursued in science involve replication of a well-established principle (such as those that demonstrate the operation of Lenz's law in physic or photosynthesis in plants), because the intention is to affirm and validate the principle as well as the procedures by which it is known. Of course, scientific knowledge is subject to constant revision, amendment, and change as new data, information, and understandings emerge, but it is constructed on what is known, and in this way the knowledge builds in integrated fashion, so that one explanation underpins another, and an expanding body of knowledge emerges (Muller, 2007).

Hence, the discourses of science among students in late adolescence to young adulthood display frequent attention to established methods in building their meanings, and the language is dense and often technically difficult, much of it using grammatical metaphor:

> *The spectrum of wavelengths of sunlight [[used in plant growth]] is called "Photosynthetically Active Radiation." PAR covers roughly the same spectrum of wavelength as visible light, approximately 400 nm to 700 nm.* (from plant physiology)
> *Solutions of ethanol can be oxidized by bacteria to form vinegar which is a solution of ethanoic acid (also called acetic acid) in water.* (from chemistry)

A cluster of scientific genres having to do with experiment or investigation can be discerned (see Christie & Derewianka, 2008; Martin & Rose, 2008; Unsworth, 2000; Veel, 1997), and certain canonical features of the discourses emerge, evident for example in statements of aim, in which material processes are very visible, typically having to do with direction of investigative behavior:

> *To test* *whether light of different colors (i.e., different wavelengths)* *affects* *plant growth.* (drawn from a study on plant physiology and used on a study sheet given 16-years-olds attending a summer school in science at the University of Technology Sydney)
> *To determine* *some properties of the rays which come from the cathode of a discharge tube.* (drawn from physics and written by Joshua, aged 17)
> *To construct* *several galvanic cells and* *investigate* *their operation.* (drawn from chemistry and also written by Joshua, aged 17)

Subsequent statements of "apparatus" or "materials" needed, "methods," "results," and/or "discussion" follow.

The language used is marked by a complete flattening of attitudinal expression, apparent, for example, in a statement of the "Risk assessment" for one experiment:

> *Risk of electrocution: charges were tiny and care was taken.*
> *Risk of dropping coil on foot: covered footwear worn, care taken.*
> *Risk of stabbing self in eye with connecting wires: care taken.*

Here, human agency is only obliquely acknowledged as in *care taken*, for, in general, human identity is removed in science writing in the interests of foregrounding the phenomena and methods of interest. This is part of deemphasizing the identity of the researcher. The universality or openness of scientific aims and methods dictates that the account of an investigation is presented in a form that allows any other researcher to repeat precisely the same investigation and get virtually the same results (allowing for small errors or variations in materials, operations, and operator).

The meanings of science are often expressed in nonverbal means, such as images, graphs, statistics, and formulas, all of them essential to the knowledge building that is involved. It is in the interplay of all these resources, verbal and nonverbal, that the scientific meanings are realized (Brookes & Etkina, 2007). Discussing the relationship of mathematics and science in multimodal science texts, O'Halloran (2007) argues that mathematics and science "form different knowledge structures which complement each other" (p. 205) in many scientific discourses.

Finally, in this review of the language of scientific experiments, I note that alongside the complex technical language, the discourse is often in other ways grammatically very simple in that simple clauses are often employed:

Thoroughly clean the flask.
Place about 200 ml of water in the flask, measuring it out with the measuring cylinder.

All this is in marked contrast with the discourses of history of the kind in Text 5.1. However, science is as much about interpretation and evaluation as is history, though its linguistic resources for expressing them are very different, because the knowledge constructed is quite different.

In summary then, experimental scientific discourse for the later years is marked by

√ use of dense technical language, often built using grammatical metaphor;
√ frequent simplicity of clauses and clause relations, part of outlining clearly defined steps;
√ use of images, graphs, statistics, or formulas;
√ use of material processes realizing actions taken;
√ absence of attitudinal expression, especially having to do with feelings;
√ an associated absence of human agency and an adoption of a rather neutral tenor;
√ use of overall schematic structures with headings and subheadings, their functions established in constant reiteration and practice, their overall purpose being to give direction to the unfolding of information.

5.3.1 Developing an Account of a Scientific Experiment

Text 5.2 is an example of a *demonstration genre* (Christie & Derewianka, 2008, p. 158), so called because it sets out a well-established scientific procedure whose results were already well known. Such genres are common in science, found both in school and undergraduate studies of science. This text was written by Joshua, aged 17. The text records an experiment undertaken to measure "mass changes" brought about by a fermentation process. It was one of a series of related experiments conducted as part of a study in chemistry, and it led on to others. I have set it out as Joshua wrote it.

Text 5.2 Fermentation of glucose. (The author is grateful to Joshua Lewis who wrote this text.)

AIM

To plan and perform a first-hand investigation to monitor the mass change during the fermentation of glucose.

METHOD

Materials: * yeast
* small beaker
* glucose (powder form)
* water
* $Na_2 HPO_4$
* rubber stopper and tube
* limewater
* digital scales
* flask
* measuring cylinder

1. Thoroughly clean the flask.
2. Place about 200 ml of water in the flask, measuring it out with the measuring cylinder. Be careful not to add more amounts of water than your digital scales can handle.
3. Use the digital scales to measure out about 5 g of yeast. Add this to the flask.
4. Also add a pinch of $Na_2 HPO_4$ as a nutrient for the yeast.
5. Fill the small beaker with enough limewater to comfortably submerge the end of the rubber tube.
6. Use the digital scales to measure out about 20g of glucose. Add this to the flask. Stir the mixture thoroughly.
7. Place the rubber stopper tube into the beaker of limewater.
8. Use the digital scales to measure the weight of the flask. Record the result.
9. Leave the flask for a number of days, recording the mass of the flask each day.

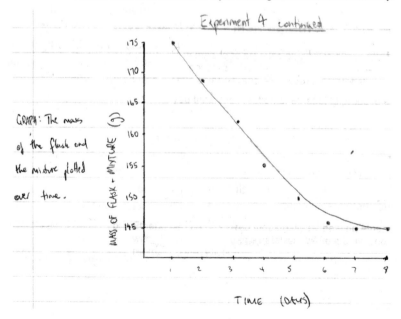

RESULTS NUMBER OF DAYS	MASS OF FLASK + MIXTURE (g)
1	175
2	168
3	162
4	155
5	150
6	146
7	145
8	145

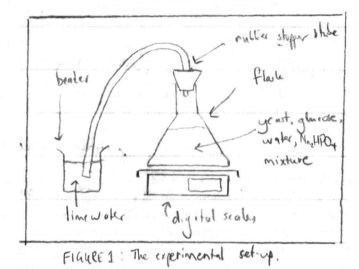

FIGURE 1 : The experimental set-up.

DISCUSSION   Sources of error:

- system in flask not anaerobic, therefore amount of fermentation may be reduced.
- other bacteria in non-sterile flask may have reduced degree of fermentation
- temperature not at 30–35°C, nor was temperature constant.

A series of follow-up questions from Joshua's teacher indicated that he intended that the results obtained should be summarized. The first such question and Joshua's answer are displayed, showing that Joshua is required to offer a formulaic summary of the chemical reaction investigated:

Write an overall equation for the fermentation of glucose

$$C_6H_{12}O_6(_{aq}) \xrightarrow{zymase} 2CH_3CH_2OH(_{aq}) + 2CO_2(_g)$$

whereas three other questions, not reproduced, asked Joshua to indicate how he would test for applications of the results of the investigation.

Turning to the field and the experiential information in Text 5.2, the notion of "planning and performing" is itself an interesting one, carrying the implication that the plan is as important as the performance. Procedure is essential, and even in a relatively advanced student such as Joshua, apprenticeship into planning and performing aspects of scientific method is at issue. In fact, so science educators affirm, attention to following the procedure continues to pertain well into university studies of science, constantly affirmed in new experimental and investigative ways. The notion of *a first-hand investigation* is also interesting for what this tells of the apparent commitment to scientific method and its language here. Such an experiment and its results might be read about in books, but the teacher's intention in this case was that Joshua have first hand experience of the phenomena of interest.

The language is relatively free of grammatical metaphor, though it is apparent in both *the mass change* and *the fermentation of glucose*. Although the language is at times reasonably simple in its references to familiar objects (*yeast, limewater, flask*), its technical significance is quite marked, for this is a specialist field that is under construction. This is apparent, for example, in the sense in which reference is made to *sources of error* in the Discussion. The notion of "error" has not, of course, to do with "mistake," but rather with the difference between the desired and actual performance of a phenomenon or system that is measured. For anyone trained in science the notion is familiar and quite fundamental to development of the desired data, though an understanding has nonetheless to be taught. The presence here of the term *sources of error*, then, reveals a student familiar with the language of a specialist field of scientific endeavor.

Turning to the textual organization of the text, the sequence of steps in conducting the experiment is simply set out, and their overall order is important in achieving what the teacher, in written notes, referred to as the "logic" of the study. In fact, the series of numbered steps in the process of constructing the experiment is, by implication, conjunctively linked in that there is an implicit sense of additive or temporal connection, or both, between steps, which helps to build the apparent logic of the study:

*"Thoroughly clean the flask **and** place about 200 ml of water in the flask, and measure it out with the measuring cylinder. Be careful not to add more*

*amounts of water than your digital scales can handle **and then** use the*
digital scales to measure out about 5 g of yeast <u>and</u> add this to the flask. "

All the selected lexical verbs realize material processes (e.g., *place, add, fill*), and the consistent use of the imperative mood reveals that the text is concerned to direct behavior: This is what one should do to investigate this phenomenon. Joshua's Figure 1 provides visual reinforcement of the steps, and the graph displays the same data as are set out in the table recording results. No attitudinal expression is apparent, though Joshua employs some modality in his Discussion:

> *system in flask not anaerobic, therefore amount of fermentation **may** be*
> *reduced*
> *other bacteria in non-sterile flask **may** have reduced degree of*
> *fermentation.*

In what ways, then, can we argue that the text reveals explanation and interpretation of a scientific experiment? There are several measures:

√ in that the text makes use of a specialist scientific language, it reveals the field that is under construction;

√ in that the text sets out an aim, it establishes an issue to be investigated and necessarily explained with respect to that field: the process of fermentation. There is, of course, a prior assumption here, which is that the issue is one worth studying; that will ideally involve some teacher intervention to develop discussion about why such a phenomenon is of interest and what kind of further understandings its investigation might open up. Ideally too, the activity of learning about fermentation will be linked to, and to some extent built upon, earlier learning of related information;

√ in that the text proposes a series of steps to be followed; using a series of material processes and the imperative mood, it provides an account of what should be done, thus also guiding the amassing of data and interpretation;

√ the text produces a series of results, displayed in the table and the graph, affirming and reaffirming what has been established;

√ finally, though avoiding any expression of feeling, the text makes limited use of modal verbs in assessing the merit of the results obtained.

Learning to understand scientific procedures and the discourses in which they are encoded is quite a difficult process, even for able students. By the secondary years, as I noted in an earlier chapter, many students find science very difficult and they are reluctant to persevere with a subject that seems re-mote from their experience, too abstruse to pursue. Adoption of constructivist pedagogies in many English-speaking countries, such as Australia, has some-times not helped, for they have too often left students adrift, unable to develop the necessary skills to handle scientific knowledge. I refer to those construc-tivist theories, which—though they differ in some ways—share a model of teaching and learning in which the teacher avoids overt instruction in favor of "facilitating" the allegedly independent learning of the students who ostensi-bly "construct" their own knowledge (Larochelle, Bednarz, & Garrison, 1998; Rohrs & Lenhart, 1995; von Glasersfeld, 1998; Wilson, 1996). In practice, without the advice, guidance, and skill of teachers, students are often left floun-dering, unable to deduce the actual knowledge bases of the subjects they study. The weaker the students, then the harder it can often be to learn the necessary scientific procedures and their meanings. A number of critiques of construc-tionism have been made (Chen, Maton, & Bennet, 2011; Christie, 2004a; Lind-strøm, 2010; Muller, 2000; Wheelahan, 2010; Young, 2008), drawing attention to the need to respect the claims of disciplinary knowledge building in the vari-ous subjects and the values of explicit teaching of these. Knowledge structures, I would add, are encoded in discourse patterns, though in science, they are often also encoded in the other resources of science, including its graphs, images, statistics, and formulas. As we teach and learn a knowledge structure, so we teach and learn the necessary discourse and associated resources to give it expression.

5.4 Constructing and Interpreting Fields in English Literary Studies in Late Adolescence to Adulthood

All school subjects value interpretation, analysis, and evaluation in varying degrees and in varying ways, apparent by the last years of schooling. Perhaps none is more committed to evaluation than is English literary study, for the engagement with producing texts that respond to other texts foregrounds eval-uation. The study of English literature is one of the humanities, and like other aspects of school subject English, it has had, by now, quite a long, often con-troversial history. In fact, a great deal has been written over the years about subject English generally, its purposes and its history. A range of points of view are represented in extant literature (Brindley, 1994; Christie, 1993; Christie & Macken-Horarik, 2007, 2011; Christie & Humphrey, 2008; Doecke, Howie, & Sawyer, 2006; Goodson & Medway, 1990; Kress et al., 2005; Locke, 2007, 2010; Misson & Morgan, 2006; Peel, Patterson, & Gerlach, 2000; Sawyer & Gold, 2004), and thus it is no part of this chapter—or indeed of this book—to review the various models of English offered in any detail. Suffice it to note that the various models or approaches to the teaching of literature have differed in many ways: for example, the literary canon (e.g., Shakespeare, Jane Austen) has sometimes been endorsed, whereas at other times, the canon has been challenged, and, under the influence of popular culture, more ephemeral popular texts, as well as films and videos, have been proposed as appropriate in the name of English studies, sometimes supplanting the literary canon, sometimes accompanying it. Though the models differ, all have this much in common: a requirement that students offer some kind of response to the text(s) studied, involving interpretation and evaluation. The knowledge differs, depending on the texts examined, purposes in considering them, and the theoretical position espoused. Often, however, and ironically, given the commitment to English studies, the linguistic resources needed to express the necessary knowledge about texts remain elusive for many students, not well explicated in many English classrooms.

As we saw in Chapter 4, students are sometimes asked to discuss main themes that are "demonstrated" in a novel, producing a *thematic interpretation* genre, where the object is to offer an interpretation of the literary text in the light of the theme, and this takes some skill in building abstract ideas, where this can often involve grammatical metaphor, though it also can involve use of abstract material processes (e.g., *explore, highlight, display, illustrate, illuminate*). Jilly, aged 17, was asked to show how the class novel illuminated themes of human understanding and empathy in relationships and wrote:

> *Mark Haddon's novel "The Curious Incident Of The Dog In The Night-time" demonstrates that people's perceptions of the world are often hindered by a lack of understanding and empathy. Christopher's individual perception of his ideal world was uniquely displayed in the novel. The novel explored many relationships of deception between characters as well as false illusions. These relationships demonstrated the physical, psychological and emotional aspects of the characters' worlds including perceptions and understandings between characters.*

Here the language of interpretive response is evident in several sources. Thus, Jilly begins by placing the novel's title in theme position, making an immediate claim about what it demonstrates:

> *Mark Haddon's novel "The Curious Incident Of The Dog In The Night-time" **demonstrates** that people's perceptions of the world are often hindered by a lack of understanding and empathy*

The second sentence then takes the notion of *perception*, just introduced as new information, and reinstates it as part of theme, giving it a different, though related significance:

> ***Christopher's individual perception of his ideal world*** *was uniquely displayed in the novel*

and this allows Jilly to go on by placing *the novel* in theme position, enabling her to make a further claim about it:

> ***The novel*** *explored many relationships of deception between characters as well as false illusions*

She now takes up the reference to *relationships* to make a claim about what they demonstrate:

> *These relationships* ***demonstrated*** *the physical, psychological and emotional aspects of the characters' worlds including perceptions and understandings between characters*

Evaluation is interwoven with the experiential information, as in

> *people's perceptions . . . are often hindered by a* ***lack of understanding and empathy;***
> *Christopher's . . . perception . . . was* ***uniquely displayed.***

Where Jilly had been asked to write in response to the text of a novel and what it revealed of characters and relationship, Elle (whose historical text we examined above) was asked to respond to two film interpretations of Shakespeare's *King Lear*. In this case, the activity called for interpretation of three different issues: the language of the text, the acting styles of the two actors who played Lear, and the film techniques involved in the films. The discourse is thus very different from that written by Jilly. Elle wrote:

> *Shakespeare's King Lear is a play [[that lends itself well to different productions and audiences]]. Its lead character is a complex one—productions highlight different character attributes according to the directors' ideologies. We see these varied interpretations in Richard Eyre's 1998 National Theatre Company film production and Peter Brooks' 1962 film. By analyzing the final scene (ACT5 Sc 3) in both of these productions, we can see how and why different interpretations are constructed.*

Here the language of interpretation differs in that Elle starts with a process of attribution, establishing the value of the play as worthy of being made into a film, where evaluative language is involved:

> *Shakespeare's King Lear is **a play that lends itself well** to different*
> *productions and audiences*

and a subsequent process of attribution establishes interest in the *lead character* in the next clause, again with some evaluative language employed:

> *its lead character is **a complex one***

and a later clause uses an abstract material process and a circumstance of angle to help establish characteristics of films:

> *productions **highlight** different character attributes **according to the***
> ***directors' ideologies.***

In two later sentences, Elle makes use of an abstract mental process of perception (*we see*, often found in interpretive texts where the young writer seeks to invite the reader to share the view adopted; Christie & Derewianka, 2008):

> ***we see** these varied interpretations*
> *by analyzing the final scene . . . **we can see**.*

In yet other contexts, students engage more directly with responding to aspects of the language of texts studied, as in the case of one student (whose identity is unknown to me) who was discussing the poem "Migrant Hostel" by the Australian poet, Peter Skrzynecki.[2] In the period after the Second World War many migrants came from Europe to Australia, and they were accommodated for differing periods in migrant hostels until they found work and better places to live. They often found the hostels uncomfortable and alienating; the poem records some of the poet's own feelings. The student makes use of two "showing" processes (*illustrates* and *demonstrated*) in discussing the poem, where his concern is to interpret and evaluate the manner in which the poet expresses his remembered feelings as a child migrant:

> *This poem (i.e., Migrant Hostel) perhaps more than any other of*
> *Skrzynecki's works **illustrates** the crisis of emotion [[experienced by many*
> *new migrants]], through the use of powerful and evocative language. This*
> ***is demonstrated** when Skrzynecki uses the metaphor of the road barrier,*
> *"A barrier at the main gate/sealed off the highway / From our doorstop,"*
> *to emphasize the pain of being excluded and partitioned off from*
> *mainstream society. As well, Skrzynecki describes the seemingly*
> *ephemeral existence of many migrant families when they first arrive in*
> *Australia: "We lived like birds of passage / Always sensing a change in the*
> *weather: / Unaware of the season / Whose track we would follow." The*

simultaneous use of imagery and simile with the phrase "we lived like birds of passage" conjures up images of nomads.

The discourse is again abstract, and the abstractions in this case have to do with feelings of alienation and loss, evident in various evaluative uses of language. Thus, the first sentence establishes a general claim about the poem and its meanings, intensifying or grading up the manner in which the poem's language is alluded to:

> *This poem **perhaps more than any other of Skrzynecki's works** illustrates the crisis of emotion experienced by many new migrants, through **the use of powerful and evocative language.***

The claim is then said to be demonstrated by reference to lines selected from the poem:

> *This **is demonstrated** when Skrzynecki uses the metaphor of the road barrier and the lines are said to emphasize **the pain of being excluded***

and a little later we are told the poet describes *the seemingly ephemeral existence* of many migrant families, and that the imagery conjures up nomads—in itself a metapohorical expression.

Evaluation is thus interspersed with experiential information, for the writer is at pains to use this evaluation as part of building an interpretation of the meanings of the poem and of what gives it "point" or significance.

In general, writers of response genres avoid much reference to self, for this is part of building the apparent detachment required in standing back from the text(s) to offer interpretation, even though such interpretation is in another sense supposed to be "personal." The skill is in using the resources of the language to foreground the theme/feeling/attitude, rather than the identity of the response writer, while appearing to appraise the text in a reasoned if sensitive way. Able students, like Rosie, are able to refer to themselves, though she does so in association with a known literary scholar, thereby giving authority to her own value position:

> *"No one in Shakespeare makes so fine an end," says Harold Bloom of Cleopatra's suicide in Scene 5, Act 2. Although the tragedy of Antony's fall has already resolved, I think this is the true climax of the play. For me, it is here that the true depth of the play becomes apparent.*

The language of response to texts is various, for much depends on the field and the purposes in discussing it. However, whether the intention is to respond to significant themes in texts as in Jilly's text, or to the visual and verbal interpretations offered in films as in Elle's case, or to the language of a poem as in the unknown student's case, or to the significance of event in a play as in Rosie's case, the language is generally marked by such features as

- ✓ the capacity to identify abstract issues and themes for interpretation, selecting sufficient details from the text(s) examined to illuminate the themes or issues, thus building symbolic readings of the text(s);
- ✓ the capacity to select appropriate language of evaluation, building interpretation by interweaving experiential and evaluative language.
- ✓ the use of dense language, sometimes built using grammatical metaphor, helping to create abstract meanings;
- ✓ frequent use of "showing" processes and associated abstract material processes that realize abstract aspects of interpretation; and
- ✓ a relative absence of reference to self in expressing evaluation, though evaluation is primarily what such texts are about.

I now turn to one student's effort at critique of a film interpretation of a Shakespearean play.

5.4.1 Writing a Critique of a Film of a Shakespearean Play

Response genres that offer critique are not very common in schooling (Christie & Derewianka, 2008; Rothery, 1994). In fact, the terms of the questions given senior students of English to answer in responding to texts generally do not really invite critique. It is partly because of this that I have chosen to discuss Eleanor's text: she seeks to be provocative in her assessment of the film she discusses, and it is of interest to see how she does this. Eleanor was invited by her teacher to write a review article on Baz Luhrmann's film[3] of *Romeo and Juliet* as part of class work in studying that play. Her critique is cleverly constructed, revealing both that she understands the original Shakespearean text and its significance in English-speaking cultural traditions and that she has facility in using her knowledge to challenge Luhrmann's interpretation of the play. The Review Article is a persuasive one in which Eleanor proposes her thesis about the film and subsequently offers arguments in support. It was accompanied by an image taken from the advertisements of the film, not reproduced here. The schematic structure may be displayed thus:

Thesis ^ Argument.

I have set out to display the elements of structure. Marked topical themes are again displayed.[4]

Text 5.3 Sex, Drugs, Rock and Roll: the New Shakespeare.

Thesis   Shakespeare's Romeo and Juliet is "The greatest love story [[the world has ever known]]." It is iconic. It embraces the meaning of true love. It combines poetry and romance to create some of the most romantic phrases [[known to man]]. Shakespeare leaves the audience shocked and heartbroken. It is one of the greatest classics of English Literature. Yet **now** a new film has been released, betraying the true play and tainting the minds of all [[who watch it]].

Transformations of Shakespeare's plays pop up a lot. Everyone seems to know [[how to change the story // to make it better]]. Some people try to make it easier to understand, some try to modernize it and some want to make it more accessible to a particular audience. Romeo and Juliet has been transformed many times, but this time, the transformation is so massive [[that it's ruined the story]].

Argument   Baz Luhrmann is a middle aged, Australian man [[trying to make some money out of film directing and acting]]. **When asked why he created the movie** he replied, "Romeo and Juliet is an iconic play. The storyline is very simple: it's about two young kids who have sex and commit suicide. But kids don't understand Shakespearean language. If you put it in modern setting with guns instead of swords, and cool cars, and drugs, it will clear up a lot of confusing Shakespeare mumbo jumbo. What I'm doing with this movie is transforming it so I can show teenagers Shakespeare in an easier way."

That's all well and good, but **[[what Luhrmann has created]]** is not just a modern transformation of Romeo and Juliet. He has created a foul film out of a beautiful play. He's changed the context of Romeo and Juliet from 15 Century Italy to a mixture of modern day Mexico City and California. This disgusting mix changes the story to focus on guns, brawls, drugs, and sex. Shakespeare would be alarmed by this exploitation of his classic tale.

The film has been created under the mask of "making the story appeal to a younger audience." It is a big hit amongst teens, eager to see this transformation. Yet is it the message [[we want to send to our children]]? **In Baz Luhrmann's version** teens are no longer seeing the true love story but rather a glorified punch-up. Each scene has a brawl, a sexual innuendo or the taking of drugs and alcohol. **Instead of showing them the story of Romeo and Juliet in a new context**, it simply promotes sex, drugs and rock and roll.

Let me give you an example. **In the original play,** Mercutio is the respectable friend of Romeo. **In Baz Luhrmann's version**, Mercutio is changed into a crass man [[who enjoys cross-dressing and drugs]]. His monologue about Queen Mab [[who visits sleepers to give them dreams]] is changed to him talking about drugs and convincing Romeo to take them. His every word is portrayed as a sexual innuendo, focused at times at Juliet's Nurse. His death occurs not from an elegant sword fight but from a barbarically violent brawl using guns and broken glass. This brutal portrayal of Romeo's respectable friend would surely make Shakespeare turn in his grave.

This is just one of the many changes that Luhrmann has made. These transformations have recreated the story and changed it into a repulsive 'new version' of one of the most beautiful love stories of all time. **In "taking the story and changing it so teenagers can understand it"** he has changed the whole focus of the story and destroyed the world's most beautiful love story. Thanks Baz, you've ruined it for me.

Because the text is written as a review article, it has some interpersonal qualities reminiscent of journalism, as in expressions like *that's all well and good*, or in the closing salutation, *Thanks Baz, you've ruined it for me*. Nonetheless, the text is constructed to offer a genuine challenge to Luhrmann's interpretation, and it builds its case by several measures, most notably deliberately setting up contrasts to demolish Luhrmann's claims as a serious filmmaker.

Thus, the Thesis is cleverly constructed in that Eleanor starts by offering warmly supportive observations about the Shakespearean play, evoking what she can reasonably assume is a cultural knowledge of it, shared with her reader. To do this, she foregrounds the play and its significance in a series of theme positions in several opening sentences, some of which consist of only one clause. Their effect is to build in short, staccato fashion, steadily expanding the evaluative significance of what is stated:

*Shakespeare's Romeo and Juliet is "**The greatest love story the world has ever known**" It is iconic*

It embraces the meaning of true love
It combines poetry and romance to create *some of the most romantic*
phrases known to man
*Shakespeare leaves the audience **shocked and heartbroken***
*It is **one of the greatest classics of English Literature.***

The writer's sense of the cultural significance attaching to the play is thus
established. By implication she is understood as suitably knowledgeable about
the field, and thus credentialed to pass judgment on the film. These matters
established, the writer introduces her negative evaluation (using a contrastive
conjunction to herald it), and she dashes the otherwise positive expectation set
up in the minds of her readers:

*Yet now a new film has been released, **betraying the true play and***
*tainting the minds of all who watch it.**

The Thesis is developed in the next paragraph by reference to *transformations of Shakespeare's plays,* and the element concludes with a closing
categorical assertion whose evaluative language is again forceful, and where
the contrastive conjunction *but* has a role as well as the marked theme (*this
time*):

*Romeo and Juliet has been transformed many times, **but this time, the***
*transformation is so massive that it's ruined the story.**

Supportive argument in the next element rests initially on a rather dismissive
reference to the director of the film:

*Baz Luhrmann is a **middle aged Australian man trying to make some***
*money** out of film directing and acting*

after which his stated reasons for making the film are reported, and Eleanor
goes on, again rather dismissively, where both a contrastive conjunction and
some negative polarity help set up a contrast:

*That's all well and good, but what Luhrmann has created **is not just a***
*modern transformation of Romeo and Juliet. He has created a foul film***
*out of a beautiful play.**

The subsequent step in the argument again sets up contrast, for we are told
that the film has been created under the mask of making the story appeal to a
younger audience:

*It is a **big hit amongst teens, eager to see this transformation.***

Again a contrastive conjunction challenges the claim made, this time with a rhetorical question:

Yet is it the message we want to send to our children?

and this aspect of the argument concludes:

Instead of showing them the story of Romeo and Juliet in a new context, it simply promotes sex, drugs and rock and roll.

Seeking to engage directly with her readers in developing her case about the violence and poor values in the film, Eleanor goes on:

Let me give you an example

where she unfolds her argument about the manner in which Mercutio, *the respectable friend of Romeo*

*is changed into **a crass man** who enjoys cross-dressing and drugs*

and of his death she writes:

*This **brutal portrayal of Romeo's respectable friend would surely make Shakespeare turn in his grave.***

The evaluative language is all negative, its force set up by the contrast in this case between what Eleanor argues is Shakespeare's intended interpretation of Mercutio and Buhrmann's interpretation.

In the final paragraph Eleanor writes of the *many changes* made by Luhrmann, though these become *transformations* in the next sentence, where again the language expresses negative evaluation and interpretation of the film but positive evaluation and interpretation of the play

*These transformations have recreated the story and changed it into a repulsive 'new version' of one of the most beautiful love stories of all time. In "taking the story and changing it so teenagers can understand it" he has **changed the whole focus of the story and destroyed the world's most beautiful love story.** Thanks Baz, you've ruined it for me.*

The success of the review article depends on two factors. First, Eleanor understands and appeals to a culturally held value attaching to Shakespeare's *Romeo and Juliet*. She demonstrates that she possesses relevant "cultural capital" and thus has the authority with which to propose her interpretation of Luhrmann's interpretation, dismissing what he has done. Second, Eleanor reveals a facility in deploying her language resources to build evaluation and judgment. Both the cultural knowledge and the facility with language in subject English are for most students quite hard won: they require practice over some years of schooling in reading, writing, and talking about literary texts and exposure to the example of others in engaging with such texts.

In summary, then, English literary studies build knowledge structures in ways different from science, for their concern is not with verifiable truths of the physical world, but with perceptions, understandings, and interpretations of literary texts, where the object is to evaluate and appraise the texts as art. The knowledge built in English is not subject to "proof" in the sense that scientific knowledge is, so that the requirement for replication of procedures, so fundamental to science, does not apply. Yet the knowledge gained and developed in English nonetheless builds, or should be built, incrementally. That is because there are practices for reading literary texts and viewing films displayed as part of English studies that require cultivation and some effort in their learning. Such practices in reading and viewing include, for example, habits of asking questions about literary pieces, techniques for identifying their meanings, including their symbolic meanings, and methods of discussing their patterns of language use, including methods of critique. All these habits and practices need to be established over some years of practice, incrementally building a knowledge base with which, as they grow older, young people can read and interpret literary texts, going on in their writing to offer analysis and interpretation.

The language of evaluation and interpretation of other texts, so prized in English literary studies, is difficult for many students, who often find it hard to understand the principles by which literary interpretation is constructed. Furthermore, the criteria for assessment often remain elusive, even invisible (Christie & Macken-Horarik, 2007, 2011; Macken-Horarik, 2002, 2006a, 2006b), so that what constitutes success is frequently not transparent. This is the more unfortunate because English studies are important, allowing access to many avenues of privilege and opportunity beyond school. Teacher intervention, enabling access to the discourses of literary discussion, is of critical importance if young people in their last years of schooling are to achieve some confidence and facility in discussing texts of many kinds. This will involve, among other matters

√ extensive shared reading and discussion of the texts studied and their meanings;

√ particular discussion of the cultural significance attaching to texts interpreted and evaluated. This is a very considerable challenge for all young people, and a special challenge for those whose cultural and language backgrounds are different from those of native speakers of English;

√ opportunity to deconstruct sample target genres for writing and active discussion of these; and

√ modeling some of the language for evaluation, including playing with different patterns of attitudinal expression to test their effects.

5.5 Conclusion

By adolescence to adulthood young people need to achieve the necessary facility in control of oral and written discourse with which to engage with the uncommonsense experience of the various school subjects valued in the English-speaking world. Such facility is expressed in control of abstraction, generalization, explanation, and argument, all variously deployed in the different school subjects. Those subjects, like the university studies from which they derive, teach different forms of theoretical knowledge, which are part of society's conversations about the world. Schooling is intended to offer an initiation into society's conversations, enabling young people to enter with understanding into the discourse patterns in which the knowledge bases of the different subjects are expressed.

In practice, although able students follow the developmental trajectory I have outlined, many others are less successful, handicapped in facing the challenges of schooling and in mastering the various discourse patterns in which the school subjects are expressed. I have suggested that a functional grammar allows us to analyze the language tasks that children and adolescents need to handle, and it can also suggest possible strategies for intervention in their learning.

Notes

1 Martin and White (2005, p. 93) acknowledge Bahktin in their use of the term "heteroglossic." They note that Bakhtin (1981, p. 93) observes that all utterances exist "against a backdrop of other concrete utterances on the same theme, a background made up of contradictory opinions, points of view and value judgments . . . pregnant with response and objections."

2 Peter Skrzynewcki is a contemporary poet, who, as a child aged four, migrated with his family to Australia from Germany in 1949. He writes on many subjects,

though themes of dislocation and of migrant experience are important for him. His collection *Immigrant Chronicle* is well known. The text cited here was written at a public examination in the last year of schooling, and the identity of the student was not revealed.

3   Although this film was released some years ago, it is still used in English classrooms in Australia. The text discussed here was written in 2008.

4   I have discussed the opening paragraph only of this text in Christie and Macken-Horarik (2011).

Language Learning   ISSN 0023-8333

CHAPTER 6

The Overall Trajectory in Language Learning in School

6.1 Introduction

This book has outlined a model of language development in schooling that attempts to explain the processes by which children and adolescents achieve a grasp of language and literacy from about age 6 or 7 to about age 17 or 18, when their formal schooling ceases. In the preschool years children learn oral language to deal with commonsense experience, and this involves mastery of a congruent grammar. The entry to school, marking the start of the first phase I have identified, takes children into learning literacy: a "second-order symbolic system" with which they learn "to reconstitute language itself into a new, more abstract mode" (Halliday, 1993, p. 109). Learning to talk, read, and write for the purposes of schooling is quite challenging for all children, even the most advantaged, and those from less advantaged backgrounds experience significant challenge. The entry to literacy establishes an early need to handle unfamiliar experience, and the first steps in writing use a very simple congruent grammar closer to the patterns of speech than to the patterns of mature written language. With time, practice, and exposure to the examples of written language in reading, children start to learn features of the grammar of writing. Their first written texts use simple lexis, and they tend to offer series of simple clauses linked by additive or temporal conjunctions; theme choices are simple unmarked themes, with some occasional uses of marked themes realized in clauses or circumstances of time. The tense choice for most writing is typically simple past. Modality is not normally used, and where attitude is expressed, it tends to be in simple processes of affect.

By late childhood to early adolescence, the second phase identified, the discourses that successful children read and write change, for the resources of the language expand as children learn to make meanings in new discourse patterns. For example, they achieve a growing control of thematic patterning, with which to shape and direct lengthening passages of written discourse, and relatedly, they show control of internal reference, helping build unity in written texts. They also learn to exploit the resource of noun group structure, thus compressing information, and circumstantial information is also often expressed in a growing number of types of prepositional phrases. The range of clause types and clause interdependencies also increases. The lexis expands, allowing children to express more nuanced meanings in which experiential and interpersonal meanings are often fused. A noncongruent grammar starts to emerge, normally expressed in nominalization, which is one aspect of learning to expand noun group structures while contributing to the developing density of written texts. This is the phase in which many children start to fall behind in their school learning, as they move from the primary to the secondary school, because the changing patterns of literate discourse become more challenging with the entry to the growing abstraction of different subject specific literacies. It is for this reason that policies of active intervention are needed in these years to halt the decline in children's school performance that often occurs.

The third phase emerges by midadolescence, and, among the successful students, this is marked by consolidation of all gains made, while the discourses of the various subjects become more specialized for building subject-specific literacies (Unsworth, 2000), so that they show much expanded lexes of the different fields, including technical language. Grammatical metaphor becomes more frequent, its impact felt, among other things, in a tendency to collapse otherwise independent clauses into large noun groups. Hence, the logical relationships between the meanings of different clauses are rendered less visible, their meanings expressed within clauses rather than between them. Attitudinal expression becomes more marked, expressed in part in an expanded lexis having to do with attitudes and values, and also to some extent in expanded uses of modality, including uses of modal adverbs. Attitudinal values can at times be overstated in this phase, as young people learn to control their language resources. Tense choices are more varied, allowing expressions of various time frames. In this phase, though the discourses differ depending on the registers and genres involved, they are generally marked by a considerable degree of abstraction, a necessary part of building the specialist fields of knowledge of the secondary years. Indeed, the knowledge structures of the different school subjects become more distinctive, and their claims on characteristic patterns of evaluation become more marked.

In the final phase, belonging to the last years of schooling, the discourses of the various school subjects all reveal abstraction, interpretation, and evaluation, expressed in different ways, depending on the field and knowledge involved.

The humanities of English literary studies and history tend to make considerable use of attitudinal expression, offering evaluation, judgment, and interpretation. The sciences make much less use of attitudinal expression, though assessment of the significance of scientific meanings is found. Successful students reveal considerable confidence in their control of the various resources, ideational, interpersonal, and textual.

As I noted in Chapter 1, the overall pattern that has been argued should be understood flexibly, because individuals progress at different rates and their life experiences and their social locations (Hasan, 2002) differentially prepare children and adolescents to deal with the language of schooling. Moreover, language development is not linear, so that, for example, in coming to terms with new and demanding ideas and information, young people may well regress, relying on earlier understandings in order to understand the new. Such a regression is perfectly understandable. On the other hand, other young people will progress very rapidly, so that, for example, by midadolescence, at around 15 years old, they can display most of the features in their oral language and literacy of others aged 17 or 18.

The movement overall is a movement from the simple and congruent to the less simple and noncongruent; from the familiar and commonsense knowledge of life toward the less familiar, uncommonsense areas of knowledge that the school subjects represent; from meanings and discourses that are elemental and of the immediate context toward meanings and discourses that are abstract and of more distant contexts. The developmental trajectory involved allows young people to embark on a journey of discovery into the knowledge structures of an English-speaking culture so that they can, at some level at least, enter into "society's conversations" about theoretical knowledge, to use Wheelahan's (2010) term.

The developmental trajectory as described is relevant for second language students as well as first language learners of English in that like mother tongue speakers, they initially use a congruent grammar in learning the discourses of schooling. In an ongoing study of junior secondary students of English in Indonesia (Emilia & Christie, 2011), for example, we have found that the students display a number of features similar to those of younger L1 children in Australia learning to write, suggesting they are following a similar developmental trajectory. For example, in writing recounts of personal experience, the children use a congruent grammar to construct sequences of mainly equal clauses, linked by simple additive and some temporal conjunctions; their thematic progression is mainly achieved using unmarked topical themes, but where marked themes occur, they are expressed in circumstances or clauses of time;

they create circumstances of time or place in prepositional phrases, and they do not use adverbial expressions, nor do they use modality; where they express attitude, it is in simple affect (e.g., *I love*); they do not use grammatical metaphor; they use only simple past tense, for varieties of tense choices are a later development. Whittaker and Llinares (2009) report on a study of content learning in the social science classrooms of Spanish-speaking students of English. Using the SF grammar, they analyze spoken and written texts from primary and secondary students of English who are learning geography and history. The register and genre choices differ from those just cited in the Indonesian study, but there are points of similarity in the written language produced by the Spanish students, including use of mainly equal or paratactic clause complexes, use of circumstances of time, place, and to some extent, manner; and limited use of modality. In general the uses of grammar appear to be congruent, as is common for a learner of a language.

In one sense, we may seem to have established the obvious point that oral language and literacy development involves a movement from the immediate and the simple toward the more remote and the more complex. So what? How does it help to think about the matter in these terms? What have we gained from the general arguments advanced in this book?

I have several answers to these questions. First, the functional grammar provides an essential *linguistic tool* with which we can trace development, noting the ways in which changes occur, and using it in a diagnostic sense to establish problems. Second, in doing this we can also trace the significant pressure points: those points at which, such are the demands in controlling literacy in particular that children and adolescents are challenged, potentially falling behind in their learning. Although all the phases I have identified are obviously important and indeed interdependent, I argue that the two phases of greatest pressure and challenge are the first phase, when children commence formal schooling, and the second, when they pass from childhood into early adolescence. The first involves the initial engagement with school oral language and in particular the second-order symbolic system of literacy; the second involves engagement with the increasingly abstract experience of late primary to early secondary school, taking children into greater abstraction, interpretation, and evaluation. Where children struggle and fail at either of these points, they are indeed in difficulties. Third, the functional grammar allows us to identify linguistic features particular to the different school subjects and their discourses; it thus helps us to identify the ways the different knowledge structures are constructed in these discourses. Fourth, once we are possessed of knowledge in all these senses, we are enabled to develop pedagogies for intervention in the learning of children and adolescents across the years of schooling.

6.2 Functionally Based Pedagogy

Pedagogies built using the functional grammar should be explicit about their goals in promoting language learning. Moreover, they should offer explicit guidance and advice to children about the English language, building a meta-language for discussing and using it. Although this is true for both oral language and literacy, the claims of learning to read and write are particularly important in schooling. All cultures, even traditional ones, have always had practices for educating their young, including in particular their patterns of talk, but it is only in literate cultures that the institution of schooling emerged. That is because teaching and learning literacy involve a range of institutionalized practices that require overt attention to the nature of the written mode and its ways of con-structing meanings. Reading and writing change consciousness about language and its uses; as reading and writing are mastered, they unlock ways of recording, knowing, valuing, interpreting, and expressing experience that are not open to those without literacy. Mastery of these ways of recording, knowing, and so on requires concentration and effort, although as any teacher reading this will also know, such ways are often also rewarding and pleasurable, even at times great fun. Early childhood education has always recognized the need for explicit teaching about literacy, at least in terms of teaching the spelling and handwrit-ing systems as well as the rudiments of how to read and write. At its best, of course, early childhood teaching has done more than these things, establish-ing an interest in, and a curiosity about, written discourse and encouraging confidence in its reading and writing, so that young children learn something of the grammatical organization of written discourse even in their first years of schooling. All this is part of learning the registers of schooling, with their requirements for participation in class discussion, and for understanding written discourse, both in reading and in writing it.

Beyond the early years, nonetheless, proficiency in language and literacy is often taken for granted, because it tends to be assumed that, the basic under-standings having been established, children will progress from late childhood into adolescence in relatively unproblematic ways. Where this occurs, what tends to be foregrounded in much teaching practice is the vocabulary of the field of knowledge of concern, though for reasons argued in earlier chapters this is never enough. That is because learning a field of knowledge is never about learning only its vocabulary, important though that is: it is about learning the meanings expressed in the discourse patterns in which relevant vocabulary is deployed. Where the attention shifts away from the discourse patterns in which meanings are expressed, the tendency is to render language invisible. The result is that by late primary school and into the secondary years, many children drop behind in their school performance, though the causes are not always explained in the terms offered in this book. These problems have been identified in various parts of the English-speaking world and discussed in Chapter 4.

What, then, will pedagogies devoted to teaching language and literacy be like, extended over the years of schooling? They will aim to teach a conscious-ness about the discourses of school subjects, exploring the meanings of their various registers and genres, and building a metalanguage for discussion and reflection on how the meanings are made.

The activities used to build the necessary consciousness will be expressed differently, of course, depending on the age group of students, their previ-ous learning experiences, and the field being taught. Two broad principles, nonetheless, should inform all pedagogical practices:

o The focus for learning should be on the text (be that spoken, written, or multimodal) and its meanings, at least as the point of departure.
o Language should be learned in use, as part of engagement with significant activities.

Genre-based pedagogy using the SF grammar, as that has emerged in Australia over the last 25 years, offers a model that can be used and adapted in schools from kindergarten to Year 12, exemplifying these two principles. For that reason I offer a brief discussion of genre-based pedagogy in the SFL genre-based tradition. I have elsewhere discussed this pedagogy, both in pri-mary and secondary schools, drawing on my own research (e.g., Christie 2002, 2005, 2008; Christie & Derewianka, 2008; Christie & Soosai, 2000–2001). Others have also documented it in several places (e.g., Feez & Joyce, 1998; Johns, 2001; Martin, 1999, 2009; Martin & Rose, 2008; Rose & Martin, in press; Unsworth, 2000, 2002). Schleppegrell (2004), writing of the Ameri-can context, has produced a related discussion of genres and genre pedagogy. Emilia (2010, pp. 45–101) has documented a successful program using genre theory to teach English to tertiary students in Indonesia while she is currently researching its teaching in Indonesian schools.

6.2.1 Genre Pedagogy in the SFL Tradition

Genre-based pedagogy, as that has been proposed by Martin and his colleagues, draws on Halliday's theories of language, text, and context, already displayed and discussed in Chapter 1, though unlike Halliday, Martin and others draw a distinction between register and genre (Figure 1.2 in Chapter 2). It will be recalled that register refers to three elements of any context of situation: field, tenor, and mode. That is to say, the meanings of any context of situation will depend on the ideational meanings (expressing the field), the interpersonal meanings (expressing the tenor and relationships of participants), and mode (the manner of organizing the text as a message). Genre refers to the overall organization of the text, where this is a condition of the context of culture.

Where a genre-based pedagogy is employed, the teacher, working closely with the students

✓ identifies a field of knowledge, a topic or both, for study;
✓ identifies its register values, considering its activities and its language;
✓ introduces the topic to the students with a particular focus on its experiential field and its importance, also considering how, if at all, it relates to other areas of knowledge previously taught and learned;
✓ devotes series of lessons to teaching and learning about the field, using any relevant resources (e.g., books, videos, films, images, class visits), and steadily building a knowledge of the field, its procedures for discussing questions, and its methods of inquiry;
✓ proposes a target genre for writing;
✓ directs any writing tasks, often by using a model of the target genre for writing, deconstructing it for discussion, and building a metalanguage for discussing the genre, its elements of structure, and their purposes; and
✓ creates opportunity throughout these steps for teaching about any relevant details of the linguistic organization of the text.

Figure 6.1 displays essentially the same teaching–learning cycle, giving it a more stylized presentation. The outer circle displays the activity of setting the context for learning, where this is reiterated but also enriched as the teaching–learning cycle proceeds: The field for work must be regularly revisited. Deconstruction of a written text involves learning the language of the field and examining the structure of the text, taking its elements apart to investigate their purpose in contributing to meaning. Extensive work on deconstruction leads to a later phase of joint construction of an example of the target genre while also doing work on the field. Finally, in the third phase, when students are confident, they move to independent construction of an example of the text type or genre involved. Talk of the language in the teaching cycle varies, depending on the age group of the students, their previous experience in working in such cycles, the field being studied, and so on. However, we can say that the talk

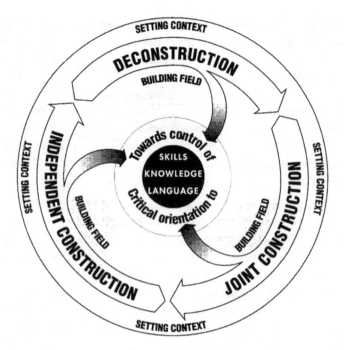

Figure 6.1 Teaching/learning cycle for mentoring genre (Martin, 2009).

typically involves detailed consideration of the overall schematic structure, its elements, and their meanings, and it can go on to consider such things as theme choices and how they help organize the text, conjunctions and their role in sequencing information, process types and their distribution in the text, technical language and its significance, among others.

6.2.2 Early Childhood Pedagogy
In Chapter 2 we examined an instance of genre-based pedagogy for early childhood, which I return to, in order to illustrate the approach involved. A very experienced teacher worked closely with Brian Gray to develop a program that followed all the principles that would become known as genre-based. In fact, Gray contributed to the emergent model that was later documented in many sources, including in a series of genre-based books for schools (Christie et al., 1990a, 1990b, 1992).

The teacher took up the field of chickens and chicken reproduction first, and over a series of lessons she involved young Aboriginal children in learning about chicken development. The question they were working with in the episode we examined was: "How do chickens grow in an egg?" The classroom talk involved a great deal of guided repetition. Previous lessons had already devoted time to observing chickens and eggs in the classroom as well as to listening to the teacher reading about chickens. Extensive talk about chickens established a shared understanding of relevant discourse patterns in which technical language of the field (*mother hen, keeping warm, incubator*, and so on) was introduced, partly from classroom observation, partly from reading the selected textbook displayed by the teacher. Habits of talking and reading about chickens were thus practiced. Hence, the necessary register values having to do with the field, the tenor, and the mode for scientific discussion of chickens were established. Later, the children participated in the shared activity of writing, where, using the field knowledge they had built up, they practiced writing a simple scientific genre, following the linguistic organization of the text as well as the formation of the various letters to write the words and sentences. Notions of *words*, *letters*, and their sounds were brought to consciousness in a series of classroom episodes that Gray, following Cazden (1977), called "concentrated language encounters": they focused the young learners on intensive engagement with important ideas while they were supported in contributing to the discourse in which those ideas were expressed.[1]

The activity grew from the initially commonsense experience of talk about eggs, and even cooking them in the classroom, but with that activity the teacher went on to guide the children into learning specialist knowledge in two senses. First, she was developing a pedagogic knowledge about how to talk, read, and write for school purposes, where the knowledge could in time be transported to other class learning activities. Second, she was developing an uncommon-sense knowledge of the field of chickens, particular to the social science program. To take terms that Halliday used in another context some years ago, the children were *learning language, learning through language, and learning about language* (e.g., Hasan & Martin, 1989).[2]

6.2.3 Genre Pedagogy in Junior Secondary Schooling

The explanation of the human digestive system discussed in Chapter 3 emerged from a research program my colleague Anne Soosai and I conducted in Melbourne in which the teacher used genre pedagogy to teach both science and English (Christie, 1999a). The teacher introduced the notion of an explanation genre by contrasting it with the report genre, examples of which the students had read and produced in earlier work in the science program. An explanation of tropical cycles was deconstructed to establish its elements and their purposes. Then the teacher chose to generate discussion of selected features of the language used to construct such a text. She focused primarily on conjunctive relations and theme and thematic progression, deeming these important to understanding text organization. One paragraph in the text (Christie et al., 1992)[3] read:

> *A tropical storm begins when air flows into an area where the air pressure is low. As this air flows in, it circles around the centre of the low pressure area. Because warm air rises, this circling air also rises up into the atmosphere in a spiral like a corkscrew. When this warm moist air gets up into the atmosphere, it cools and forms rain clouds. These rain clouds and spiraling winds are what cause a storm at sea.* (p. 12)

Talk of the conjunctive relations led at one point to the following exchanges:

> T: *OK, what is the next conjunction that you can find?*
> Max: *"As."*
> T: *Yes and what's that, time or reason?*
> Max: *Time.*
> T: *OK. "As the air flows in" means that moment doesn't it? What's the next thing? Yes, somebody said that here.*
> Kylie: *"Because."*
> T: *Yes, "Because." Right. Is that time or reason?*
> Kylie: *Reason.*
> T: *Because the warm air rises, the circling air always rises. It's telling us why something happened.*

Talk of conjunctions and their functions was quite a new aspect of learning science, though constant reference to the text in which conjunctions had relevance proved illuminating to the 14-year-old students involved. The notion of theme was a completely new idea, though once they were alerted to looking for it, the students became quite adept at recognizing topical themes and their purposes. Referring again to the same text extract the teacher pointed to topical themes on an overhead transparency and asked students to comment on the purpose of the first one:

> *A tropical storm begins when air flows into an area where the air pressure is low.*
> *As this air flows in, it circles around the centre of the low pressure area.*
>
> T: *OK. What do you notice about that . . . there, about that theme? [Points to it]*
> Daniel: *You get more information about the sentence before.*
> T: *Yes, you get some more information so it's linking back to the sentence before and giving some information.*

The later discussion established all the topical themes and their role in the unfolding of the text. Once these matters had been explored, the teacher turned, in a subsequent lesson, to the nature of the human digestive system, establishing that this was the field for exploration and devoting time to building a sense of that field and its language.

The brief details given from the classroom talk about conjunctions and theme are reproduced here because I want to make the point that the teacher needs always to make selective judgment about what aspects of the language for writing can be usefully foregrounded in learning to write genres. Over the years of schooling, many features of the grammar of the language can be usefully explored and learned, building an incremental knowledge about the language, useful for promoting skilled reading and writing. The important point to note is that such teaching–learning activity arises in a context of use while working with a passage of discourse. This is the reverse of much time-honored and, hopefully, discredited teaching of the past that would, for example, have students focus on strings of conjunctions produced as lists remote from contexts of use. Genre theory will always start with the discourse, explore it, engage with its meanings, even play with its ideas, before moving to some teaching and learning about selected language features that help create it. I now turn to some aspects of teaching about functional grammar.

6.3 Teaching Aspects of the Functional Grammar

Returning for the moment to early childhood education, with which I started the above discussion of genre pedagogy, it is useful to note that Feez (2010, 2011), whose work on Montessori's early childhood education draws on both Vygotsky's psychology and Halliday's SFL theory, offers an account of early childhood education much in the tradition of the model provided in the classroom with Aboriginal children. Feez shows how Montessori, whose work was particularly directed to helping poor and underprivileged children, saw the educational program as initiating the young into the important values, principles, and bodies of knowledge of a Western culture. Among the many areas of the curriculum of concern, Montessori saw language, language games, and language learning as central to the activities of teaching and learning. Language enrichment in talk, in play, including play with its sounds in rhyme and rhythm, and in handling objects and naming them, all are used to build a developing consciousness of language. In addition, in a Montessori classroom talk and play develop around storybooks, letters, factual books, maps, encyclopedias, and other resources, building from very early a sense of how to discriminate different registers and genres. A language for talking about language is also taught early while children play with letter pieces in a movable alphabet, forming them into different words. Different word groups are early identified using different colors, constituting different parts of speech or "structure words" that the children can name and talk about. I well remember visiting Feez when she was teaching in a Montessori classroom and being asked by a child of about six to look at the list of adjectives she had created. She was, I found, capable of initiating and maintaining an animated conversation about adjectives and why they were interesting. Young children experience no difficulty mastering a metalanguage, provided they see it as relevant and interesting to their purposes. (See Feez, 2010, for a much longer discussion.)

Whereas Feez, following Montessori, has shown that teaching the traditional parts of speech or structure words is a useful aspect of building school knowledge of language and literacy, Williams (1998, 2005b) has demonstrated that the functional grammar and some of its terms can be successfully used with very young children. Williams (1998) reports a reading program developed with 6-year-old children reading Browne's *Piggybook* (1986), and he records the ways in which the children learned to identify different processes as they read and reread the tale, exploring and interpreting its meanings while developing a metalanguage for talking about them and also developing enhanced reading skills. Williams (2007) later reported more extensive research programs teaching the functional grammar to older children in the last years of primary school, revealing, for example, how they learned about different process types and their roles in making meaning as well as how to explore English clauses and their organization, enabling them to reflect quite deeply on how language was used. Although optimistic about the possibilities for using the SF grammar for teaching children, Williams (2005b) concludes that more research needs to be done, examining, among other things, how to "sequence the introduction of grammatical features for maximal benefit" to learners, how to enable children to move between functional and structural descriptions of words, and how to "enable children to 'think grammatically' in editing and critiquing text" (p. 307). French (2010), one of the classroom teachers who worked with Williams, has offered a detailed discussion of their work with primary children teaching them the functional grammar. It has sometimes been suggested, she argues, that primary aged children are not ready developmentally to learn about grammar, though she demonstrates how successful they can be. In a more recent study (French, in press), she reports how Year 2 students were taught about direct and indirect speech as an aspect of reading literary texts. She concludes that the children developed an enhanced understanding of the differences between passages that recorded speech and those that did not and that this contributed to improved expressiveness in their own oral reading of texts as well as improving their understanding of punctuation in their writing.

Many of the aspects of functional grammar that Williams and French record introducing to very young children are relevant for all ages, though the manner in which they are introduced and the detail in which they are taught and learned will depend on the ages of students and their prior experience. In fact, over the years of schooling many aspects of the language should be reintroduced, the better to improve learning over the developmental phases I have identified. This is why teachers need a considerable knowledge of the functional grammar so that they can make informed judgments about when to introduce some items and when to revisit them at later points. The point here is reminiscent of Bruner's (1960) notion of the spiral curriculum, for he argued that basic ideas should be repeatedly revisited, building on them in greater detail as students advance. In similar fashion, Muller has argued for learning sequences in which "topics are repeated across learning levels, but differently" (Muller, 2007, p. 81), whereas the notion of "return with a difference" is also explored by Adoniou and Macken-Horarik (2007) with respect to teaching ESL (see also Christie & Macken-Horarik, 2011). I use the metafunctions to explore aspects of the functional grammar that can be introduced and revisited at various stages of schooling.

6.3.1 Experiential Meanings

An important way to explore the resources in which experiential meanings are expressed is to examine transitivity processes, tracing the patterns that emerge, so that one can comment on their role in the text. The point can be sharpened if we examine two different text types with a view to getting at how differently they draw on the language system. This can induce a consciousness about the way meanings are made, enabling children and adolescents to reflect on information read or written. I use an extract from a story written for teaching purposes, and contrast this with an extract from a text on hemophilia introduced in Chapter 4.

Consider the following extract from a story written about the Wild Child of Aveyron (Christie & Soosai, 2000), where MATERIAL PROCESSES (WAS DISCOVERED), mental processes (liked), *relational* processes (*was*), and verbal processes (were told) are identified. Participants might also be identified and discussed, though in the interests of not overcrowding the text, I have not identified them. I do however, identify the circumstances (about two centuries ago) expressed in prepositional phrases, as they provide useful information.

About two centuries ago, a wild boy WAS DISCOVERED in the woods of
Aveyron in France. He *was* filthy, *had* long matted hair and WORE no
clothes. He became known as the "Wild Child of Aveyron." Very strange
stories were told of the Wild Child. He LIVED in the woods like an animal.
He ATE potatoes, turnips and carrots, and nuts such as chestnuts and
walnuts, but he WOULDN'T EAT meat. He DRANK a lot of water and he liked
TO PLAY in water. He *had* no family or friends, and he LIVED an isolated
life. He *had* many scars on his body and it was thought he HAD BEEN
ATTACKED and BITTEN by animals. (p. 22)

In reading such a text with their teacher, students can explore such questions as

- What processes construct actions?
- What processes construct being or having?
- What processes construct thinking?
- What processes construct talking?
- How are the processes distributed across the text and which appear the most often?
- What kinds of circumstances are present?

Table 6.1 sets out a possible table for class work and discussion.

Setting out the processes this way allows students to see that there are
mainly material or action processes (e.g., *was discovered in the woods, wore no
clothes, lived an isolated life*), required to build aspects of a story, whereas the
relational processes (*he was filthy, had long matted hair*) help to tell something
about a character. Mental or thinking processes tell either what others think of
that character (*he became known*) or what he thinks himself (*he liked to play*).
Finally, the presence of one verbal process (*very strange stories were told*)
reveals there is not much telling in this text extract, though the one that is there
helps to build information about the character.

Table 6.2 sets out circumstances in the text. Most of the circumstances have
to do with place, and some identify places the character was found (e.g., *in the
woods of Aveyron*), whereas others identify places on his body (*many scars on
his body*). Of the other circumstances, there are only single examples of time
(*about two centuries ago*), matter (*of the Wild Child*), role (*as the "Wild Child of
Aveyron"*) and manner (*like an animal*). Clearly the circumstantial information
is primarily about places, and discussion might be developed about why this
is so.

If we turn to one extract from Text 4.4 (originally presented in Chapter 4),
selected here because it is a scientific text, we can see the difference in the

Table 6.1 Processes in the story about the wild child

Process	Type	Function
A wild boy was discovered	Material or action	Express doing
He wore no clothes		
He lived in the woods		
He ate potatoes, etc.		
He wouldn't eat		
He drank a lot of water		
To play in water		
He lived an isolated life		
He had been attacked		
[He had been] bitten		
He was filthy	Relational or being	Express being or having
[he] had long hair		
he had no friends		
he had many scars		
He became known	Mental or thinking process	Express thinking
He liked to play		
It was thought		
Very strange stories were told	Verbal	Express telling

Table 6.2 Circumstances in the story about the wild child

Circumstances	Type	Function
about two centuries ago	Time	Tells when
in the woods of Aveyron	Place	Tells where
in the woods		
in water		
on his body		
of the Wild Child	Matter	Tells what about
as "the Wild Child of Aveyron"	Role	Tells the role given
like an animal	Manner	Tells how

distribution of processes. Material and relational processes are shown as above, and <u>causative</u> processes (a defective gene <u>causes</u>) and <u>existential</u> processes (<u>there is</u> a defective gene) are displayed differently.

> Hemophilia *is* a hereditary disease [[in which <u>there is</u> a defective gene [[that <u>causes</u> the owner of this gene TO BE UNABLE TO CLOT efficiently]].
> The deficiency CAN BE CARRIED by both the X and the Y (female and male)

Table 6.3 Processes in text extract on hemophilia

Process	Type	Function
Hemophilia is a hereditary disease [[in which there is a defective gene [[that causes the owner of this gene to be unable to clot efficiently]].	Relational	Expresses definition
The deficiency can be carried by both the X and the Y (female and male) chromosome	Material	Express doing
It only seems to affect the Y or male chromosome		
[They are] concerned with creating a blood clot		
One of these is missing		
The "chain" is broken		
The body is unable to create clots.		
Hemophilia occurs		
[This] prevents the body from creating strong blood clots.		
There is a defective gene	Existential	Express being
There are 13 main proteins or factors, concerned with creating a blood clot.		
[Which] causes the owner of this gene	Causative	Express causing
[This] results in low levels of fibrin		

chromosome, but it only SEEMS TO AFFECT the Y or male chromosome. There are 13 main proteins or factors, CONCERNED with CREATING a blood clot. When even one of these IS MISSING, the "chain" IS BROKEN and therefore the body IS UNABLE TO CREATE clots. Hemophilia OCCURS when there is a defect in one or more of the blood coagulation protein factors which results in low levels of fibrin, which in turn, PREVENTS the body from CREATING strong blood clots.

Table 6.3 displays the processes. Several of them occur within clause embeddings, and for that reason I have displayed them twice, both inside and outside the embeddings.

Material or action processes are again the most numerous, involved with building the activities within the body with hemophilia (e.g., *the deficiency can be carried*; *it seems to affect the Y or male chromosome*). One relational process occurs with the important role of defining (*hemophilia is a hereditary disease*), whereas two existential processes build being (*there is a defective gene*; *there is a defect*). Two causative processes (*that causes the owner of the gene . . .* ; *which results in low levels of fibrin*) also occur, having an important function in establishing causal links between phenomena discussed. The overall distribution of process types is revealed as very different from that in the text on the Wild Child of Aveyron, for indeed the meanings constructed are quite different. What is also of interest is the apparent absence of circumstances in the text on hemophilia: There is only one, and that is a circumstance of place: *when there is a defect **in one or more of the blood coagulation protein factors***. In my observation, science fields typically generate few circumstances, and those that appear are mainly those of place. It seems that the experiential meanings of science are built very much in the processes and their participants. Students might also discuss why this is so and what it tells us about the meanings made in science.

Talk of transitivity can also, of course, lead to discussion of the ways in which grammatical participants are constructed in discourses, and among other matters this can take students into examining how noun group structures are built. The Wild Child text has simple nouns, but the science text has quite dense ones. Teaching how the noun group is constructed can be helpful, using notions of *Headwor*d (Halliday & Matthiessen, 2004), and revealing how this can be expanded, first, in a premodifying sense:

a hereditary	*disease*
Premodifier	Headword

and, second, in a postmodifying sense:

a disease	*[[in which there is a defective gene [[that causes the owner of this gene to be unable to clot efficiently]]]].*
Headword	Postmodifier

Playing with noun group structures is a useful activity for the primary years, though it can also be introduced with secondary students. It should be used to help children see ways to compress information into their written texts. Equally, learning to interpret dense noun groups is an important task for reading, because a great deal of experiential information can be compressed in such groups.

It will be recalled that Amy, whose text on Nelson Mandela we examined in Chapter 3, could exploit the resource of noun groups very effectively, for she asked the rhetorical question:

What are heroes?

and went on:

*Heroes are **people [[who help others, [[who put themselves in danger // to save other people]]]].***

Displaying such items with the embedded and enclosed clauses noted helps to unpack the construction of the noun groups, telling a lot about how we constantly choose to compress meanings (though the choice is not conscious, unless we choose to make it so!). Teachers might, or might not, choose to take this step of identifying the embedded clauses, and in any case much depends on the purposes for teaching it and the background of the students. One other example I display here, again taken from an earlier chapter in this book:

*The digestive system is **a system [[that helps break down food // absorb the nutrients from food // as well as eliminate waste.]] The nutrients [[that are absorbed from your food]]** are used for growth and tissue maintenance, or burnt off as energy.*

Before I leave these examples, note how considerable can be a noun group as in Elle's text in Chapter 5:

***The information on the death and burial practices for other members of Spartan society** is relatively scarce.*

Not for nothing is English often said to be a language that likes to nominalize!

The structures of noun groups can be examined in other ways, as in the many examples where an embedded clause functions in place of a noun, often found in relational identifying processes as in

The most interesting thing [[I learned]]	*was*	*[[that the convicts weren't always kept in jails]].*
Value	Process: relational Identifying	Token

but also found in relational attributive processes that build description:

[[what Bas Luhrman has created]]	*is not*	*just a modern transformation of Romeo and Juliet.*
Carrier	Process: relational Attributive	Attribute

(Note: I have labeled the participants in full in the last two examples, following Halliday & Matthiessen, 2004. Teachers may well decide that they will simply use the term *participant* in all such cases.)[4]

Similar work can be done on the prepositional phrases creating circumstances, some of which contain embedded clauses:

They	*fight*	*for [[what is right]].*
Actor	Process: material	Circumstance: purpose

and

It (i.e. the symbol of the mockingbird)	*makes a strong point (i.e. emphasizes)*	*about [[what is innocence and sin]].*
Sayer	Process: verbal	Circumstance: matter

Similar work can be done on adverbial groups, which ideally appear by late childhood:

Ever since the colonization of Australia	*Aborigines*	*have been treated*	*extremely poorly.*
Circumstance: duration	Recipient	Process: material	Circumstance: manner

(Note: This rather awkward way of labeling the participant [as Recipient] is proposed by Halliday and Matthiessen [2004]. It is sometimes hard to find appropriate terms. In many cases it is sufficient for teacher to refer only to *participants*, leaving out the complexities of different labels.)

and

In other parts of Africa	*people*	*were fighting*	*against their oppressors*	*violently*
Circumstance: place	Actor	Process: material	Circumstance: cause	Circumstance: manner

Verbal group structures in which processes are expressed can also be explored, where this also takes students into the English tense system, which is often difficult for second language speakers, though I have found that L1 students can display confusion in using it in writing.

6.3.2 Logical Meanings and Conjunctive Relations

Logical meanings, together with the experiential meanings just reviewed, represent another aspect of the meanings termed *ideational*, and for that reason I introduce them here. The conjunction system, readily available in speech to native speakers, requires teaching to second language learners, though L1 children and adolescents often need assistance with it in their reading and their writing. Conjunctions build different kinds of logical relationships between clauses, hence contributing in important ways to the ideational meanings of texts. Like all the other matters discussed in this chapter, some of the strategies considered are more relevant than others, depending on the language abilities and knowledge of the students involved. Nonetheless, students can usefully be taught to recognize clauses and clause interdependencies, and this can be established by taking cause complexes from their own reading and writing and displaying these to illustrate that there is a dependency.

Where children in their first years of writing tend to use simple additive clause connections:

> *Robyn slept in the fold up bed **and** I slept in the stretcher*

and temporal connections:

> ***When it is twenty-one days*** *the little chick cracks open the egg with his egg tooth*

they tend as they grow older to produce clauses of reason:

> *I woke up excited, **for today we were going to The Rocks and Hyde Park Barracks.***

By late childhood, they can produce a varied range, always depending on the field and the genre, of course, including clauses of condition:

> *If you put something thin on the floorboards* *the pests would slide it through the cracks on the floor*

purpose:

> *we soon left the barracks **to drive back to school***

concession:

> *Nelson believed that **although the white population oppressed them** both races should live equally and in harmony*

and many others.

Talk of clause interdependencies can bring to consciousness aspects of sentence patternings, always useful for children in the late primary and secondary years:

> *Hemophilia occurs* (initiating clause)
> *when there is a defect in one or more of the blood coagulation protein factors* (dependent clause of time)
> *which results in low levels of fibrin* (dependent nondefining clause)
> *which in turn prevents the body from creating strong blood clots* (dependent nondefining clause)

One important value in developing some facility in understanding clauses and clause interdependencies is that this knowledge can be used to assist children to link their clauses into more coherent sequences of written text. For example, some junior secondary students of English in Indonesia wrote descriptive reports about the city of Bandung (from Emilia & Christie, 2011). One student, about 12 years old, wrote:

> *Bandung is the capital city of West Java. Bandung is known as Paris van Java. Beside that, Bandung is the fourth largest city in Indonesia. And, Bandung has many cultures.*

Such an opening shows considerable promise: Its grasp of a relevant vocabulary is good, and the writer had understood that in writing a report on his own city he should introduce it by offering general statements about the city, which he should elaborate later in the text. Yet in other ways the opening is clumsy, and after some discussion in a workshop with teachers, the following version was produced, for modeling with such a young writer:

Bandung, which is the capital city of West Java, is known as Paris van Java. It is the fourth largest city in Indonesia and it is famous for its fine buildings, its Sundanese cultural arts and crafts, its music and its rich traditions.

An important challenge that lies beyond mastery of clauses and clause interdependencies is learning to handle the resources of grammatical metaphor, which as we have seen in earlier chapters, often cause otherwise interdependent clauses to collapse, buried within noun group structures. I say more of that below when discussing speech and writing. First I turn to interpersonal/attitudinal meanings.

6.3.3 Interpersonal/Attitudinal Meanings

The resources of the interpersonal metafunction are learned early in speech, for they are a necessary part of learning to engage in interaction with others. As we saw in Chapter 2, young children need to learn the oral language of schooling, where this is a considerable challenge for many who must learn the encoded ways of exploring and elaborating upon meanings that school discourse ideally requires and rewards. Intensive small group talk around useful activities in which children are scaffolded in their learning are most appropriate in this regard. Genre pedagogy as outlined above provides a model for developing talk in this sense. Capacity to express attitude, ideas, values, and opinion should indeed be fostered through talk, reading, and writing. Literacy, of course, brings its particular challenges in mastery of the interpersonal and attitudinal values. Looking at the developmental evidence that has emerged over earlier chapters, it seems that in early childhood the most commonly expressed attitude in writing involves simple affect:

We all had fun.

whereas appreciation emerges a little later:

I clobbered my poor innocent brother.

The various subject-specific literacies that emerge with some distinctiveness by adolescence require skill in handling discourse that often enmeshes attitudinal and experiential values:

In retrospect, the censorship laws were definitely useful in many ways. Harper Lee's use of a mockingbird as her central symbol of innocence in the story is very effective.

and students must also learn to discuss values and meanings that are "shown" in varying ways:

> *This quote* [from the novel *The Catcher in the Rye*] *shows that Holden is not taking this advice seriously.*

By midadolescence able students can often overstretch in terms of their attitudinal expression, so keen is their interest in exploiting their language to achieve effects, though this tendency is more often marked in the humanities than in the sciences. The tendency is apparent particularly in efforts to express evaluation. For example, a student in midadolescence writes about a character in a novel she has read, where the metaphor used to describe the character is rather excessive:

> *Lara is an unbelievably strong person. I would describe her as an army tank in emotional traumas.* (from Christie, 2010, p. 156)

Another student, writing a story set in Paris, strains to establish a sense of atmosphere, where the experiential and interpersonal/attitudinal language are also rather excessive, the resources of intensity sometimes overused, and the series of clauses a little confused:

> *A warm summer air, so easily associated by many with the chirruping of swallows, lazy swaying of leafy tress and merry frolicking of children had only in the last few minutes begun to dissipate into the sharp icy chill of European evenings—regardless of what time of year it happened to be. In the short of things, the still frantic Avenue de Champs-Elysées bustling with fashionably dressed shoppers and astute looking business men and women was actually very far from singing birds, laughing children—although the street was admittedly lined with straight rows of green foliage.* (from Christie & Derewianka, 2008, p. 50)

Such expressions in the writing of adolescents are, of course, defensible, for they are evidence that the young writers involved are exploring how to write about different fields of experience, engaging in what I call "flexing their linguistic muscles" as they test their abilities. We can even say that the writers are striving to achieve verbal art, though they are not completely successful. Among the many challenges of language and literacy learning of great importance for adolescence generally is the challenge of achieving adequate control of attitude. Attitudinal expression is essential to building all the associated capacities in interpretation and argument, abstraction and evaluation that,

I have argued throughout this book, are fundamental to the many valued areas of knowledge in English-speaking cultures. They are important even in their absence in the sciences, where, as we have seen, attitudinal expression is flattened, so that learners need to understand why it is removed in scientific genres, though modality often has some relevance.

By late adolescence, among successful students, evaluative expression is generally better controlled, so that experiential and interpersonal/attitudinal resources produce texts that are attitudinally measured, if often quite forceful, their meanings dependent partly on well selected lexis, partly on judicious uses of conjunction, intensity, and modality, as their writers take a stance (Hood, 2010) in what has become academic writing. For example:

> It can be argued that religious authority equated to political power in Sparta. An example of such power is provided in an account of an incident in which King Cleomenes refused to go into battle (which was a criminal offence), but got off trial by saying that the omens were bad so he could not fight. If a Spartan King had a reasonable religious excuse he could be forgiven for losing battles and refusing battles. Thus, it can be argued that for kings at least, religion also had a higher status than the legal system.

> Such religious connection was important in gaining loyalty and obedience in the political arena, for the divine status of the Kings was a sign of military elitism. Spartan society according to Xenophon depended on the king and was loyal to the King, even believing that if an untitled person occupied the royal seat military disaster and famine would ensue.

and

> Shakespeare's Romeo and Juliet is "The greatest love story the world has ever known." It is iconic. It embraces the meaning of true love. It combines poetry and romance to create some of the most romantic phrases known to man. Shakespeare leaves the audience shocked and heartbroken. It is one of the greatest classics of English Literature. Yet now a new film has been released, betraying the true play and tainting the minds of all who watch it.

The success of such passages of discourse, it will be clear, depends on the total patterns of linguistic resources in which they are expressed. Such patterns are learned, though not always fully consciously, among L1 students in particular. Yet the facts that the patterns are learned and that, using a functional grammar, we are able to identify their elements, name them, and talk about them give grounds for arguing that intervention in bringing them to consciousness facilitates developmental growth among L1 students. The case for assistance for L2 students is obvious, for they need to make considerable conscious efforts to master English for the purposes of schooling, an issue of concern at all levels of schooling including the last years. By late adolescence, as students learn the various subjects found in school, they are actually engaged in working with academic discourses, whose nature remains demanding, even for those students who choose to go on to further studies beyond school.

All this brings me to say a little about modality in English. I have noted in earlier chapters that modality achieves limited expression in the school language of children in the primary years. By late childhood to adolescence it appears, typically first expressed in modal verbs and rather later in modal adverbs and adjectives. The fact that it is a development of the adolescent years is consistent with the fact that attitudinal expression generally is much more a feature of mid- to late adolescence than of childhood, at least in writing: It is in the adolescent years that capacity to express judgment, interpretation, evaluation, and opinion becomes more important. Developing maturity in life, as in schooling, we can argue, depends on a steadily enhanced capacity to address issues, weigh up evidence, judge the values of courses of action, and interpret phenomena and actions, depending on the field of endeavor involved. Modality is but one of the resources used in developing capacity in these senses, and because it is often said to be a troubling resource for learners, especially second language learners, it merits some attention for its relevance in the latter years of schooling, when, as I have noted, young people are required to handle many examples of academic discourse.

Ventola (1997) reports a study on the problems of Finnish academic writers coming to terms with writing English academic discourse. Her observations are pertinent to the context of teaching school English, though her research work was with adults. That is because contemporary schools in English-speaking societies have many second-language users coming to terms with expression of opinion, attitude, and judgment in the various traditions of the different school subjects. In fact, Ventola's observations about sources of difficulty for adult Finns writing academic English and her recommendations about areas where they need what she calls textual training are worth reporting here because they accord with sources of difficulty identified at different points in this book. Adult Finns, she argues, need training in such areas as "awareness of cultural differences in writing, global and local structuring of texts, theme-rheme pro-gression patterns, reference as a system for indicating text participants and text reference, connectors (i.e., conjunctions) and metatext (i.e., overall textual structure), unpacking heavy nominalization and modality" (Ventola, 1997, p.

167). The area of modality causing most difficulty for Finns, according to Ventola, is that aspect having to do with probability, because the Finnish language handles questions of probability rather differently from the English language. Ventola concludes:

> In academic writing it is extremely important that one is able to "strike just the right tone"—writers who are too assertive when interpreting their own research results can be seen as arrogant. But not being assertive enough does not help the marketing of the research. Young novice writers in particular . . . must be taught how to move smoothly and in a contextually appropriate way from subjective to objective meaning making in both spoken and written texts. (p. 176)

Similar observations might well be offered for secondary students of English who are very much involved in achieving an apprenticeship in academic English. They are not always asked to report their own research, perhaps, but they are asked to write discourse, typically drawn from other sources they have needed to access before writing various persuasive and interpretive texts. Striking the right tone in such contexts is critically important, as, for example, does Elle in writing her history text. At several points in the first elements she makes extensive use of language that is metaphorically modal in that it assesses the probability or reliability, or both, of the evidence she uses:

> *According to Herodotus, Spartans worshipped their kings as Gods. This **is associated with suggestions that the practice of "dual kingship" arose from the sons of Zeus, the Dioscuri.** We already know of their strict obedience and dedication to the gods, so **it can be assumed** that the Spartans would see the kings as means of divine communication. **It is believed** that the kings passed messages down from the oracles to the rest of society, in a sense elevating the king's position to one close to that of the gods.*

All such expressions tend to qualify Elle's observations so that she is seen to be behaving responsibly in establishing evidence. Finally, after producing quite a long text, she concludes in a manner that asserts a position without qualification, because she has reviewed the evidence in the previous elements of the text:

> *In summary, religion occupied an important place in Spartan life. In particular the Spartan kings were seen as "quasi-gods," that is almost as significant as the gods, and with divine powers. The kings performed many*

of the duties of high priests and drew on religious beliefs and practices to support their military campaigns, often allowing religious beliefs to drive military decisions. Their deaths were observed with much ritual, in contrast to those of ordinary people.

Learning to strike the right tone is a problem for many students, though the functional grammar can be used to guide teaching them, as Marshall (2006) demonstrates in quite another context. She outlines the case in Australia of a 17-year-old girl of a non-English-speaking background who entered a college for senior students aiming to attend university. In her English literary studies, the student needed, among other matters, to develop a capacity to write genres responding to literary texts; her first efforts at discussing a sensitive poem about grief were totally misplaced. She wrote in a conversational tone, using much of the grammar of idiomatic speech, and so inept was the piece she wrote that she was failed, to her great consternation. Marshall reveals how, over one year, she used the functional grammar to guide the girl, developing a better sense of the culturally valued response to grief that was required and shaping her language to create an appropriate passage of written discourse.

Because she had only one year in which to assist the student and little time to develop a very detailed metalanguage with the girl, Marshall simplified the terms with respect to the SF grammar and register and genre theory, though she used them to inform her teaching. For example, she used register theory to talk about an appropriate relationship with the audience for writing, entering with some sensitivity into the feelings expressed in the poem. She also used nominalization in particular to demonstrate how expressions the girl wanted to write could be reexpressed, creating larger structures more characteristic of written language, and this helped build an understanding of the developing density in the texts the girl wrote. Considerations of textual organization, reference, and coherence allowed Marshall to go on to teach about theme and thematic development as well as the overall schematic structure of the target genre. On the evidence Marshall provides the girl made good progress over the year, achieving an appropriate understanding of how to write a response genre for the purposes of her English matriculation examination. Importantly, as Marshall also shows, the girl herself achieved a much enhanced understanding of the English language in a manner that would serve her well in her life generally.

6.3.4 Textual Meanings and Periodicity
Textual meanings involve the organization of discourse, and as we have seen in earlier chapters, this metafunction is realized in particular in theme and

thematic progression as series of clauses unfold. Theme is "what comes first in the clause," and this can be made a talking point for classroom work. For example, why write:

When we arrived at The Rocks we were split into two groups and walked off with the tour guide

when we could have written the following?

We were split into two groups and walked off with the tour guide when we arrived at the Rocks.

Such questions can lead to discussion of the choices involved here, how the meaning is changed depending on where the dependent clause is placed, and why such a time clause is often placed first in narratives and other story genres. This kind of activity can commence in the primary school, though I have also used it in junior secondary classrooms. Playing with theme can lead to creation of tables providing sets of paradigms, offering alternative meanings, as in these few examples (Christie & Soosai, 2001, pp. 104–105), developed in class work, using prepositional phrases that create circumstances:

Subject as topical theme	Prepositional phrase/Circumstance as topical theme
Many people have learned English over the years.	*Over the years many people have learned English.*
Australia became a federal nation in the year 1901.	*In the year 1901 Australia became a federal nation.*
They drove carefully in case of accident.	*In case of accident they drove carefully.*
They played the football match despite the heavy rain.	*Despite the heavy rain they played the football match.*
They ate their meal in complete meal.	*In complete silence they ate their meal.*

Similar activities can be used for circumstances expressed using adverbial groups:

Subject as topical theme in the first clause	Adverbial group/circumstance as topical theme in the first clause
The soldiers were fighting bravely // as they defended the city.	*Bravely the soldiers were fighting as they defended the city.*

The cricket team practices very regularly // so they can win their matches.	*Very regularly the cricket team practices // so they can win their matches.*
The teacher sets homework very rarely // and everyone is surprised.	*Very rarely does the teacher set homework // and everyone is surprised.*

Discussion of such contrasting examples enables a great deal of talk about language, including developing a metalanguage for reflecting on it and the choices it offers. Talk about how to organize paragraphs in writing led to the diagram shown in Figure 6.2, showing a sequence of topical theme choices, expressed either in nouns or in pronouns (from Christie & Soosai, 2001, p. 100).

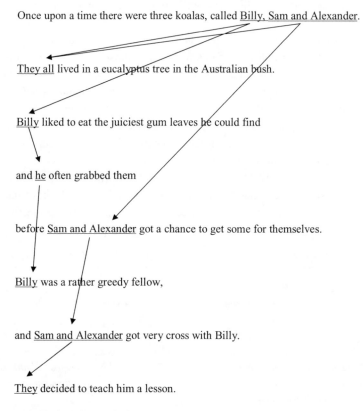

Once upon a time there were three koalas, called Billy, Sam and Alexander.

They all lived in a eucalyptus tree in the Australian bush.

Billy liked to eat the juiciest gum leaves he could find

and he often grabbed them

before Sam and Alexander got a chance to get some for themselves.

Billy was a rather greedy fellow,

and Sam and Alexander got very cross with Billy.

They decided to teach him a lesson.

Figure 6.2 Topical theme choices, expressed either in nouns or in pronouns.

This was constructed as part of building an understanding of how patterns of thematic progression work, where visual display facilitates understandings. In fact, in this context, I note the wonderful facility now available to teachers and students in using PowerPoint presentations, CD-ROMs, interactive whiteboards, and the like for teaching a great deal about how language works, not only its thematic patterns. Important research and development work lies ahead for teachers willing to work on these possibilities.

In the classrooms where I worked, the paragraph in Figure 6.2 was modeled on an overhead projector. It was discussed and the students (in the first and second years of secondary school) were asked, working in pairs, to complete the narrative, written as for young primary school readers. This was part of a series of lessons that examined themes in different genres. Thematic patterns should be practiced and extensively discussed in the second phase of language development I have identified, for they are often elusive, apparently difficult to master. For many students they need continuing attention throughout the secondary years.

One further matter about theme I shall mention, because of my experience teaching teachers of English as a foreign language, most of them from Southeast Asia. They told me that notions of active and passive voice had proved difficult to teach. I suggest that voice is made easier if we think about its values for making different entities thematic. Active voice allows us to place some entity—person, object, or place—in theme position. However, if we choose to use the passive voice we create a rather different meaning because something else is made thematic. The important point in examining voice in this sense is to consider its impact on what is made the focus of information. The reason we have the passive voice is that it enables us to shift the focus of the information, changing what becomes the theme—the point of departure for the message of the clause. This is a matter worthy of class discussion and reflection.

Passive voice	Active voice
Nelson Mandela was sent to prison.	*A South African judge sent Nelson Mandela to prison.*
When Australia or any of the allied countries achieved a victory, it was widely publicized and they were celebrated. . . . if the allies suffered a loss, it was only briefly mentioned.	*When Australia or its allies achieved a victory, the government published news of it widely, but if they lost a battle the government only briefly mentioned it.*

Passive voice	Active voice
Ever since the colonization of Australia Aborigines have been treated extremely poorly.	*Ever since the colonization of Australia, white people have treated Aborigines extremely poorly.*
Care was taken. [From a scientific text]	*I took care.*

In contrasting such pairs as those displayed, it is necessary to encourage children to think less about these matters in terms of "rules" (which has often been the tendency in much traditional teaching) and rather more in terms of choice: how do we alter meaning by choosing to change the voice? What does this tell us about the freedoms we enjoy in making meanings in discourse? When is it a good thing to use the passive voice (e.g., in some science writing, though there are many other contexts)? How do people sometimes hide their identities behind the passive voice? Is that a good thing or a bad thing? What does all this tell us about agency in language?

A grasp of theme and of thematic progression is a useful step toward thinking about the overall textual organization of any passage of discourse. Ideally, information flows through a text so that the listener in speech or the reader in writing is alerted to the manner in which information is introduced, foregrounded, developed, and then often revisited in a manner that gives a sense of a periodic progression of ideas. In Chapter 3 we looked at Amy's talk (Text 3.2) about Nelson Mandela, and in Chapter 4 we looked at a history text (Text 4.1) explaining the introduction of censorship in Australia in World War II. Both texts revealed a sense of the overall flow of ideas, and in the case of Text 4.1, I demonstrated the flow of ideas by introducing notions of macroTheme, hyperTheme, and periodicity. Introducing students to such traditional terms as the "topic sentence" is a useful way to proceed with opening up talk of overall periodic development in a passage of discourse, though once terms such as *theme* and *thematic development* have been introduced, it is a relatively easy step to introduce *macroTheme* and *hyperTheme*.

Figure 6.3 sets out the overall structure of an expository genre written by a boy in Indonesia aged about 14 years (from Emilia, 2011). Uniforms have apparently been a sensitive issue in Indonesian schools in recent times, and after extensive class work on how to write expositions, the boy in question produced a text in which he discussed his views of uniforms. It will be clear that he has followed a pattern given him by his teacher, such that having once stated his opinion or thesis in his opening macroTheme, he has developed the text by very visibly signaling each new hyperTheme that looks back to the

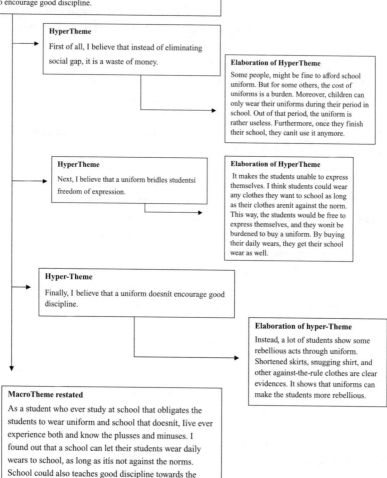

Macro-Theme

Nowadays, almost every school in Indonesia obligate their students to wear uniform. It is said that uniform gives the students a sense of identity and teaches good discipline to them. It is also said that by wearing uniform, it will eliminate social gap among students. **For these reasons,** schools made rules about uniform. However, I believe that those reasons are not an excuse for making such a rule. Iím assured that uniform is unnecessary, because it is a waste of money. Bridles studentsi freedom to express themselves and fails to encourage good discipline.

HyperTheme

First of all, I believe that instead of eliminating social gap, it is a waste of money.

Elaboration of HyperTheme

Some people, might be fine to afford school uniform. But for some others, the cost of uniforms is a burden. Moreover, children can only wear their uniforms during their period in school. Out of that period, the uniform is rather useless. Furthermore, once they finish their school, they canít use it anymore.

HyperTheme

Next, I believe that a uniform bridles studentsí freedom of expression.

Elaboration of HyperTheme

It makes the students unable to express themselves. I think students could wear any clothes they want to school as long as their clothes arenít against the norm. This way, the students would be free to express themselves, and they wonít be burdened to buy a uniform. By buying their daily wears, they get their school wear as well.

Hyper-Theme

Finally, I believe that a uniform doesnít encourage good discipline.

Elaboration of hyper-Theme

Instead, a lot of students show some rebellious acts through uniform. Shortened skirts, snugging shirt, and other against-the-rule clothes are clear evidences. It shows that uniforms can make the students more rebellious.

MacroTheme restated

As a student who ever study at school that obligates the students to wear uniform and school that doesnít, Iíve ever experience both and know the plusses and minuses. I found out that a school can let their students wear daily wears to school, as long as itís not against the norms. School could also teaches good discipline towards the students without uniform. It doesnít matter whether there is uniform or not, good discipline could still be taught and students can still have a sense of identity.

Figure 6.3 MacroTheme and hyperThemes in uniforms text.

macroTheme and then looks forward to elaboration, before he finally restates the macroTheme in the conclusion. This manner of representing the flow of information reveals the schematic structure of the genre involved, providing a way to uncover how patterns in the discourse direct the flow of information and of argument. Making very visible the bare bones of the structure of patterns of discourse in this way is thus very valuable for all students. In my view the Indonesian student did very well organizing his text.

I have now reviewed aspects of the teaching of functional grammar by reference to each of the metafunctions: experiential, logical, interpersonal/attitudinal, and textual. It remains at this point to say a little more about the differences between speech and writing, which I also addressed in Chapter 2.

6.3.5 Speech and Writing

The functional grammar provides teachers with a very useful tool for thinking about the differences between speech and writing. As we have seen, the primary mode is speech, and in early childhood, children rely on the grammar of speech as they commence their school learning. It takes native speakers all the years of a primary education, at least, to master the essential tools of literacy—the writing, spelling, and punctuation systems, as well as some aspects of the grammar of writing. Such aspects include achieving some control of

o thematic progression across texts to create text unity, where this also involves control of reference;
o conjunctive relationships, allowing the capacity to produce and sequence series of interconnected clauses types, depending on field and genre;
o noun group structure, allowing the capacity to expand and elaborate on information;
o prepositional phrase structures, also allowing the elaboration of information;
o some attitudinal expression, typically in simple lexis, while modal verbs may also appear; and
o enhanced lexical density.

For the most part, these are all achieved using a congruent grammar, though, as we saw in earlier chapters, by late childhood many children start to achieve some control of nominalization, which is a form of grammatical metaphor. This ultimately takes children into new ways of expressing information that secondary schooling rewards. In fact, the secondary years require and use the noncongruent grammar of written language with all its compression, abstraction, interpretation, explanation, and argument. These are all features of the discourses of the uncommonsense areas of knowledge that the various school subjects represent. It is these features in particular that cause difficulties for young learners in late childhood and early adolescence, both native and nonnative speakers of the language.

Grammatical metaphor, it will be recalled from Chapter 3, often leads to sentences like the following, found in a biology textbook:

Organs [[specialized for sequential stages of food processing]] form the mammalian digestive system.

A good teacher will always find ways to take a passage such as this and reexpress it in the language of speech, creating five clauses and signaling connectedness between items of information through use of the conjunctive system:

"Mammals digest their food
and they do this in a series of stages in a sequence
by using a number of different organs
and each organ has a special role
in order to process the food."

Such deconstruction of written language into speech should be a constant feature of classrooms across all ages in schooling, facilitating frequent shifts between the two modes and, also, when appropriate, allowing discussion of the strengths and values of both modes. Above I discussed noun group structures as they operate to form grammatical participants in discourse. Discussion of noun group structures can lead to talk of nominalization, allowing students to reflect on why it occurs and why it is useful. In addition, teaching activity can involve children and adolescents in jointly creating noun group structures, sometimes using nominalization to do so. Although such activity is relevant for teaching and learning in all school subjects, the English classroom provides an additional context in which to involve children in oral and written storytelling, as we saw in Chapter 2. Oral storytelling is a useful skill in any case, and time spent developing it in class is in itself valuable, and the written versions created by students can become a source for examining such matters as

o What information about the context is given in the written version that is not found in the spoken version (or at least not in the same detail)? What language is used to create this contextual information?

- o What information about feelings and attitudes is found in the written version and how does this compare with what was in the spoken version? What language items are used to express attitude? How is attitude expressed in spoken language?
- o What have you learned about the differences between speech and writing? Here, where a metalanguage for discussion has been already established, students could discuss the different nominal groups, or the changes in verbal groups and the processes they realize, or the prepositional phrases creating circumstances, or the conjunctions used, or they could discuss the thematic progression, looking at what is made thematic as the story unfolds.

All such activities can lead in several directions, depending on what the teaching goals might be. For example, such an activity could lead to class discussion about the origins of writing systems and where and how they appeared in the world. This enables students of non-English backgrounds to contribute talk about their writing systems. Alternatively the activity could turn away from storytelling to considering other kinds of written language of a factual kind. Why, for example, is a lot of factual language often difficult to read out loud, when compared with the written language of a narrative? What might this tell us about the nature of language and its uses?

Much of what I have suggested of possible strategies for using the functional grammar and genre theory has come from my own research and many others in the SFL community. Such suggestions as I have made for using the functional grammar do not exhaust the possibilities. Excellent recent resources on the functional grammar and schooling include *A New Functional Grammar* (Derewianka, 2011) and *Working Grammar: An Introduction for Secondary English Teachers* (Humphrey, Love, & Droga, 2011). Apart from these, *Exploring English Grammar: From Formal to Functional* (Coffin, Donohue, & North, 2009) is an excellent volume that makes a case for a functional grammar in contrast with the more formal traditions known by many people.

Other recent sources of related activities for teaching genres and the language found within them, especially for primary and junior second language users, are found in the work of John Polias and Brian Dare, at their Lexis Education website.[5] Apart from work in Australia (Polias, 2009a, 2009b, 2009c; Custance, Dare, & Polias, 2011), Polias has worked extensively with members of the Hong Kong Department of Education, developing programs for teaching English in English medium schools in Hong Kong, in which he has introduced the functional grammar and genre pedagogy (Hong Kong Department of Education, 2011).

6.4 The Overall Trajectory in Language Development for Schooling

The trajectory for language development I have described in this book is drawn primarily from observation of children and adolescents in Australian schools. Moreover, most of the texts I have used were from native speakers of English, though they were not necessarily privileged students, some of them from disadvantaged backgrounds. The observations were all made in classrooms involving students for whom English was a second language, who, though their background experiences no doubt differed from those of the native speakers, nonetheless needed to master the discourse patterns that were required for learning the forms of knowledge valued in an English-speaking culture. The developmental trajectory moves from an initial proficiency in speech, established before school, in which the patterns of language use a congruent grammar. This capacity in speech is challenged by the entry to school, with its consequent demands both in starting to learn literacy and in learning patterns of classroom talk: Although the grammar used is still congruent, the need to master literacy and some emergent uncommonsense knowledge of schooling puts pressure on children's language learning. Mastery of theme and reference is important for learning to read coherent texts while also learning to write simple genres.

By late childhood to adolescence, when children move from the primary to the second school years, their language and literacy are again challenged by the need to come to grips with a changing curriculum in which subjects are more clearly differentiated and in which the grammatical organization of the language becomes more noncongruent, most notably in the emergence of nominalization. The available range of clauses and clause interdependencies is enlarged, though the distribution of clauses, as with all other areas of language, depends on the register and genre values involved. Thematic progression becomes increasingly important as young people learn to handle longer passages of written discourse, and the overall organization of different genres is important for learning the various subject-specific literacies. Attitudinal expression becomes more nuanced, partly in expanded vocabulary and partly in growing use of some modality. By midadolescence, young people have a good control of dense written language both for reading and for writing. Attitudinal expression, although very important for realizing interpretation, judgment, and opinion, develops in this stage, though it is not necessarily well controlled, as young people overreach to achieve effect. The final years of late adolescence to adulthood see a generally stronger control of lexicogrammatical resources, including evaluative resources.

The functional grammar provides powerful linguistic evidence for the developmental trajectory that has been described, though as I have stressed throughout the book, it does not follow that all children and adolescents travel at the same rate and in the same way. Life experience varies enormously, and, for reasons discussed earlier in the book, children and adolescents are very differentially prepared for the challenges of schooling. However, the functional grammatical analyses discussed in this book allow us to uncover the capacities in language children need to succeed in school and to intervene in their learning, teaching them explicit knowledge about language to enable them to progress.

I am sometimes asked whether I think it is possible or desirable to bring to consciousness *all* that we do in language as we speak, listen, read, or write. The question seems an odd one to me, because I actually doubt that anyone is ever totally conscious of the choices one makes in language. However, like other SFL theorists, when talking of education, I argue the importance of a pedagogy that is explicit about its goals and explicit about language usage. The latter has never meant teaching and learning all that might, or could, be known about language at any time. A good pedagogy is always selective about the knowledge of language taught, though once having taught it, teachers and students need to retain the knowledge, the better to build incrementally across the years of schooling. Above all, teachers and teacher educators need a good knowledge of the functional grammar so that they can make considered decisions about what knowledge to teach, and when to teach it, in the education of the young.

Notes

1 There was no Deconstruction stage in this teaching episode, because the children were very young, just taking their first steps in mastering literate behavior.
2 This statement about language development was one adopted from Halliday for the national Language Development Project in Australia, which I coordinated from 1987 to 1992.
3 This was one of a series of books for genre teaching that emerged after research work in the 1980s investigating genres in schools in various parts of Australia. The series is listed in the references.

4 For those who are interested in going further with the analysis of participants, I note the following: In an identifying process, the two participants involve two entities, one of which represents the other, so that one is the *Token* of the other, termed the *Value*; for example, *Sydney* [Token] *is the capital of Australia* [Value]. The former represents the latter. In the case of attributive processes, one participant termed the *Carrier* is said to "carry" or "hold" some characteristic or *Attribute*. Hence *Sydney* (Carrier) *is a beautiful city* (Attribute). Halliday and Matthiesen (2004, pp. 210–248) offer a long discussion.

5 http://www.lexised.com/writing.htm

References

Adams, M. J. (1994). *Beginning to read: Thinking and learning about print.* Cambridge, MA: MIT Press.

Adoniou, M., & Macken-Horarik, M. (2007). Scaffolding literacy across ESL: Some insights from ACT classrooms. *TESOL in Context, 17*(1), 5–14.

Aidman, M. (1999). *Biliteracy development through early and mid-primary years: A longitudinal case study of bilingual writing.* Unpublished doctoral dissertation, University of Melbourne.

Bakhtin, M. M. (1981). *The dialogic imagination* (C. Emerson & M. Holquist, Trans.). Austin: University of Texas Press.

Bazerman, C. (1988). *Shaping written knowledge: The genre and activity of the experimental article in science.* Madison: University of Wisconsin Press.

Bernstein, B. (1971). *Class codes and control, Vol. 1: Theoretical studies towards a sociology of language.* Boston: Routledge and Kegan Paul.

Bernstein, B. (1975). *Class, codes and control, Vol. 3: Towards a theory of educational transmissions.* Boston: Routledge and Kegan Paul.

Bernstein, B. (1990). *Class codes and control, Vol. IV: The structuring of pedagogic discourse.* New York: Routledge.

Bernstein, B. (2000). *Pedagogy, symbolic control and identity: Theory, research, critique* (Rev. ed.). Lanham, MD: Rowman & Littlefield.

Brindley, S. (Ed.). (1994). *Teaching English.* New York: Routledge & the Open University.

Brookes, D. T., & Etkina, E. (2007). Using conceptual metaphor and functional grammar to explore how language used in physics affects students learning. *Physical Review Special Topics: Physics Education Research, 3*(1), 1–16.

Browne, A. (1986). *Piggybook.* New York: Dragonfly Books.

Bruner, J. (1960). *The process of education.* Cambridge, MA: Harvard University Press.

Butt, D. (2004). How our meanings change: School contexts and semantic evolution. In G. Williams & A. Lukin (Eds.), *The development of language: Functional perspectives on species and individuals* (pp. 217–240). New York: Continuum.

Campbell, N. A., Reece, J. B., Meyers, N., Urry, L. A., Cain, M. L., Wasserman, S. A., & Jackson, R. B. (2009). *Biology.* Sydney: Pearson Education Australia.

Carnegie Council on Advancing Adolescent Literacy. (2010a). *Advancing adolescent literacy: The cornerstone of school reform.* Retrieved from http://carnegie.org/publications/search-publications/pub/365/

Carnegie Council on Advancing Adolescent Literacy. (2010b). *Time to act: An agenda for advancing adolescent literacy for college and career success*. Retrieved from http://carnegie.org/publications/search-publications/pub/365/

Cazden, C. (1977). Concentrated versus contrived encounters: Suggestions for language assessment in early childhood. In A. Davies (Ed.), *Language and learning in early childhood* (pp. 40–54). London: Heinemann.

Cazden, C. (1983). Adult assistance to language development: Scaffolds, models and direct instruction. In R. Parker & F. Davis (Eds.), *Developing literacy* (pp. 3–18). Newark, DE: International Reading Association.

Cazden, C. B. (2001). *Classroom discourse: The language of teaching and learning* (2nd ed.). Portsmouth, NH: Heinemann Educational.

Chan, E., & Unsworth, L. (2011). Image-language interaction in online learning environments: Challenges to student. *Australian Educational Researcher*, *38*(2), 181–202.

Chen, R.T.-S., Maton, K., & Bennett, S. (2011). Absenting discipline: Constructivist approaches in online learning. In F. Christie & K. Maton (Eds.), *Disciplinarity: Functional linguistic and sociological perspectives* (pp. 129–150). New York: Continuum.

Chomsky, N. (1962). *Aspects of the theory of syntax*. Cambridge, UK: Cambridge University Press.

Chomsky, N. (1974). Discussing language. In H. Parret (Ed.), *Discussing language* (pp. 27–54). The Hague, the Netherlands: Mouton.

Chomsky, N. (1981). An interview with Noam Chomsky about linguistics. *Mark These Linguistics: The English Magazine*, *7*, 4–6.

Chomsky, N. (2002). *On nature and language*. A. Belletti & L. Rizzi (Eds.). New York: Cambridge University Press.

Chomsky, N. (2006). *Language and mind* (3rd ed.). Cambridge, UK: Cambridge University Press.

Christie, F. (1984). Varieties of written discourse. In *Deakin University Children Writing B.Ed. Study Guide. Course Study Guide, Section 1* (pp. 11–66). Geelong, Victoria, Australia: Deakin University Press.

Christie, F. (1985). Language and schooling. In S. Tchudi (Ed.), *Language, schooling, and society: Proceedings of the International Federation for the Teaching of English seminar, 1984* (pp. 110–120). Portsmouth, NH: Boynton Cook Publishers.

Christie, F. (Ed.). (1990). *Literacy in a changing world*. Melbourne: ACER.

Christie, F. (1991). *The construction of knowledge in the junior social science classroom: Towards the development of an educational linguistics*. Funded by the Australian Research Council. Melbourne: University of Melbourne.

Christie, F. (1993). The "received tradition" of English teaching: The decline of rhetoric and the corruption of grammar. In B. Green (Ed.), *The insistence of the letter: Literary studies and curriculum theorizing* (pp. 75–106). London: Falmer Press.

Christie, F. (1994). *On pedagogic discourse* [Report of a research activity funded by the Australian Research Council 1990–2]. Melbourne: University of Melbourne.

Christie, F. (1995a). Pedagogic discourse in the primary school. *Linguistics and Education, 3*(7), 221–242.

Christie, F. (1995b). *The teaching of English literature in secondary school English: A case study* [Report 1 of a research study into the pedagogic discourse of secondary school English, 1993–4]. Melbourne: University of Melbourne.

Christie, F. (1995c). *The teaching of story writing in the junior secondary school* [Report 2 of a research study into the pedagogic discourse of secondary school English, 1995–7]. Melbourne: University of Melbourne.

Christie, F. (1996). *The pedagogic discourse of secondary school social sciences: Geography* [Report of a research study funded by the Australian Research Council 1995–7]. Melbourne: University of Melbourne.

Christie, F. (1998). *Teaching knowledge about language in the junior secondary English writing program* [Report 1 of a study funded by the Australian Research Council 1998–2000]. Melbourne: University of Melbourne.

Christie, F. (1999a). *Teaching knowledge about language in the junior secondary English literacy program* [Report 2 of a study funded by the Australian Research Council 1998–2000]. Melbourne: University of Melbourne.

Christie, F. (Ed.). (1999b). *Pedagogy and the shaping of consciousness: Linguistic and social processes*. London: Continuum.

Christie, F. (2000). Pedagogic discourse in the post-compulsory years: Pedagogic subject positioning. *Linguistics and Education, 11*(4), 313–332.

Christie, F. (2001). Pedagogic discourse in the post-compulsory years: Pedagogic subject positioning. In J. Cumming & C. Wyatt-Smith (Eds.), *Literacy and the curriculum: Success in senior secondary schooling* (pp. 94–103). Melbourne: Australian Council for Educational Research.

Christie, F. (2002). *Classroom discourse analysis. A functional perspective*. New York: Continuum.

Christie, F. (2003a). Initial literacy: Extending the horizon. In J. Bourne & E. Reid (Eds.), *World yearbook of language education* (pp. 91–108). London: Kogan Page.

Christie, F. (2003b). Writing the world. In N. Hall, J. Larson & J. Marsh (Eds.), *Handbook of early childhood literacy research* (pp. 287–298). London, Thousand Oaks, & New Delhi: Sage/Paul Chapman.

Christie, F. (2004a). Authority and its role in the pedagogic relationship of schooling. In L. Young & C. Harrison (Eds.), *Systemic functional linguistics and critical discourse analysis: Studies in social change* (pp. 173–201). New York: Continuum.

Christie, F. (2004b). Revisiting some old themes: The role of grammar in the teaching of English. In J. A. Foley (Ed.), *Language education and discourse: Functional approaches* (pp. 145–173). New York: Continuum.

Christie, F. (2005). *Language education in the primary years*. Sydney: University of New South Wales Press.

Christie, F. (2006). Literacy teaching and current debates over reading. In
    R. Whittaker, M. O'Donnell, & A. McCabe (Eds.), *Language and literacy:
    Functional approaches* (pp. 45–65). New York: Continuum.

Christie, F. (2007a). Literacy and current debates over reading. In R. Whittaker, M.
    O'Donnell, & A. McCabe (Eds.), *Language and literacy: Functional approaches*
    (pp. 45–65). London and New York: Continuum.

Christie, F. (2007b). Ongoing dialogue: Functional linguistic and Bernsteinian
    sociological perspectives on education. In F. Christie & J. R. Martin (Eds.),
    *Language, knowledge and pedagogy: Functional linguistic and sociological
    perspectives* (pp. 3–13). London and Washington: Continuum Press.

Christie, F. (2008). Genres and institutions: Functional perspectives on educational
    discourse. In M. Martin-Jones, A. M. de Mejia, & N. Hornberger (Eds.),
    Encyclopedia of language education, Vol. 3: Discourse and education (2nd ed.,
    pp. 29–40). New York: Springer.

Christie, F. (2010). The ontogenesis of writing in childhood and adolescence. In
    D. Wyse, R. Andrews, & J. Hoffman (Eds.), *The Routledge international handbook
    of English, language and literacy teaching* (pp. 146–158). New York: Routledge.

Christie, F. (2011). Manuscript in preparation.

Christie, F., & Cléirigh, C. (2008). On the importance of showing. In C. Wu,
    C. Matthiessen, & M. Herke (Eds.), *Proceedings of the International Systemic
    Functional Congress 35: Voices around the world* (pp. 13–19). Sydney: Macquarie
    University.

Christie, F., & Derewianka, B. (2007). *Key indicators of development in adolescent
    writing* [Final report of a study funded by the Australian Research Council,
    2004–2006].

Christie, F., & Derewianka, B. (2008). *School discourse: Learning to write across the
    years of schooling*. New York: Continuum.

Christie, F., Freebody, P., Martin, J. R., Luke, A., & Walton, C. (1991). *Teaching
    English literacy: A project of national significance on the preservice preparation of
    teachers for teaching English literacy*. Darwin: Northern Territory University and
    Department of Education and Employment.

Christie, F., Gray, B., Gray, P., Macken, M., Martin, J. R., & Rothery, J. (1990a).
    Language: A resource for meaning: Procedures, Books 1–4, and *Teacher Manual*.
    Sydney: Harcourt Brace Jovanovich.

Christie, F., Gray, B., Gray, P., Macken, M., Martin, J. R., & Rothery, J. (1990b).
    Language: A resource for meaning: Reports, Books 1–4, and *Teacher Manual*.
    Sydney: Harcourt Brace Jovanovich.

Christie, F., Gray, B., Gray, P., Macken, M., Martin, J. R., & Rothery, J. (1992).
    Language: A resource for meaning: Explanations, Books 1–4, and *Teacher Manual*.
    Sydney: Harcourt Brace Jovanovich.

Christie, F., & Humphrey, S. (2008). Senior secondary English and its goals: Making sense of "The Journey." In L. Unsworth (Ed.), *New literacies and the English curriculum* (pp. 215–237). New York: Continuum.

Christie, F., & Macken-Horarik, M. (2007). Building verticality in subject English. In F. Christie & R. Martin (Eds.), *Language, knowledge and pedagogy: Functional linguistic and sociological perspectives* (pp. 156–183). London: Cassell Academic.

Christie, F., & Macken-Horarik, M. (2011). Disciplinarity and the case of school subject English. In F. Christie & K. Maton (Eds.), *Disciplinarity: Functional linguistic and sociological perspectives* (pp. 175–196). New York: Continuum.

Christie, F., & Martin, J. R. (Eds.). (2007). *Language, knowledge and pedagogy: Functional linguistic and sociological perspectives*. New York: Continuum.

Christie, F., & Maton, K. (Eds.). (2011). *Disciplinarity: Functional linguistic and sociological perspectives*. New York: Continuum.

Christie, F., & Misson, R. (Eds.). (1997). *Literacy and schooling*. London: Routledge.

Christie, F., & Simpson. A. (Eds.). (2010). *Literacy and social responsibility*. London: Equinox.

Christie, F., & Soosai, A. (2000–2001). *Language and meaning* (Vols. 1–2). Melbourne: Macmillan Education.

Christie, F., & Unsworth, L. (2005). Developing dimensions of an educational linguistics. In R. Hasan, C. Matthiessen, & J. J. Webster (Eds.), *Continuing discourse on language: A functional perspective* (Vol. 1; pp. 217–250). London: Equinox.

Cloran, C. (1994). *Rhetorical units and decontextualization: An inquiry into some relations of context, meaning and grammar*. Monographs in Systemic Linguistics, Nottingham University.

Cloran, C. (1999). Contexts for learning. In F. Christie (Ed.), *Pedagogy and the shaping of consciousness* (pp. 31–65). London: Continuum.

Coffin, C. (1997). Constructing and giving value to the past: An investigation into secondary school history. In F. Christie & J. R. Martin (Eds.), *Language, knowledge and pedagogy: Functional linguistic and sociological perspectives* (pp. 196–230). New York: Continuum.

Coffin, C. (2004). Learning to write history: The role of causality. *Written Communication, 21*(3), 261–289.

Coffin, C. (2006). *Historical discourse*. London: Continuum.

Coffin, C., Donohue, J., & North, S. (2009). *Exploring English grammar: From formal to functional*. New York: Routledge.

Cumming, J., & Wyatt-Smith, C. (Eds.). (2001). *Literacy and the curriculum: Success in senior secondary schooling*. Melbourne: Australian Council for Educational Research.

Custance, B., Dare, B., & Polias, J. (2011). *How language works: Success in literacy and learning*. Adelaide: Government of South Australia, Department of Education and Children's Services.

Daly, A., & Unsworth, L. (2011). Analysis of multimodal texts. *Australian Journal of Language and Literacy, 34*(1), 61–80.

Delpit, L. (2006). *Other people's children. Cultural conflict in the classroom.* New York: The New Press. (Original work published 1995).

Derewianka, B. (2003). Grammatical metaphor in the transition to adolescence. In A. M. Simon-Vandenberg, M. Taverniers, & L. Ravelli (Eds.), *Grammatical metaphor* (pp. 185–220). Philadelphia: John Benjamins.

Derewianka, B. (2011). *A new grammar companion for teachers.* Sydney: Primary English Teachers' Association.

Doecke, B., Howie, M., & Sawyer, W. (Eds.). (2006). *Only connect: English teaching, schooling and community.* Kent Town, South Australia: Wakefield Press and the Australian Association for the Teaching of English.

Droga, L., & Humphrey, S. (2002). *Getting started with functional grammar.* Berry, New South Wales: Target Texts.

Eggins, S., & Slade, D. (2005). *Analyzing casual conversation.* London: Equinox.

Emilia, E. (2010). *Teaching writing: Developing critical learners.* Bandung, Indonesia: Rizqi Press.

Fang, Z., & Schleppegrell, M. J. (2008). *Reading in secondary content areas: A language-based pedagogy.* Ann Arbor: The University of Michigan Press.

Feez, S. (2010). *Montessori and early childhood.* Thousand Oaks, CA: Sage Publications.

Feez, S. (2011). Discipline and freedom in early childhood education. In F. Christie & K. Maton (Eds.), *Disciplinarity: Functional linguistic and sociological perspectives* (pp. 151–171). New York: Continuum.

Feez, S., & Joyce, H. (1998). *Text based syllabus design.* Sydney: National Centre for English Language Teaching & Research.

Freedman, A., & Medway, P. (1994a). *Genre and the new rhetoric.* London: Taylor & Francis.

Freedman, A., & Medway, P. (Eds.). (1994b). *Learning and teaching genre.* Portsmouth, NH: Boynton/Cook.

French, R. (2010). Primary school children learning grammar: Rethinking the possibilities. In T. Locke (Ed.), *Beyond the grammar wars: A resource for teachers and students on developing language knowledge in the English/literacy classroom* (pp. 206–230). New York: Routledge.

French, R. (in press). Learning the grammatics of quoted speech: Benefits for punctuation and expressive reading. *Australian Journal of Language and Literacy.*

Gibbons, P. (2004). Changing the rules, changing the game: A sociocultural perspective on second language learning in the classroom. In G. Williams & A. Lukin (Eds.), *The development of language: Functional perspectives on species and individuals* (pp. 196–216). New York: Continuum.

Goodson, I., & Medway, P. (Eds.). (1990). *Bringing English to order.* Bristol, PA: Falmer Press.

Gray, B. (1985). Helping children to become language learners in the classroom. In M. Christie (Ed.), *Aboriginal perspectives on experience and learning: The role of language in Aboriginal education* (pp. 188–209). Geelong, Victoria: Deakin University Press.

Gray, B. (1999). Accessing the discourses of schooling: English language and literacy development with Aboriginal children in mainstream schools. Unpublished doctoral dissertation, University of Melbourne.

Green, J., & Dixon, C. (Eds.). (1994). Santa Barbara Classroom Discourse Group [Special issue]. *Linguistics and Education, 5.*

Halliday, M. A. K. (1975). *Learning how to mean: Explorations in the development of language.* Baltimore, MD: Arnold.

Halliday, M. A. K. (1985). *Spoken and written language.* Geelong, Victoria: Deakin University Press.

Halliday, M. A. K. (1993). Towards a language-based theory of learning. *Linguistics and Education, 5*(2), 93–116.

Halliday, M. A. K. (1995). Language and the theory of codes. In A.R. Sadovnik (Ed.), *Knowledge and pedagogy: The sociology of Basil Bernstein* (pp. 127–144). Norwood, NJ: Ablex.

Halliday, M. A. K. (2002). Introduction: A personal reflection. In J. Webster (Ed.), *On grammar: The collected works of M.A.K. Halliday* (Vol. 1, pp. 1–14). New York: Continuum.

Halliday, M. A. K., & Hasan, R. (1985). *Language, context and text: Aspects of language in a social-semiotic perspective.* Geelong, Australia: Deakin University Press.

Halliday, M. A. K., & Martin, J. R. (1993). *Writing science: Literacy and discursive power.* Washington, DC: Falmer Press.

Halliday, M. A. K., & Matthiessen, C. (1999). *Construing experience through meaning: A language-based approach to cognition.* New York: Cassell.

Halliday, M. A. K., & Matthiessen, C. (2004). *An introduction to functional grammar* (3rd ed.). New York: Arnold.

Halliday, M. A. K. & Webster, J. J. (Eds.). (2009). *Continuum companion to systemic functional linguistics.* New York: Continuum.

Hammond J., & Gibbons, P. (2005). Putting scaffolding to work: The contribution of scaffolding in articulating ESL education. *Prospect: An Australian Journal of TESOL, 20*(1), 6–30.

Hart, B., & Risley, T. R. (2002). *Meaningful differences in the everyday experiences of young American children.* Baltimore, MD: Paul Brookes Publishing. (Original work published 1995).

Hasan, R. (1989). Semantic variation and sociolinguistics. *Australian Journal of Linguistics, 9*(2), 221–276.

Hasan, R. (1992). Meaning in sociolinguistic theory. In K. Bolton & H. Kwork (Eds.), *Sociolinguistics today: International perspectives* (pp. 80–119). New York: Routledge.

Hasan, R. (1995). The conception of context in text. In P. Fries & M. Gregory (Eds.), *Discourse in society: Systemic functional perspectives* (pp. 183–283). Norwood, NJ: Ablex.

Hasan, R. (2002). Ways of meaning, ways of learning: Code as an explanatory concept. *British Journal of Sociology of Education, 23*(4), 537–548.

Hasan, R. (2004). Analyzing discursive variation. In L. Young & C. Harrison (Eds.), *Systemic functional linguistics and critical discourse analysis: Studies in social change* (pp. 15–54). London: Continuum.

Hasan, R. (1973/2005). Code, register, and dialect. In J. J. Webster (Ed.), *Language, society and consciousness: The collected works of Ruqaiya Hasan* (Vol. 1, pp. 160–193). [Reprinted from *Class, codes, and control* (Vol. 2): *Applied studies towards a sociology of language* (pp. 253–292), by B. Bernstein (Ed.), 1973, Boston: Routledge and Kegan Paul].

Hasan, R. (2005). *Language, society and consciousness: The collected works of Ruqaiya Hasan* (Vol. 1). J. J. Webster (Ed.). London: Equinox.

Hasan, R. (2009). Language in the processes of socialization: Home and school. In J. J. Webster (Ed.), *Language, society and consciousness: The collected works of Ruqaiya Hasan* (Vol. 2, pp. 119–179). London: Equinox.

Hasan, R., & Martin, J. R. (Eds.). (1989). *Language development: Learning language, learning culture. Meaning and choice in language: Studies for Michael Halliday.* Norwood, NJ: Ablex.

Hasan, R., Matthiessen, C., & Webster, J. J. (Eds.) (2005). *Continuing discourse on language: A functional perspective* (Vol. 1). London: Equinox.

Hasan, R., Matthiessen, C., & Webster, J. J. (Eds.). (2007). *Continuing discourse on language: A functional perspective* (Vol. 2). London: Equinox.

Heath, S. B. (1983). *Ways with words.* Cambridge, UK: Cambridge University Press.

Hong Kong Department of Education. (2011). *English language materials.* Retrieved from http://www.edb.gov.hk/index.aspx?nodeID=5476&langno=1

Hood, S. (2009, September). *Challenging dominant orientations to genre in EAP: An SFL perspective on research writing.* Paper presented at the Australian Systemic Functional Linguistics Association Conference, Brisbane.

Hood, S. (2010). *Appraising research: Evaluation in academic writing.* New York: Palgrave Macmillan.

Hood, S., & Martin, J. R. (2007). Invoking attitude: The play of graduation in appraising discourse. In R. Hasan, C. Matthiessen, & J. J. Webster (Eds.), *Continuing discourse on language: A functional perspective* (Vol. 2, pp. 739–764). London: Equinox.

Humphrey, S., Love, K., & Droga, L. (2011). *Working grammar: An introduction for secondary English teachers.* Melbourne: Pearson.

Hyland, K. (2000). *Disciplinary discourses: Social interactions in academic writing.* London: Longman.

Hyon, S. (1996). Genre in three traditions: Implications for ESL. *TESOL Quarterly*, *30*(4), 693–722.

Johns, A. (2001). *Genre in the classroom*. Mahwah, NJ: Erlbaum.

Kress, G. (1997). *Before writing: Rethinking the paths to literacy*. New York: Routledge.

Kress, G. (2003). *Literacy in the new media age*. Routledge: London.

Kress, G., Jewitt, C., Bourne, J., Franks, A., Hardcastle J., Jones, K., & Reid, E. (2005). *English in urban classrooms: A multimodal perspective on teaching and learning*. New York: Routledge/Falmer.

Labov, W. (1969). *The logic of non-standard English*. Georgetown Monographs on Language and Linguistics, 22. Washington: Georgetown University Press. (Reproduced in P. P. Giglioni (Ed.), *Language and social context*. Harmondsworth: Penguin.)

Larochelle, M., Bednarz, N., & Garrison, J. (Eds.). (1998). *Constructivism and education*. Cambridge, UK: Cambridge University Press.

Lemke, J. L. (2001). Multimedia literacy demands of the scientific curriculum. In J. Cumming & C. Wyatt-Smith (Eds.), *Literacy and the curriculum: Success in senior secondary schooling* (pp. 170–181). Melbourne: Australian Council for Educational Research.

Lemke, J. L. (2002). Multimedia semiotics: Genres for science education and scientific literacy. In M. J. Schleppegrell & M. C. Colombi (Eds.), *Developing advanced literacy in first and second languages: Meaning with power* (pp. 21–44). Mahwah, NJ: Erlbaum.

Lindstrøm, C. (2010, June). *Mapping the hierarchy: Advancing the theoretical and practical understanding of the hierarchical knowledge structure of physics*. Paper presented at the Sixth Basil Bernstein International Symposium, Brisbane, Australia.

Locke, T. (2007). Constructing English in New Zealand: A report on a decade of reform. *Educational Studies in Language and Literature*, *7*(2), 5–33.

Locke, T. (Ed.). (2010). *Beyond the grammar wars: A resource for teachers and students on developing language knowledge in the English/literacy classroom*. New York: Routledge.

Macintyre, S. (2004). *A concise history of Australia*. Cambridge, UK: Cambridge University Press.

Macken-Horarik, M. (2002). "Something to shoot for": A systemic functional approach to teaching genre in secondary school science. In A. M. Johns (Ed.), *Genre in the classroom: Multiple perspectives* (pp. 17–42). Mahwah, NJ: Erlbaum.

Macken-Horarik, M. (2003). Appraisal and the special instructiveness of narrative. *Text*, *32*(2), 285–312.

Macken-Horarik, M. (2006a). Knowledge through "know how": Systemic functional grammatics and the symbolic reading. *English Teaching: Practice and Critique*, *5*(1), 102–121.

Macken-Horarik, M. (2000b). Recognizing and realizing "what counts" in examination English: Perspectives from systemic functional linguistics and code theory. *Functions of Language, 13*(1), 1–35.

Macken-Horarik, M. (2008). Multiliteracies and "basic skills" accountability. In L. Unsworth (Ed.), *New literacies and the English curriculum: Multimodal perspectives* (pp. 283–308). New York: Continuum.

Malinowski, B. (1923). The problem of meaning in primitive languages (Supplement 1). In C. K. Ogden & I. A. Richards (Eds.), *The meaning of meaning*. London: Kegan Paul.

Malinowski, B. (1977). *The language of magic and gardening*. Bloomington: Indiana University Press. [Reprinted from *Coral gardens and their magic* (Vol. 2), by B. Malinowski, 1935, London: Allen and Unwin]

Marshall, S. (2006). Guiding senior secondary students towards writing academically valued responses to poetry. In R. Whittaker, M. O'Donnell, & A. McCabe (Eds.), *Language and literacy: Functional approaches* (pp. 251–263). New York: Continuum.

Martin, J. R. (1985). Process and text: Two aspects of human semiosis. In J. D. Benson & W. S. Greaves (Eds.), *Systemic perspectives on discourse* (Vol. 1, pp. 248–74). Norwood, NJ: Ablex.

Martin, J. R. (1992). *English text: System and structure*. Philadelphia and Amsterdam: Benjamins.

Martin, J. R. (1999). Mentoring semogenesis: "Genre-based" literacy pedagogy. In F. Christie (Ed.), *Pedagogy and the shaping of consciousness* (pp. 123–155). New York: Continuum.

Martin, J. R. (2003). Making history: Grammar for interpretation. In J. R. Martin & R. Wodak (Eds.), *Re/reading the past. Critical and functional perspectives on time and value* (pp. 19–57). Amsterdam: John Benjamins.

Martin, J. R. (2009). Genre and language learning: A social semiotic perspective. *Linguistics and Education, 20*(1), 10–21.

Martin, J. R. (in press). Writing and genre studies. In C. A. Chapelle (Ed.), *The encyclopedia of applied linguistics*. Oxford: Wiley-Blackwell.

Martin, J. R., & Rose, D. (2007a). Designing literacy pedagogy: Scaffolding democracy in the classroom. In R. Hasan, C. Matthiessen, & J. J. Webster (Eds.), *Continuing discourse on language: A functional perspective* (Vol. 2, pp. 251–280). London: Equinox.

Martin, J. R., & Rose, D. (2007b). *Working with discourse: Meaning beyond the clause* (2nd ed.). New York: Continuum.

Martin, J. R. & Rose, D. (2008). *Genre relation: Mapping culture*. London: Equinox.

Martin, J. R., & White, P. R. R. (2005). *The language of evaluation: Appraisal in English*. New York: Palgrave Macmillan.

Maton, K., & Moore, R. (Eds.). (2010). *Social realism, knowledge and the sociology of education: Coalitions of the mind*. New York: Continuum.

Mehan, H. (1979). *Learning lessons: Social organization in the classroom*. Cambridge, MA: Harvard University Press.

Michaels, S. (1986). Narrative presentations: An oral presentation for literacy with first graders. In J. Cook-Gumperz (Ed.), *The social construction of literacy* (pp. 95–116). Cambridge, UK: Cambridge University Press.

Misson, R., & Morgan, W. (2006). *Critical literacy and the aesthetic: Transforming the English classroom*. Urbana, IL: NCTE.

Mohan, B. A. (1986). *Language and content reading*. Reading, MA: Addison-Wesley.

Moore, M. F. D. (2008). *Bringing knowledge back in: From social constructivism to social realism in the sociology of education*. New York: Routledge.

Moore, R. (in press). *Basil Bernstein, the thinker and the field*. London: Routledge.

Morais, A., Neves, I., Davies, B., & Daniels, H. (Eds.). (2001). *Towards a sociology of pedagogy: The contribution of Basil Bernstein to research*. New York: Peter Lang.

Muller, J. (2000). *Reclaiming knowledge: Social theory, curriculum and education policy*. New York: RoutledgeFalmer.

Muller, J. (2001). *Reclaiming knowledge: Social theory, curriculum and education policy*. New York: RoutledgeFalmer.

Muller, J. (2007). On splitting hairs: Hierarchy, knowledge and the school curriculum. In F. Christie & J. R. Martin (Eds.), *Language, knowledge and pedagogy: Functional linguistic and sociological perspectives* (pp. 65–86). New York: Continuum.

Muller, J., Davies, B., & Morais, A. (2004). *Reading Bernstein, researching Bernstein*. New York: RoutledgeFalmer.

Myhill, D. (2008). Towards a linguistic model of sentence development in writing. *Language and Education, 22*(5), 271–288.

Myhill, D. (2009). Becoming a designer: Trajectories of linguistic development. In R. Beard, D. Myhill, J. Riley, & M. Nystrand (Eds.), *Handbook of writing development* (pp. 402–414). London: Sage.

National Commission on Writing. (2003). *The Neglected "R." The need for a writing revolution*. Retrieved from http://www.writingcommission.org/prod_downloads/writingcom/writing-school-reform-natl-comm-writing.pdf

National Commission on Writing. (2006). *Writing and school reform*. Retrieved from http://www.writingcommission.org/

National Inquiry into the Teaching of Literacy. (2005). *Teaching reading*. Retrieved from http://www.dest.gov.au/nitl/report.htm

O'Halloran, K. (2007). Mathematical and scientific forms of knowledge: A systemic functional multimodal grammatical approach. In F. Christie & J. R. Martin (Eds.), *Language, knowledge and pedagogy: Functional linguistic and sociological perspectives* (pp. 205–238). New York: Continuum.

O'Halloran, K. (2011). The semantic hyperspace: Accumulating mathematical knowledge across semiotic resources and modalities. In F. Christie & K. Maton (Eds.), *Disciplinarity: Functional linguistic and sociological perspectives* (pp. 217–236). New York: Continuum.

Olson, G. B., Land, R., Anselmi, T., & AuBuchon, C. (2010). Teaching secondary English learners to understand, analyze and write interpretive essays about theme. *Journal of Adolescent and Adult Literacy, 54*(4), 245–256.

Painter, C. (1999). *Learning through language in early childhood.* New York: Cassell.

Painter, C. (2007). Language for learning in early childhood. In F. Christie & J. R. Martin (Eds.), *Language, knowledge and pedagogy: Functional linguistic and sociological perspectives* (pp. 131–155). New York: Continuum.

Painter, C. (2009). Language development. In M. A. K. Halliday & J. J. Webster (Eds.), *Continuum companion to systemic functional linguistics* (pp. 87–103). New York: Continuum.

Painter, C., Derewianka, B., & Torr, J. (2007). From microfunction to metaphor: Learning language and learning through language. In R. Hasan, C. Matthiessen, & J. J. Webster (Eds.), *Continuing discourse on language: A functional perspective* (Vol. 2, pp. 563–588). London: Equinox.

Paltridge, B. (1997). *Genre, frames, and writing in research settings.* Philadelphia: John Benjamins.

Peel, R., Patterson, A., & Gerlach, J. (2000). *Questions of English: Ethics, aesthetics, rhetoric and the formation of the subject in England, Australia and the United States.* New York: RoutledgeFalmer.

Perera, K. (1984). *Children's writing and reading: Analyzing classroom language.* New York: Blackwell.

Plum, G. (1988). *Text and contextual conditioning in spoken English: A genre-based approach.* Nottingham: University of Nottingham.

Polias, J. (2009a). *Developing the language of personal, social and humanities education.* Adelaide, South Australia: Lexis Education.

Polias, J. (2009b). *Doing, talking and writing science: How students are apprenticed into the world of science through language and visuals.* Adelaide, South Australia: Lexis Education.

Polias, J. (2009c). *Exploring how meanings are made in mathematics.* Adelaide, South Australia: Lexis Education.

Qualifications and Curriculum Development Agency. (2010). *Assessing Pupils' Progress (APP).* Retrieved from http://www.qcda.gov.uk/assessment/354.aspx

Reddy, M. (1993). The conduit metaphor: A case of frame conflict in our language about language. In A. Ortony (Ed.), *Metaphor and thought* (2nd ed., pp. 164–201). New York: Cambridge University Press.

Rohrs, H., & Lenhart, V. (Eds.). (1995). *Progressive education across the continents. A handbook.* Frankfurt: Peter Lang.

Rose, D. (2004). Sequencing and pacing of the hidden curriculum: How Indigenous learners are left out of the chain. In J. Muller, B. Davies, & A. Morais (Eds.), *Reading Bernstein, researching Bernstein* (pp. 91–107). New York: Routledge-Falmer.

Rose, D. (2007). Towards a reading based theory of teaching. In L. Barbara & T. Berber Sardinha (Eds.), *Proceedings of the 33rd International Systemic Functional Congress, São Paulo: PUCSP, 36–77*. Retrieved from http://www.pucsp.br/isfc/ proceedings

Rose, D. (2009). Writing as linguistic mastery: The development of genre-based literacy pedagogy. In R. Beard, D. Myhill, J. Riley, & M. Nystrand (Eds.), *The Sage handbook of writing development* (pp. 151–166). Thousand Oaks, CA: Sage.

Rose, D. (2010). Beating educational inequality with an integrated reading pedagogy. In F. Christie & A. Simpson (Eds.), *Literacy and social responsibility* (pp. 101–115). London: Equinox.

Rose, D., & Martin, J. R. (in press). *Learning to write, reading to learn: Genre, knowledge and pedagogy in the Sydney School*. London: Equinox.

Rosen, H. (1973). *Language and class: A critical look at the theories of Basil Bernstein*. London: Falling Wall Press.

Rothery, J. (1994). *Exploring literacy in school English: "Write it Right" Resources for Literacy and Learning*. Sydney: New South Wales Department of School Education Metropolitan East Regions Disadvantaged Schools Program.

Sadovnik, A. (Ed.). (1995). *Knowledge and pedagogy: The sociology of Basil Bernstein*. Norwood, NJ: Ablex.

Sadovnik, A. R. (2008). Schools, social class and youth: A Bernsteinian analysis. In L. Weis (Ed.), *The way class works* (pp. 315–329). New York: Routledge.

Sawyer, W., & Gold, E. (Eds.). (2004). *Reviewing English in the twenty first century*. Melbourne: Phoenix Education.

Schleppegrell, M. J. (2004). *The language of schooling: A functional linguistics perspective*. Mahwah, NJ: Erlbaum.

Schleppegrell, M. J. (2005). *Helping content area teachers work with academic language: Promoting English language learners' literacy in history*. Santa Barbara, CA: UC Linguistic Minority Research Institute.

Schleppegrell, M. J. (2007). The linguistic challenges of mathematics teaching and learning: A research review. *Reading and Writing Quarterly, 23*(2), 139–159.

Schleppegrell, M. J. (2011). Supporting disciplinary learning through language analysis: Developing historical literacy. In F. Christie & K. Maton (Eds.), *Disciplinarity: Functional linguistic and sociological perspectives* (pp. 197–216). London: Continuum.

Schleppegrell, M., Achugar, M., & Oteíza, T. (2004). The grammar of history: Enhancing content-based instruction through a functional focus on language. *TESOL Quarterly, 38*(1), 67–93.

Schleppegrell, M., & Go, A. L. (2007). Analyzing the writing of English learners: A functional approach. *Language Arts, 84*(6), 529–538.

Simon-Vandenbergen, A. M., Taverniers, M., & Ravelli, L. (Eds.). (2003). *Grammatical metaphor*. Philadelphia: John Benjamins.

Snow, C., & Biancarosa, G. (2003). *Adolescent literacy and the achievement gap: What do we know and where do we go from here?* New York: Carnegie Corporation.

Strickland, D. S., & Alvermann, D. E. (Eds.). (2004). *Bridging the literacy achievement gap, Grades 4–12*. New York: Teachers College Press.

Stubbs, M. (1983). *Language, schools and classrooms* (2nd ed.). London: Methuen.

Tardy, C. (Ed.). (2011). The future of genre in second language writing: A North American perspective [Special issue]. *Journal of Second Language Writing, 20*(1).

Thompson, G. (2004). *Introducing functional grammar* (2nd ed.). London: Arnold.

Trudgill, P. (1983). *Sociolinguistics: An introduction to language and society* (Rev. ed.). Harmondsworth: Penguin.

Unsworth, L. (Ed.). (2000). *Researching language in schools and communities: Functional linguistic perspectives*. New York: Cassell.

Unsworth, L. (2002). *Teaching multiliteracies across the curriculum: Changing contexts of text and image in classroom practice*. Philadelphia: Open University Press.

Unsworth, L. (Ed.). (2008). *New literacies and the English curriculum: Multimodal perspectives*. New York: Continuum.

Veel, R. (1997). Learning how to mean—scientifically speaking: Apprenticeship into scientific discourse in the secondary school. In F. Christie & J. R. Martin (Eds.), *Genres and institutions: Social processes in the workplace and school* (pp. 161–195). London: Cassell Academic.

Ventola, E. (1997). Modalization: Probability—An exploration into its role in academic writing. In A. Duszak (Ed.), *Culture and styles of academic discourse* (pp. 157–179). New York: Mouton de Gruyter.

Vinson, T. (2010). The social context of literacy acquisition: Achieving good beginnings. In F. Christie & A. Simpson (Eds.), *Literacy and social responsibility* (pp. 71–86). London: Equinox.

Von Glasersfeld, E. (1998). Why constructivism must be radical. In M. Larochelle, N. Bednarz, & J. Garrison (Eds.), *Constructivism and education* (pp. 23–28). Cambridge, UK: Cambridge University Press.

Wells, G. (1993). Reevaluating the IRF sequence: A proposal for the articulation of theories of activity and discourse for the analysis of learning and teaching in the classroom. *Linguistics and Education, 5*(1), 1–37.

Wheelahan, L. (2010). *Why knowledge matters in the curriculum: A social realist argument*. New York: Routledge Taylor & Francis Group.

Whittaker, R., & Llinares, A. (2009). CLIL in social science classrooms: Analysis of spoken and written productions. In Y. Ruiz de Zarobe & R. M. Jiménez Catalán

(Eds.), *Content language integrated learning: Evidence from research in Europe* (pp. 215–234). London: Multilingual Matters.

Williams, G. (1995). *Joint-book reading and literacy pedagogy.* Unpublished doctoral dissertation, Macquarie University, Sydney, Australia.

Williams, G. (1998). Children entering literate world: Perspectives from the study of textual practices. In F. Christie & R. Misson (Eds.), *Literacy and schooling* (pp. 18–46). London: Routledge.

Williams, G. (1999). The pedagogic device and the production of pedagogic discourse: A case example in early literacy education. In F. Christie (Ed.), *Pedagogy and the shaping of consciousness: Linguistic and social processes* (123–155). London: Cassell.

Williams, G. (2005a). Semantic variation. In R. Hasan, C. Matthiessen, & J. J. Webster (Eds.), *Continuing discourse on language: A functional perspective* (Vol. 1, pp. 457–480). London: Equinox.

Williams, G. (2005b). Grammatics in schools. In R. Hasan, C. Matthiessen, & J. J. Webster (Eds.), *Continuing discourse on language: A functional perspective* (Vol. 1, pp. 281–310). London: Equinox.

Williams, G. (2008). Language socialization: A systemic functional perspective. In P. A. Duff & N. H. Hornberger (Eds.), *Encyclopedia of language and education, Vol. 8: Language socialization* (2nd ed., pp. 57–60). New York: Springer.

Williams, G., & Lukin, A. (Eds.). (2004). *The development of language: Functional perspectives on species and individuals.* New York: Continuum.

Wilson B. G. (1996). *Constructivist learning environments: Case Studies in instructional design.* Englewood Cliffs, NJ: Educational Technology Publications.

Young, M. F. D. (2008). *Bringing knowledge back in: From social constructivism to social realism in the sociology of Education.* New York: Routledge.

Index

abstraction, 3, 28, 72, 96, 103, 109, 112, 113, 118 124, 137, 146, 150, 177, 185, 188, 190, 209, 220

academic writing, 21, 210, 212, 232, 238

Achugar, M., 74, 237

Adams, M. J., 69, 225

adolescent literacy, 106, 225, 226

Adoniou, M., 199, 225

adverbial groups, 6, 11, 16, 17, 92, 103, 205

agency, 97, 109, 112, 113, 118, 137, 139, 146, 154, 155, 168, 169, 217, 236

Aidman, M., 27, 29, 225

Alvermann, D. E., 106, 238

anecdote genre, 75

Anselmi, T., 135, 235

appraisal, 21

attitudinal expression, 78, 85, 92, 96, 98, 169, 173, 184, 220, 223

AuBuchon, C., 135, 235

Bakhtin, M. M., 185, 225

Bazerman, C., 136, 225

Bednarz, N., 174, 232

Bennett, S., 236

Bernstein, B., 34, 35, 36, 136, 149, 151, 167, 225, 230, 231, 233, 235, 236, 237

Biancarosa, G., 238

Bourne, J., 232

Brindley, S., 174, 225

Brookes, D. T., 168, 225, 231

Bruner, J., 199, 225

Butt, D., 72, 225

Cain, M. L., 225

Campbell, N. A., 96, 98, 225

Carnegie Council on Advancing Adolescent Literacy, 106, 107, 225, 226

Cazden, C., 40, 41, 49, 195, 226

Chan, E., 72, 226

Chen, R. T. S., 174, 226

Chomsky, N., 5, 30, 226

Christie, F. vii, viii, ix, x, xi, 10, 17, 18, 21, 29, 31, 34, 40, 42, 48, 50, 53, 61, 66, 69, 81, 82, 88, 93, 104, 108, 113, 116, 123, 124, 125, 126, 127, 128, 136, 137, 141, 151, 153, 155, 168, 169, 174, 177, 179, 184, 185, 189, 192, 194, 195, 196, 199, 207, 209, 214, 215, 226, 227, 228, 229, 230, 234, 235, 237, 238, 239

circumstance, 6, 7, 14, 15, 16, 22, 57, 58, 67, 109, 110, 116, 188, 144, 164, 177, 203, 205, 206, 214

circumstantial information, 7, 15, 16, 86, 87, 93, 94, 103, 188, 200

clauses, 6, 7, 8, 11, 17, 18, 19, 23, 24, 25, 26, 27, 30, 45, 46, 52, 56, 57, 60, 62, 65, 66, 68, 70, 73, 79, 81, 82, 87, 88, 89, 90, 94, 97, 100, 101, 102, 103, 111, 114, 122, 123, 135, 140, 152, 154, 155, 157, 169, 181, 188, 198, 204, 205, 206, 207, 208, 214, 220, 221, 223

clause interdependencies, 17, 188, 206, 207, 208, 223

dependent clauses, 18, 45, 57, 68, 79, 88, 94, 102, 188

equal and unequal clauses, 18

embedded clauses, 18, 19, 60, 68, 70, 79, 82, 100, 101, 157, 204, 205

Cléirigh, C., 124, 153, 228

Cloran, C., 35, 229